D1470299

PROGRESSIVE
Manufacturing

Managing Uncertainty
While Blazing
a Trail to Success

Soli J. Engineer, CPIM

FOREWORD BY GEORGE W. PLOSSL

J.ROSS
PUBLISHING

APICS.
**THE EDUCATIONAL SOCIETY
FOR RESOURCE MANAGEMENT**

Copyright ©2005 by Soli J. Engineer

ISBN 1-932159-29-0

Printed and bound in the U.S.A. Printed on acid-free paper
10 9 8 7 6 5 4 3 2 1

Library of Congress Cataloging-in-Publication Data

Engineer, Soli J.
  Progressive manufacturing : managing uncertainty while blazing a trail
to success / by Soli J. Engineer.
    p. cm.
  Includes bibliographical references and index.
  ISBN 1-932159-29-0 (hardback : alk. paper)
  1. Manufacturing industries—Management. 2. Production management. 3.
Organizational change—Management. 4. Manufacturing
industries—Technological innovations—Management. 5. Manufacturing
industries—Quality control. I. Title.
  HD9720.5.E54 2004
  670′.68′5—dc22   2004005589

This publication contains information obtained from authentic and highly regarded sources. Reprinted material is used with permission, and sources are indicated. Reasonable effort has been made to publish reliable data and information, but the author and the publisher cannot assume responsibility for the validity of all materials or for the consequences of their use.

All rights reserved. Neither this publication nor any part thereof may be reproduced, stored in a retrieval system or transmitted in any form or by any means, electronic, mechanical, photocopying, recording or otherwise, without the prior written permission of the publisher.

The copyright owner's consent does not extend to copying for general distribution for promotion, for creating new works, or for resale. Specific permission must be obtained from J. Ross Publishing for such purposes.

Direct all inquiries to J. Ross Publishing, Inc., 6501 Park of Commerce Blvd., Suite 200, Boca Raton, Florida 33487.

Phone: (561) 869-3900
Fax: (561) 892-0700
Web: www.jrosspub.com

DEDICATION

To my mother, Dhun, and my father, Jimmie. If only more parents could be as loving, caring, nurturing, and selfless as they were, the world would be a much better place.

And to two wonderful ladies, my dearest Meher and my sweet darling Vahishta, who chose to share a part of their lives with me.

While they have all passed on, I am a better person for having known them — I am truly blessed!

TABLE OF CONTENTS

Section II: Products and Services

FOREWORD

Unlike other books on industrial planning and control, this one contains a wealth of information on the people factor. It is the most important of the three elements required for success in any commercial business — knowledgeable people, saleable products or services, and efficient processes.

Techniques and computer systems are covered in business English, explaining what they can and cannot do. Buzzwords, with which the field abounds, are avoided. Seemingly complex concepts are related to common activities and ideas. Explanations of the inner workings of powerful techniques are easy to understand.

The myths of popular terms like "push and pull" systems are debunked, as are fallacies of comparing techniques (like material requirements planning) with concepts and processes (like just in time and total quality management). The book illustrates why commonly accepted beliefs and methods should be challenged.

Specific ways are presented to reduce lead times, the most important variable in procurement, processing, and distribution. Means of improving customer service and productivity while reducing inventory investment are shown. Real-life case examples are used to illustrate ways of simplifying plant and office activities. Included are work breakdown structure and improvement curve theory, used effectively in aerospace firms but ignored in most commercial businesses.

Humor and appropriate anecdotes make this book very readable. It will be useful to people at all levels of organization in manufacturing and distribution businesses or in firms advising or working with them.

George W. Plossl

A SPECIAL ACKNOWLEDGMENT

It is not very often that one has the opportunity to meet a person who helped pioneer an entire profession. George W. Plossl was one of the pioneers of the material management profession as it exists today, and I had the honor and privilege of knowing him. George was a prolific author and an educator, and during his lifetime assisted several organizations with their efforts to improve productivity. He was also one of the founding members of APICS.

While reading two of his books, *Orlicky's MRP* and *Managing in the New World of Manufacturing,* I sensed some of his frustration with the current state of affairs in the areas of manufacturing and material management. It was the kind of frustration that I had been feeling for several years, which eventually prompted me to write this book.

I decided that I had to meet George, and so I wrote to him. Soon after, we scheduled a meeting for late summer of 2003. George and his wonderful wife, Marion, welcomed me into their home for the entire day.

Although we knew each other for only a few short months, George and I developed a special friendship, and I would call him whenever I needed his advice. Not only did he always make time to answer my questions, but the perfectionist in him dissected some of my work to help improve it. He also agreed to write the foreword to this book. For all of this I am truly grateful.

George was also kind enough to present me with an autographed copy of his book *Production and Inventory Control Applications.* In a personal note, he referred to me as a "fellow laborer in the field of improving productivity in business." I feel privileged that he included me in such an elite category.

Although George has passed on, his teachings will continue to help the manufacturing industry for a long time. I will remember and respect him as a straight shooter and a "fellow laborer in the field of improving productivity in business."

Soli J. Engineer

ACKNOWLEDGMENTS

The thought of writing this book had been germinating in my mind for about 12 years. For one reason or another, primarily due to my work schedule, the book was always put on the back burner. Finally, in 2003, I decided to take a sabbatical from my consulting practice and work on the book.

Given that this book is comprised of several experiences, many of which I gained while working for a large organization during the 1980s and 1990s, I would like to thank my management for affording me the opportunity and my colleagues and teammates for their patience and perseverance. I learned a lot during those years, sometimes by trial and error. In particular, I would like to thank my friend Mark Whitaker, to whom I reported for some of those years. He stepped back and allowed me to try different approaches — some of which initially seemed a bit off the wall but eventually proved to be the right thing to do. I know he experienced a few nail-biting moments, but he stood by me through it all. I could never forget those days. I would also like to thank Jim Ashton and Dick Fagan for teaching me the proper use of certain concepts relating to project management — concepts such as work breakdown structure and improvement curve theory, to name just a few.

My family and friends have been a constant source of encouragement, and the occasional kick in the pants I received from them was just what the doctor ordered. I am grateful for their support. Specifically, I would like to thank Ruby Homawala and Nazreen Cooper for taking time out of their busy schedules to help with editing the text and creating charts. I could not have completed the manuscript on time without their help.

Last but not least, I would like to express my gratitude to the folks at J. Ross Publishing, Inc. Specifically, to Sandy Pearlman for the excellent job of editing the work, Steve Buda for his ongoing support and encouragement, and Drew Gierman for affording me, a first-time author, this opportunity.

ABOUT THE AUTHOR

 **Soli J. Engineer** is President of SJE Consultants & Associates, a management consulting firm. With more than 25 years of global business, manufacturing, and management experience, his expertise lies in effective senior management, production and inventory management, manufacturing engineering, value analysis, ISO 9000, and the implementation of management information systems. He educates, advises, and assists organizations worldwide using his extensive knowledge and ability to simplify concepts and methodologies so that they are easily understood.

Soli earned a Master's Degree in Business Administration from the University of Houston and a Master's Degree in Electrical Engineering from Texas A&I University, Kingsville.

He is a published author and speaker, an active member of APICS, Certified in Production and Inventory Management, and has taught several certification courses.

ABOUT APICS

APICS — The Educational Society for Resource Management is a not-for-profit international educational organization recognized as the global leader and premier provider of resource management education and information. APICS is respected throughout the world for its education and professional certification programs. With more than 60,000 individual and corporate members in 20,000 companies worldwide, APICS is dedicated to providing education to improve an organization's bottom line. No matter what your title or need, by tapping into the APICS community you will find the education necessary for success.

APICS is recognized globally as:

- The source of knowledge and expertise for manufacturing and service industries across the entire supply chain
- The leading provider of high-quality, cutting-edge educational programs that advance organizational success in a changing, competitive marketplace
- A successful developer of two internationally recognized certification programs, Certified in Production and Inventory Management (CPIM) and Certified in Integrated Resource Management (CIRM)
- A source of solutions, support, and networking for manufacturing and service professionals

For more information about APICS programs, services, or membership, visit www.apics.org or contact APICS Customer Support at (800) 444-2742 or (703) 354-8851.

*Free value-added materials available from
the Download Resource Center at www.jrosspub.com*

At J. Ross Publishing we are committed to providing today's professional with practical, hands-on tools that enhance the learning experience and give readers an opportunity to apply what they have learned. That is why we offer free ancillary materials available for download on this book and all participating Web Added Value™ publications. These online resources may include interactive versions of material that appears in the book or supplemental templates, worksheets, models, plans, case studies, proposals, spreadsheets and assessment tools, among other things. Whenever you see the WAV™ symbol in any of our publications, it means bonus materials accompany the book and are available from the Web Added Value Download Resource Center at www.jrosspub.com.

Downloads available for *Progressive Manufacturing: Managing Uncertainty While Blazing a Trail to Success* consist of improvement curve calculations, a cost rollup exercise, and PowerPoint slides that illustrate how to effectively establish and achieve improvement objectives.

INTRODUCTION

*Lord grant me the Serenity to accept
the things I cannot change,
the Courage to change the things I can,
and the Wisdom to know the difference.*

Serenity Prayer

Managing any business is akin to juggling without gravity. What is the one thing on which all jugglers rely? The certainty that when they toss a ball in the air, it *will* come down. With sufficient practice, they are able to predict when and where the ball will land.

In the realms of manufacturing, project management, and life in general, this is not always the case. Yes, at times, the proverbial ball will descend as expected; occasionally, it may stay suspended in the air, and we have to *make* it come down; and sometimes it will fall with such force that we are not able to catch it at all.

Several factors that dictate the fate of the ball are within our control, and in many instances, we are able to make the ball "behave." Some issues can be anticipated, controlled, and, if necessary, changed. Some cannot, and we must be flexible enough to work through them. This is not unlike the Serenity Prayer. Unfortunately, in our business and personal lives, we often lack the wisdom to know the difference between what we can and cannot change.

Occasionally, we try to control things that are beyond our control and we let slide certain issues that can be easily controlled, invariably resulting in efforts to pull imaginary rabbits from fictitious hats.

Some years ago, Holiday Inn used "The best surprise is no surprise" as its advertising motto. This is exactly what we should be striving for in the management of any project or business. Every day, life presents us with numerous challenges just by the basic nature of its uncertainty. We do not need to add to these challenges and complicate our lives further. Our objective should be to minimize these uncertainties by simplifying the work at hand and to anticipate and prepare ourselves for the ones we cannot eliminate.

Over the past few decades, Western manufacturers have appeared to be searching for solutions to their inventory, delivery, cost, and quality woes. In an effort to help us meet these challenges, several consultants and experts (some self-proclaimed) in the field of production and inventory management have professed a variety of philosophies. After 30-odd years, a whole new vocabulary of buzzwords and acronyms has developed, but the woes linger on.

I often feel that some of the pundits have lost sight of the real objective. For many, racing down the buzzword highway on the latest and greatest bandwagon appears to be the order of the day.

The real objective for any business should be to succeed and grow. This is best achieved by serving its customers. The basic ingredients that lead to such success are discipline, attention to detail, and common sense. Sometimes it is easy for an organization to become complacent as long as its bottom line continues to be in the black. During economic downturns, if the profits turn to losses, the intuitive reaction is to raise prices and/or to trim the workforce. We must recognize that we are entering a new age where, in every type of business, customers expect goods and services cheaper, faster, and of exceptional quality. While it is important for any business to price its products and services competitively, continually raising prices is not the preferred way to stay in business. In order to create more headroom, we must look at ways to drop the floor, instead of continually raising the ceiling. The best way to drop the floor is to eliminate every kind of waste and any activity that does not add value to products or services. Reducing head count should be considered only as a last resort.

Over the years, I have learned much from knowledgeable professionals with whom I have had the privilege to work and from books on manufacturing and management principles. Authors such as Warren Bennis, Bill Creech, W. Edwards Deming, Peter Drucker, Joseph Orlicky, Tom Peters, George Plossl, and Peter Scholtes, to name just a few, have written books that I have found to be informative, enjoyable, and truthful. I have used these principles and procedures quite successfully to implement processes that have cut cycle times, product costs, and nonvalue-added work, while making significant improvements in product and service quality. Often, in order to achieve these results, I had to veer off the beaten path and challenge some traditionally accepted theories. I still use them in my consulting life today.

I describe my thoughts and methods in this book to encourage you to pepper theoretical knowledge with sound judgment and common sense, in the hope that you, in turn, will think of innovative ways to arrive at elegant solutions for your organization. Most of the ideas in this book focus on highly engineered and customized low-volume products. These are the ones that provide the greatest challenge. High-volume repetitive products with relatively constant demand are more forgiving.

I also include some examples of situations that I have encountered during my career. They relate to both manufacturing and service organizations. Where possible, I provide analogies between managing a production facility and things we do in our everyday lives.

In the context of this book, the word "manufacturing" is used in a generic sense. It includes machining, fabrication, and assembly operations.

In several instances, where I recognized that other authors have already done a very good job of explaining certain concepts, I resisted rehashing the details in this book. In such cases, I cite their books as a reference. It is my opinion that as far as the theory behind production and inventory control and computerized material requirements planning is concerned, no one comes close to presenting it as accurately and comprehensively as George Plossl and Joseph Orlicky. I believe they are part of an elite group of people who pioneered the basic concepts in this field. Likewise, in the fields of quality improvement, management principles, and statistical process control, I am a firm believer in the teachings of Dr. W. Edwards Deming. His fourteen points for management are invaluable. In the same vein, Tom Peters' book *Thriving on Chaos* has been a major source of inspiration for me to veer off the beaten path, to question traditional practices, and to try new methods for improvement.

While individuals at all levels of an organization will find parts of this book to be helpful, I believe middle and upper-level managers will gain the most from it. They are usually the ones to establish policy and direction for an organization. Students in the field of manufacturing and materials management will also benefit from this book. It can serve as a reference to help them gain insight into the practical applications of theories, concepts, and procedures taught in schools.

Experience gained from our mistakes over the last three decades has shown us that we can improve upon traditional methods. What keeps us from taking the leap to change are the boundaries we set around ourselves — boundaries created by our mental paradigms. I firmly believe that as long as we keep on rehashing the tried-and-true ideas, no significant improvement will be realized.

In this book, I show only a handful of examples of how progress can be achieved by keeping an open mind and by questioning tradition. It will be up to others to question several traditional philosophies that my own paradigms have kept me from challenging. I eagerly look forward to their ideas.

It is my sincere hope that you find this book to be enlightening, helpful, and, at times, humorous. I wish you success with your own efforts toward "juggling without gravity."

This book has free materials available for download from the Web Added Value™ Resource Center at www.jrosspub.com.

SECTION I:
PEOPLE

*The greatest danger for most of us is not
that our aim is too high and we miss it,
but that it's too low and we reach it.*

Michelangelo

1

CHANGE:
THE BIGGEST HURDLE!

*Insanity: doing the same thing over and over again
and expecting different results.*

Albert Einstein

A wise person once noted that the only human to like change is a wet baby. How true! Let's face it, most people dislike change. People would like to be left alone to continue doing what they have been doing, in the same manner in which they have been doing it. Some of us are more open to change than others. Even the most die-hard proponents of change are reluctant when it comes to certain aspects of their lives. Although I am an avid proponent of change, especially when it comes to organizational and productivity improvements, the thought of moving makes me cringe. I will travel to any place and stay there for extended periods of time, but I must eventually return to my home.

Most humans are creatures of habit and resist change. Yet, by its very nature, life is unpredictable and change is imminent — and sometimes painful. This is true in our personal lives as well as at work. The degree of pain is often directly proportional to the degree of resistance to the change.

In spite of the fact that most people resist change, change is inevitable in life and often involuntary. Some of the more drastic changes that can be experienced are the loss of a loved one, a serious accident, or losing one's job. Being human, we are seldom prepared for such changes. In fact, we lull ourselves into believing that "This happens to others. It won't happen to me."

Traumatic as these changes can be, most humans possess a resilience which enables them to rationalize the reason for the change (sometimes a simple but heavyhearted c'est la vie!), weigh their options, and eventually bounce back. Some people take longer than others to recover, and some require external help, while others do not.

In our professional lives, things are not much different. During the course of our professional careers, we are sometimes required to change jobs, change bosses, or change the way we perform our work. We accept some changes more readily than we do others. If we perceive a change to be in our favor, we are more receptive to it than if we view it as threatening our organizational stature or existence. A change in salary is, after all, a change, but no one would fight getting a healthy pay raise.

I believe that this reluctance to change is a result of the human tendency to keep from entering perceived antigravity situations. We like to believe that since nothing untoward has happened to us while following the age-old processes, chances are good that if we continue in the same manner, nothing untoward will happen in the future either. The current processes may be tedious and time consuming, but we can live with that; we always have! Besides, if we change the way we have always done things, there is no telling what rude surprises could be in store for us. So we try to continue living with a known evil. Why rock the boat?

AN ANALOGY

Imagine repeatedly tossing a coin above your desk, waiting for it to land on its edge. There is a reason why the probability of a coin landing on either of its two flat surfaces (heads or tails) is 50%. Any other outcome is against the laws of physics. The *only* way to enable a coin to land on its edge is to *change* something. The coin could be made much thicker, so that the edge would be wide enough to support it. Or you could toss it at the beach, where the loose sand could support it on its edge. The first case would involve changing the design of the coin, whereas the second would require a change in the process and environment.

Ironically, many of our business practices are analogous to a coin toss. For example, each year we set financial objectives that exceed the performance of the prior year, but we neglect to recognize that *something* must be changed in order to achieve them. We assume that the objectives will be met by people working harder and more diligently. If this is indeed true, then why didn't we achieve the same objectives last year? Were people not working hard enough? Were they sandbagging?

A PROFESSIONAL RUT

In organizations for which we work, as in life, we develop certain habits, and when given sufficient time, we tend to fall into a rut. We *must* do certain things in a certain way, at a certain time of the day, week, or month. Very often, when asked why we perform a certain task the way we do, the answer is "This is how I have always done it" or "This is how I was taught to do it." Sometimes, when asked why a certain task needs to be performed at all, people have a horrified, questioning look on their faces that says "Are you for real? I've been doing this for 20 years." But when they are probed more deeply, very often the answer is "I don't really know why this task needs to be performed" or "I really don't want to bring it up with my supervisor."

With the passage of time, we sometimes forget why we were hired in the first place. Production planners begin to believe their *job* is to write work orders, buyers begin to believe their *job* is to write purchase orders, and so on. Very often, a major portion of the *job* becomes paper shuffling. All of a sudden, the perceived *job* becomes a deeply etched rut that we find hard to get out of. Sometimes people even forget that they work for an organization altogether; this happens when they start believing that they work for their boss (or department).

FOR WHOM DO YOU WORK?

One of my favorite questions to ask people I interview at my clients' facilities is "For whom do you work?" More often than not, the reply will be the boss's name, sometimes the name of the department, and occasionally (but not often enough in my opinion) the name of the company. People often confuse to whom they report with for whom they really work. A person may *report* to one individual today and a different one tomorrow or next month or next year, but he or she would continue to *work* for the same organization. This may sound like splitting hairs, but I have seen cases where it has resulted in robotic departments, if not entire robotic organizations. It is more prevalent in smaller organizations, especially ones that are owned by a single individual, but it is quite easy for larger companies to fall prey to it too. Very often, managers actually believe that their subordinates work for *them*. It is not unusual to hear a manager or supervisor say, "That person works for me." Bill Creech alludes to this in his book, *The Five Pillars of TQM.*

This tendency says a lot about the general culture within an organization. It could result from the boss or manager being dictatorial, or it could be that the overall management philosophy is dictatorial: "You're not paid to *think*, you're paid to *do*." It could also result from the employees' reluctance to stick their necks out and take risks. It is so much easier and safer to do as one is told and not take unnecessary chances. A person could look like a fool if his or her ideas don't work. What's worse, the boss could start wondering about that person's competence.

I'm being facetious, but some people really do operate this way. This often stems from the supposed leaders within the organization who have failed to develop a culture of openness and sharing of ideas. When people actually *believe* that they work for their immediate manager and not for the parent organization, they tend to mouth the manager's thoughts and ideas and suppress their own. This is unhealthy for *any* organization — and it is certainly unhealthy for the people who continue to suppress their own thoughts.

TYPES OF CHANGES

It is not feasible to imagine, let alone list, *every* type of change that people could encounter in their business lives. A few of the common ones are discussed below.

Different Manager

Every time a different person is brought in to manage a department, the people within the department should expect to have to adjust to that person's philosophy, pet projects, and basic quirks. Every person has his or her own individual management style, and this style is what becomes the driving force in any department. Also, when people are involved, personalities come into play. An employee may or may not like the new manager or may have certain traits that the manager may or may not view as favorable.

Changes in management can have a significant effect on the performance of any organization. Someone once told me that given sufficient time, people within a department are likely to take on the personality of their manager. Although I do not believe this to be universally true, I have seen it happen in quite a few cases. One instance that I will not soon forget took place in a division of a large company for which I worked.

Personal Experience

Sam, the new division manager, was a smart, well-educated individual and an extrovert by nature. When he moved into this position, the employees were a bit wary at first. They just did not know what to make of him. Sam believed in encouraging cross-departmental interaction among the employees within the division. He would do so by conducting in-house meetings and off-site retreats and on several occasions having informal meals where the employees from different departments were encouraged to socialize and learn more about each other.

This created camaraderie among the employees, and within a few months, the imaginary departmental walls that existed began to crumble. People were excited about their work and would go out of their way to share new ideas with co-workers in other departments, even though some of them worked in different cities.

Roughly three years later, Sam was promoted to another job. He was replaced by John, an equally well-educated and very smart individual — except that John lacked some basic social skills. He had a difficult time relating with the employees, which, coupled with the fact that he was a miser and could not justify spending money for dinners and off-site meetings to help the workforce socialize, didn't help matters. He even had difficulty understanding why he was made division manager. He would actually tell us, "I have a degree in metallurgy — I'm not sure what I'm doing here." As one might imagine, this attitude from our perceived leader didn't exactly excite the employees to the point where they were ready to set the world on fire. To make matters worse, the economy had just started on a downswing and many people were concerned about losing their jobs. Within a few months, the departmental walls started to crop back up and morale took a nosedive. A little more than a year later, John was transferred to another job, but he had made certain that the person who replaced him had his work cut out for him.

Some companies believe in frequently moving their upper-level managers around in order to allow them the opportunity to learn more about different operations within the organization. While this may be good for the managers, it can play havoc with the various departments and divisions that they manage, if done too frequently. The company in the above example was notorious for moving managers from one job to another every two to three years, which created a lack of much needed stability for the workforce. Although it is a good idea to cycle managers through different jobs because it gives the managers a broader perspective of the company and is good for the divisions because it helps infuse new and fresh ideas into the organization, each manager's term of service in any job should last longer than two or three years.

Change in Work Assignment

A change in work assignment could involve a promotion, a demotion, or a lateral move. Most people would not fight a promotion. Why should they? It usually entails more money and an increase in importance, prestige, and perceived organizational clout. I say "perceived" organizational clout because many people rate the degree of clout a person has in the organization by the number of people who report to him or her. In my experience, I have found that this is not necessarily true. As a result, many individuals in a supervisory or management position with people reporting to them resent being asked to perform as individual contributors. They perceive such a change as a reduction in clout or a demotion and try to fight it. When the change goes through anyway, some of them get hurt feelings and go into hiding by crawling into a shell or blending in with the tapestry. This is often a result of misplaced priorities. People need to realize and keep in mind why they are employed by the organization. It is to do what is required (within the bounds of morality and governmental laws) to help the organization succeed. Very often, people tend to lose sight of this and let feelings of self-gratification win over rational thought.

My personal experience has shown that the greatest clout I had within the organization I worked for was when I was an individual contributor. To me, it is much more challenging and emotionally rewarding to be able to get a group of people who do not report to you to agree on certain issues. Getting direct reports to agree with you is not necessarily a true test of leadership. Many individuals agree with their managers just because it is the lesser of possible evils and one way to keep the boss happy and off their backs.

Change in Location

A change in location could be as simple as changing offices or as involved as a move to another city or another country. Not everyone can be expected to comply with such changes, depending, for instance, on family commitments.

Change in Work Processes

More often than not, people who have been in a job for a long time begin to believe that the tasks they have been performing, along with the way in which they have been performing them, are essential and must be performed. They seldom stop to question whether it still makes sense to perform a particular task. It is difficult to get a person out of this rut.

Sometimes it is a result of personal insecurities: "If I don't perform this task, I may have nothing to do and I may lose my job, so why rock the boat?" As a result, some people continue to perform inane tasks just to ensure a paycheck at the end of the week or month. At other times, it results from people not knowing any better. Take, for example, a new hire brought in to replace a retiring veteran. Invariably, the new person will be placed under the veteran's tutelage to enable a smooth transition. What is the veteran going to teach the rookie? You guessed it — the same methods that he or she used for perhaps 20 years. Because the rookie is too new to question the veteran, the inefficiencies are perpetuated.

Often enough, these tendencies may arise from the "how we did it at XYZ Corp." syndrome. I can explain this best by sharing an experience at a client's facility.

Personal Experience

Jerry, a real entrepreneur, owned Gizmos, Inc. He started the company by approaching two competitors and offering to build their products for them. Both companies had been considering subcontracting their manufacturing so that they could concentrate on their core business. One of the conditions stipulated by both customers was that Jerry hire some of their workforce. Jerry agreed. While the normal hiring process of advertising and interviewing candidates from other organizations was used to fill a few of the positions, the majority of the workforce at Gizmos, Inc. consisted of veterans from the two competitors.

After three consecutive years of losing money and five general managers, Jerry finally decided to hire me as a consultant to help Gizmos, Inc. become profitable. The first thing I noticed after talking to most of the employees was that even though they were happy to have a job, they had a chip on their shoulder about how "things should be done" at Gizmos, Inc. The fact that they used to work for competing organizations prior to being hired by Gizmos, Inc. didn't help matters any; in their minds, they were still competitors.

The activities at Gizmos, Inc. were anything but orchestrated. In fact, if you were to listen closely to the "sound" of the organization, it was a lot like an orchestra tuning its instruments on stage just before a concert — cacophony! In the case of an orchestra, the ultimate objective of tuning instruments is to ensure a harmonious result, but this certainly was not the case at Gizmos, Inc. What was missing was teamwork and leadership — a "Gizmo spirit" just didn't exist. What blew my mind was that it was allowed to go on for three years!

I began with my usual three-pronged approach toward improvement — addressing issues pertaining to people, products, and processes (which is also how I have structured this book). It was obvious to me that the first order of business was people related. I had to start inculcating a "Gizmo spirit" within the organization before addressing the products and processes. Without that, it would have been an exercise in futility!

It took the better part of a year to bring a semblance of unity and teamwork to the workforce.

LEADERSHIP AND TEAMWORK

Much has been written and much has been said about leadership and teamwork. Instead of boring you with yet another iteration of the same theories, I will share an example with you. If you care to read more on these topics, I recommend two books by Peter Scholtes: *The Leader's Handbook* and *The Team Handbook*. Both books contain a wealth of information along with specific dos and don'ts.

Before getting into the example, I feel obliged to provide a brief version of my interpretation of these terms. In a nutshell, a good leader is a person who can encourage others to work toward a specific goal, as opposed to a manager, who traditionally dictates what needs to be done. Leaders work toward implementing visions, while managers work toward implementing specific tasks.

Joel Arthur Barker[1] offers an excellent definition of a leader: *A leader is a person you will follow to a place you wouldn't go by yourself.*

Teamwork is usually described as a group of people working together toward a common goal. However, the dictionary[2] meaning of teamwork reveals a caveat that is often ignored: teamwork is joint action by a group of people in which individual interests are subordinated to group unity and efficiency. The caveat is that "individual interests are subordinated," a "minor" detail that often is missed.

Example

Jim was the manufacturing engineer/project manager for a certain line of products. One of the objectives for the production group was to continually reduce the cost of a new product that recently had been introduced. The assembly hours were a large component of the cost of the product. As a result, Tom, the shop supervisor, would diligently keep track of the actual hours spent on every subassembly. Periodically, Tom and Jim would compare the actual hours with the estimated hours they had agreed on. They had already achieved a sizeable reduction in the actual hours and were finally at the target that was set for them by management — 850 hours per unit. In spite of this, Jim was certain that they could reduce the hours even further. Tom, on the other hand, was reluctant to make any further cuts due to several concerns: "What if something goes awry and I need more time? What if some operations take more time than we had planned? I can't take the risk of incurring unfavorable labor variances."

Jim empathized with his concerns, but he also knew that further reductions were possible, so he made Tom an offer: "Tom, what if I were to create an additional step on the routing for the final assembly of the finished product, and we treat it as a reserve or a savings account? Every time we see a reduction in hours on any subassembly, we reduce the hours required for the subassembly and add the reduction to the savings account. If a certain subassembly requires more time than our estimates, we can draw from the savings account and transfer those hours to that subassembly. This way, the total hours for the unit would not change from 850 hours, and the various subassemblies would have realistic times allocated to them.

"Let's do this for three months. If at the end of three months we see a positive balance of hours in the savings account, it would represent excess hours that we have not needed to use. Would you agree to cut 90% of the hours still showing in the savings account at the end of three months?"

Tom replied, "Let me see if I understand. If I haven't used up the savings account in three months, I probably don't need those hours. And if we keep 10% of the excess in the savings account, I still have something to draw from. Yeah, that makes sense. Let's go with it."

At the end of the first three months, Tom and Jim were able to cut another 32 hours from the total of 850 hours. They followed the procedure every three months for the remainder of the year and were able to reduce the total by a few more hours.

I was impressed by the way Jim handled the situation. He could have easily taken the approach of a bull in a china shop and entered into desk-pounding arguments with Tom. Instead, he chose to empathize with Tom's concerns and presented Tom with a logical yet creative solution to help allay his fears. Tom had no reason not to accept Jim's offer.

Jim took the right approach and good things happened. Also, Jim's offer to Tom was so logical and reasonable that Tom could not refuse it.

This underscores some of my beliefs and philosophy: If we do the right things, good things will happen, and it is hard for anyone to argue with common sense.

Cause for Concern

A cause for concern is a general lack of understanding of the concept behind leadership and teamwork. Quite often, managers are too quick to create teams and assign individuals to leadership roles. They believe that using an imaginary Excalibur on individuals and a simple "I hereby dub thee team leader" immediately transforms them into team leaders. They use a similar approach when forming teams. The common misconception is that if the right words are used, the right things will happen, which often proves not to be the case. We are prone to our penchant for instant gratification. Teams and leaders must be *developed* — and that takes time, care, and nurturing. These variables are often left out of the formula for achieving success. When things don't pan out as hoped for, some people are quick to disband the team with a "Yeah, we tried the team concept, but it doesn't lend itself very well to our line of work."

WHAT DOES IT TAKE TO EFFECT CHANGE?

Simple as it may seem, the philosophy of doing the right things raises a number of important questions for the CEO of any company: "How do I know what the *right things* are?" "What sort of *good things* should I expect to come from the effort?" "What is involved in doing the right things?" "How much will it cost?" "How long will it take?" "How do I know that I need to make any changes in the first place?"

Two basic ingredients are required for any organization that expects to achieve significant results by changing the way it conducts business. If an organization is large, a third ingredient could be called for. The first ingredient is the presence of a change agent — a person high enough in the organization, usually the CEO, who must commit to a continuous and unrelenting, sometimes gut-wrenching, effort toward improvement. The second ingredient is a guide or a coach to help point the way — unless, of course, the CEO is knowledgeable and confident enough to proceed solo. The coach should be a trustworthy person who has the vision to see the benefits that are achievable and the knowledge and conviction to drive toward them. Notice that I did not say that the coach must be able to *quantify* the potential benefits at the outset. This is seldom possible. I am always wary of individuals who promise an x% improvement in any metric the first time they walk through the door — that just smells too much like snake oil.

It is rare for an effective coach to emerge from within the organization. I say this because, to a certain extent, employees within any organization develop a set of blinders, which often get in the way of clarity of thought and the strength of the message that may need to be conveyed, especially to higher ups in the organization. Some people develop blinders that are virtually opaque — except for a narrow slit through which they see their organizational world. Others develop a translucent or semi-transparent variety, but it is very rare to encounter an employee, however knowledgeable, who is completely unaffected by his or her environment and is willing to consistently speak up in spite of the possibility of losing his or her job. Office politics can be a powerful deterrent to truth and free speech!

More often than not, one has to look outside the organization for an effective coach. This person usually comes in the form of a consultant. A good consultant can be a valuable short-term asset for any business that wants to improve its quality and processes. Two adjectives used in the previous statement, "good" and "short-term," are key to a successful relationship with any consultant. A good consultant is one who will tell the CEO what he or she *needs* to hear instead of what the CEO *wants* to hear — even if it means that the consultant may summarily be shown the door. A good consultant also will be a good teacher who will show the organization ways to work autonomously in the long run and not constantly be dependent on external help. Short term can range from a few months to a couple of years, depending on the size of the project.

The third ingredient, which may or may not be required depending on the size and geographic spread of an organization, is a project manager (or a group of project managers). The project manager would certainly come from within the organization, and his or her charter would be to execute the plan laid out by the CEO and the coach. The project manager would get his or her knowledge from the coach and authority from the CEO.

Notice that nowhere in the above explanation was the word "easy" used. There is no doubt that such efforts consist of several tedious, detail-oriented steps and involve hard work. The secret is to start small, highlight the successes along the way, and find ways to *enjoy* doing it. Success breeds on itself; when the employees see minor improvements in their daily grind, they will find it easier to sustain the effort for the long haul.

Management's Responsibility

Any organization that expects to improve its operations must involve its workforce in the decision-making process. The workforce must believe that the "team" consists of everyone within the walls of the organization. Only then can the spirit of cooperation flourish. The onus of encouraging employee involvement sits squarely on the shoulders of the most senior member of the organization — the owner or CEO. This person must initiate and set this culture with his or her direct reports so that they in turn will adopt it with their direct reports and so on down the organization. Employees must feel comfortable sharing their thoughts and concerns without fear of criticism or retribution. They must believe that they are an *integral* part of the organization and not just another commodity. Employees must be encouraged to question why a certain task is performed in a certain way and, sometimes, whether or not a task needs to be performed at all. This is an effective way to keep from falling into a rut. Such an environment can only exist if the CEO or the owner believes in the culture of continuous improvement, encourages it, and constantly *lives* it.

Employees' Responsibility

The road to effecting change is by no means a one-way street. While management has its set of responsibilities, so does the workforce. Once the employees understand and agree to a change, they are responsible for providing the necessary effort and cooperation required for its successful implementation.

Sometimes this is easier said than done. Occasionally, some employees may not be willing to get on board with the program and are quite vocal when it comes to expressing their disagreement. They have a few choices available to them; they can choose to:

- Grin and bear it — hoping that they like what develops
- Talk to management — and try to convince them to take a different route
- Find some positives — and build on them
- Quit

The ones to watch out for are those who exercise tacit resistance to the change effort. They will nod their heads in agreement at meetings, but when they return to their desks, it's back to the "same old, same old." Of course, in such cases, excuses abound, such as "I guess I didn't understand what you said" or "Oh, you mean we're going with the new method as of right now?" Simply by dragging their feet, these people can cause serious delays and disruptions.

PARADIGMS

No discussion on change would be complete without addressing paradigms. Before I read Joel Arthur Barker's book,[1] I had developed my own definition of a paradigm: an imaginary fence we build around ourselves that influences our thoughts and actions. It is similar to the proverbial "box" that we are often encouraged to think outside of. Mr. Barker offers a more eloquent definition: *A paradigm is a set of rules and regulations (written or unwritten) that does two things: (1) it establishes or defines boundaries; and (2) it tells you how to behave inside the boundaries in order to be successful.*

Mr. Barker begins his book by presenting a paradigm shift[1] that pertains to watches. He explains how the huge market share that was held by the Swiss dwindled from the late 1960s to the early 1980s. What caused this was the advent of the electronic quartz movement. Ironically, although the Swiss invented the movement, they could not "see" it as a replacement for their high-precision mechanical movements. Seiko and other Japanese watchmakers saw merit in the electronic quartz movement, adopted it, and by the early 1980s, Japan held the major market share for watches.

In recent years, we have experienced two other major paradigm shifts in the making. With the advent of wireless technology and the speed at which it is progressing, we could be witnessing the slow demise of landline telephones. Newspaper articles indicate that it is not uncommon for people to opt to give up their conventional telephones for the cellular kind. I believe that not too long from now, once technology has progressed to the point where cellular telephones become globally affordable, landlines will become historical relics.

The field of photography is another area where I believe we are experiencing a paradigm shift, one that I got caught up in. Photography is one of my hobbies and I consider myself a serious amateur. Until a few years ago, I belonged to the ranks of the purists and could not see myself moving away from conventional cameras and film. An article that I read helped open my mind to digital photography. The article was addressed to photographers like me, the purists, and it explained how even the great Ansel Adams worked much of his "magic" in the darkroom and not just with the camera. That got me thinking. While the process of enhancing "raw" photographs has not really changed, the equipment has. Darkrooms, optical enlargers, mechanical masks, and chemicals have given way to digital technology. A few years ago when my work required me to travel like a nomad, I grew tired of toting my 35-mm camera and auxiliary lenses, so I decided to buy a small digital camera. It takes good pictures and is really convenient to carry on business trips. I find myself using my "old" camera less and less. Just a few years ago, I could not have imagined myself with a digital camera. However, when I want to take "serious" photographs, I still use my 35-mm camera, probably because the purist in me is not completely dead yet.

My point is that our old habits and rituals become so ingrained that sometimes we cannot see past our noses. Changing old habits is truly one of the most difficult undertakings in life.

The next two chapters are devoted to what I believe to be some of the critical people-related elements that must exist for change to occur and to last.

NOTES

1. Joel Arthur Barker, *Paradigms: The Business of Discovering the Future,* HarperCollins, New York, 1993, pp. 15–19, 32, 163.
2. *Webster's New World Dictionary, Third College Edition.*

This book has free materials available for download from the Web Added Value™ Resource Center at www.jrosspub.com.

ORGANIZATION

Discipline without freedom is tyranny;
freedom without discipline is chaos.

Cullen Hightower

Two important characteristics that separate one company from another are the way the organization is structured and the culture within the organization. The traditional method for organizing a company's workforce is to group individuals by skill and function into discrete "departments." Engineers responsible for product design are part of the design-engineering department, buyers are grouped under the purchasing department, and so on.

How did this departmental philosophy originate? I believe the root cause is our penchant for pigeonholing — everything. Human beings like to see things cut-and-dried and packaged in neat little bundles. If it works with hay, we can make it work with people.

In large organizations, departmentalizing can provide a simple way to keep track of head count, expenses, and capacity. It can also help with easy identification of resource skills from which we can draw. Certainly a noble thought with potential merit to it.

Over time, the departmental philosophy began to take on an identity of its own. For many individuals, the department to which they belong becomes a "home." Their thoughts and actions are directed toward the department's goals and objectives, and the department is the place to which they return after having fought their daily battles with people from *other* departments. Often, the overall organization's goals and objectives take a back seat to those of the department.

The effects of such a mind-set are detrimental to the culture of any organization. Lack of overall direction, intracompany competition, and reduced motivation and trust within the organization give rise to fear.

A common fallacy is the belief that if the performance of every component of an entity is optimized, then the performance of the parent entity also will be optimized. This usually is not the case. The real objective should be to optimize the performance of the parent entity or organization. If that results in suboptimizing the performance of some of its components or departments, so be it. An example relates to production scheduling. Traditional philosophy has been to optimize the output of *every* work center in the hope that it will provide the best result for the entire facility. However, this has proven to be a good method for building unnecessary inventory. Eliyahu Goldratt cited an excellent example of this in his book *The Goal*. He explained that in order to optimize the output of a production facility, the bottleneck work center should be optimized.

When it was finally recognized that the departmental mind-set was hindering organizations from achieving their true potential, something had to be done to enable people to work together — to work as a *team*. Initially, there were still reservations about totally dismissing the departmental concept. This gave rise to matrix management in the 1970s and 1980s. Conceptually, companies would continue to organize by departments, but for certain projects, individuals would be cherry-picked from different departments and for the duration of those projects form a cross-functional project team. The team would functionally report to a person dubbed a team leader, but organizationally, each individual on the team would continue to report to his or her department manager or supervisor. The hope was that this would help decouple individuals from the day-to-day grind of meeting departmental objectives and get them to work together more closely.

While people used all the right words, in many instances, body language, which kept alluding to the departmental concept, gave them away. I know, because several years ago, I had the privilege of participating in this circus. Even though the department managers knew that one or more of their direct reports were expected to concentrate on the team's objectives, they could not let go of them. The basic message was "I know you have been assigned to the project team, but we still have to meet our core objectives. The show must go on." As a result, the efforts of the individuals on the team were diluted, and while the team's goals were seldom met, the department's goals also began to suffer, which was a great source of frustration. After a few more feeble attempts, the general conclusion was "This team concept is good, but it hasn't worked for us." Group involvement teams and quality circles of the early 1980s serve as textbook examples of this approach.

To make matters worse, project assignments began to be misused, especially "special project" assignments. They began to be used as a mechanism to shunt perceived nonperformers out of their mainstream job functions. To this day, many consider a special project assignment to be the beginning of the end of their careers — the handwriting on the wall, the kiss of death!

Over time, several organizations saw the fallacy of these approaches and took corrective steps. They changed from the departmental philosophy or function-oriented organization to a project-oriented approach. However, the general trend is still to organize by function.

KEEP IT SHALLOW

Regardless of how an organization is structured, it is the depth of the structure that usually dictates the level of bureaucracy or flexibility in any company. A deeper structure will consist of a greater number of hierarchical levels, resulting in greater bureaucracy. In many cases, it has been proven that the preferred way to organize is by project, but if a functional structure *must* be adopted, it must be kept shallow.

Few things could be worse for an organization than to be structured by department *and* have multiple levels of management. The departmental mindset ends up creating fiefdoms, and the multiple levels effectively serve to choke communication and flexibility.

Having a group of specialists who cannot operate without the stamp of approval from multiple levels of management is a recipe for rigidity and stagnation in an organization. It leads to organizational rigor mortis, which sets in when people forget why they are employed by the organization; instead, they live in a dream world in which they belong to a certain department and require a "green light" from above to permit them to take the slightest diversion from the beaten path.

MISSION

The first order of business for any organization should be to point all heads in the same direction. From the CEO down to the lowest rank in an organization, all employees must know and understand the reason why they come to work each day. This objective or *mission* is generally described in a mission statement, and it is meant to serve as the drumbeat for the organization. Most management consultants will spout the importance and benefits of having a mission statement. Some agencies even offer to write mission statements for organizations. I find this to be fundamentally wrong! I can certainly understand explaining guidelines to help formulate a mission statement, but I cannot understand someone else telling me what the mission of my organization should be. There is even software to help an organization write its own mission statement. Just insert the appropriate catchwords and the program will create an impressive-sounding mission statement for you.

Over the past decade or so, the concept of a mission statement has waxed and waned in popularity. This is because, ironically, the underlying *mission* of the mission statement has been violated. In many instances, it ends up being just a collection of words, often buzzwords and too many of them, printed in fancy type, on fancy paper, mounted in a fancy frame, and displayed in a prominent location for all to see. Instead of using it as a tool to help focus an organization's workforce, it is used as a marketing tool to wow potential customers — if you can't baffle 'em with brilliance, befuddle 'em with bullshit!

Example

During a recent visit to my dentist, I noticed an elaborate, wordy mission statement hanging on a wall in the reception area. I decided to test its effectiveness. When the dental hygienist escorted me to one of the exam rooms, I asked her to recite the mission statement to me. She started to walk back to the reception area, signaling for me to follow, and said, "Come, I'll show it you." "I was wondering if you have it memorized," I replied. "Oh I couldn't do that," she answered. "None of us can — it's too long. It's Dr. Smith's baby; he insisted we should have one, so there it is."

Credo of the Organization

A mission statement should be used to describe the credo of an organization — its basic beliefs. When we encounter tough decisions, it should point us to the correct answer. If a mission statement is to be effective, everyone in the organization should understand it, believe in it, and *live* it — *every day*. For this to be possible, the mission statement must be short, achievable, and written in plain, simple words. It does not need to be prominently displayed, but it does need to be recalled and referred to, on a regular basis. When employees are not quite sure which route to pursue, it should guide them in making the correct decision. This must apply to every level of management within the organization.

The best way to inculcate such a culture within an organization is for the senior members to practice it. When employees at lower levels of the organization see that the CEO takes the mission statement seriously, they in turn will feel more comfortable adopting it. If used properly, it can be an extremely powerful tool for any organization. If misused, however, it can generate mistrust in the workforce and will be a detriment to morale.

I have seen some good mission statements and some that are just plain terrible. The terrible ones tend to ramble on and on. They contain so much detailed information that the *real* message gets lost in the rhetoric. At best, they are vague, and hardly anyone in the organization can memorize them, let alone understand them. A mission statement that does not clearly and concisely depict a company's "reason for living" undermines the very concept of having one in the first place. It *creates* an environment of antigravity! A proper mission statement creates a sense of "Aha!" within the workforce instead of "Huh? What?"

It is important to note that a mission statement is not meant to be a set of objectives.[1] However, when departmental and individual objectives are developed, or when processes are established, they *must* support the corporate mission. The example that follows depicts a case where an organization's pay scheme drove the employees in a direction that was totally contrary to the corporate mission.

Example

James owns a heavy-duty truck dealership in Texas. The dealership sells trucks made by three different manufacturers, one of which is Big Wheels, Inc. A few years ago, James invited me to review the operations at the dealership and to make recommendations for improvement.

My first question for James was "Do you perceive some problems, and if so, what are they?" After all, why would anyone hire a consultant if they thought everything was hunky-dory in their organization?

"Well, the biggest problem that I see is with the service group," James explained. "Trucks that we repair invariably come back within a few days because we forgot to do something to them. Plus, we are *always* late delivering the vehicles back to the customers — sometimes by weeks! The customers are not happy with the quality of work, and hardly a week goes by that I don't get a letter or a phone call from one of them. I keep telling the guys to pay attention to quality and timeliness, because we really need to keep the customers happy, but for one reason or another, it's not happening. I'm really concerned about this."

The dealership employs roughly 70 people, and I offered to talk to everyone and have them fill out a questionnaire that I developed. I told James that I would share my thoughts with him once I completed my chats with the employees. Of course, individual employee feedback would be kept confidential, but the general opinion of the workforce would be shared with James. With help from my associate Arthur Watkins, we were able to accomplish this in about a week.

One of the questions that we asked was "What, as you perceive it, keeps you from doing a good, quality job?" The most frequent response was "Time. We are not allowed enough time to do a good job."

This dealership operated on a "flat rate" pay scheme. "Flat rate" is the accepted term in this industry. The manufacturer, Big Wheels, Inc., decides how long a given repair task should take by averaging the time it takes nationwide. Most of us have had some experience with this. If you take your car to the dealer to replace the water pump, you are given an estimate that is accurate to the penny. This is because the dealership knows how much it will charge for the parts and how long it should take to replace them.

Let's say that the time allowed to replace a water pump is 1.5 hours. Based on the flat rate pay scheme, regardless of how long a technician actually takes to replace a water pump, he or she will only get paid for an hour and a half. If a technician takes two hours, that's just too bad; if a technician can do the job in an hour, that's great, because he or she can then move on to the next job that much sooner.

You can probably guess what was really happening at the dealership. The technicians would race through the jobs in an effort to earn more money. Hardly any tests were performed to make sure that the work was completed properly. Even simple checks like making sure that hoses did not leak were bypassed in a rush to get to the next job. The emphasis was on speed and not quality.

These problems were further exaggerated when it came to warranty work. The underlying assumption was that if a truck was still within the manufacturer's warranty, it was relatively new and the work should be performed in less time than a truck that was out of warranty.

During my interviews, one of the technicians complained that Big Wheels, Inc. did not allow enough time to diagnose a malfunctioning air conditioner that was still under warranty. Big Wheels allowed 40 minutes for diagnosis, but sometimes that was not enough. "So what do you do in that case?" I asked.

"I just take the truck back to the parking lot and move on to the next job," the technician explained. "I don't get paid for anything more than 40 minutes for that job. But if I could hook up our laptop computer to the truck and take it for a road test, I certainly could figure out what's wrong."

"And how long would that take you?" I had to ask.

"About an hour," the technician continued, "but I don't get paid for the 20 minutes that I would go over, so I don't do it."

I couldn't resist asking, "What happens to the truck? How does it ever get fixed?"

"Don, the manager of the service department, has to decide what he wants to do," the technician said. "He usually has to go back to Mr. Smith, the regional service manager for Big Wheels, and get him to agree to allow more time for the job. Don's pretty good at that. He usually gets us more time, but sometimes the truck has to sit on the lot until Mr. Smith comes by, and he visits us just once a week."

Whew! No wonder the customers are getting mad, I thought to myself.

James and I had known each other for more than ten years. Before I started my management consultancy, I worked for an organization that bought several trucks from his dealership. In those days, I was his customer, and we developed an honest and respectful working relationship. When I was done with my analysis of the various issues facing the dealership, it was time for me to talk to James.

"James, what do you want out of this dealership?" I asked.

"I want us to remain in business and to grow," he answered.

"What do you suppose could help you achieve that?" I said.

"Gotta keep the customers happy," he replied, "and I can only do that by providing the best damn customer service possible. That's the best way I know to get a leg up on the competition, but the guys on the floor obviously don't understand that."

"James," I said, "I believe I know what's causing this."

His eyes narrowed as he said, "Okay, lay it on me."

"Look," I explained, "on the one hand, you're pointing toward the customer as the focal point for the dealership, and on the other, you are waving a financial 'carrot' in front of your technicians, but in a totally different direction. How would you describe the mission of the dealership?"

"I want us to provide exceptional customer service," James replied.

After I explained how the flat rate pay scheme was working against his mission, he said, "We could change the pay scheme to a fixed hourly rate based on a technician's level of experience, but how will I get the technicians to be productive and keep from goofing off? With flat rates, the technicians keep working, and the more hours they log, the more money the dealership makes. What would motivate them to work hard with fixed hourly rates?"

"James, you have been using flat rates as a substitute for good management in the service group," I explained. "Besides, your philosophy about the dealership making more money if the technicians make more money makes no sense. Instead, the employees should understand that if the dealership makes more money, they stand to share a piece of the pie, perhaps in the way of a profit-sharing plan."

Within two months after our talk, James abolished flat rates and switched to hourly pay. He also formalized the dealership's mission statement: *Provide exceptional customer service!*

THE RIGHT PEOPLE IN THE RIGHT JOBS

We have all encountered individuals who fit their job function like a square peg in a round hole. Invariably, an employee who performed exceptionally well in the position of an individual contributor is rewarded with a promotion to a supervisory or management job. Yet, the person knows little or nothing about managing people, and very little effort if any goes into educating the person in the art of people management or leadership.

I have seen perfectly competent people in one job function moved to a totally different and unrelated function just because someone quit. I call this the "warm body/open position syndrome": a position opens up within the organization and a warm body is asked to fill it. This is more prevalent in small, privately owned businesses. For example, the owner of a business may go to his or her most trusted confidant and ask the person to play the role of shop supervisor. The confidant may say, "But I don't know much about running a shop. What exactly do you want me to do?" The owner's response might be "I know, but I really need someone I can trust in this position. Just do your best; I'm sure you'll figure it out in a few weeks." Talk about a recipe for failure!

Personal Experience

The general manager of an organization asked one of his trusted buddies, who was an excellent estimator and buyer of sheet metal, to supervise the assembly shop. The guy knew *nothing* about assembly operations and perhaps even less about supervising people. As a result, he felt intimidated to assign work, check production status, or even *talk* to the assemblers. He spent most of his time in his office, shuffling paper. All of a sudden, not only did the assembly shop have an incompetent supervisor, but the fabrication shop did not have a decent estimator/buyer either — a double whammy!

Three months went by, and while the shop was falling behind on the work, overtime was escalating. The general manager couldn't believe that his trusted friend would let him down, and his frustration turned to disgust. After another month, the individual was sent back to his position as a buyer. The last I heard, the relationship between the general manager and his buddy still had not healed.

GOOD PEOPLE

Most people would agree that the key to the success of any organization is its workforce. The journey toward long-term success must start with employing good people. For the purposes of this discussion, a *good* person is one who is:

- Honest
- Dependable
- Happy to work within the organization
- Concerned for the well-being of the entire organization (co-workers, suppliers, and customers)
- Willing to:
  - ☐ Subordinate individual interests to enhance group unity and efficiency[2]
  - ☐ Learn new skills
  - ☐ Adapt to changing circumstances
  - ☐ Make suggestions for improvement

The importance of good hiring practices cannot be stressed enough. Very often, an individual is hired without conducting a proper interview or thoroughly checking references. The mind-set seems to be to hire a "very good buyer" or a "very good production planner" based on education and past experience listed on the resume. Later it may turn out that the person learned his or her job at another business and only knows how to perform it the way it was done there; any changes to what he or she has "always done" just will not work! All too often, 25 years of experience is confused with one year of experience 25 times. Another potential pitfall is confusing education with intelligence. Someone once said, "Some people are educated beyond their intelligence," and we have all encountered such individuals.

Two important points to remember:

- A good employee can be taught to be a good buyer or planner far more easily than a good buyer or planner can be taught to be a good employee!
- A person cannot be expected to have an honest smile for a customer on his or her face if that person does not have an honest smile in his or her heart!

I have found that the existing workforce in most organizations is made up of people who fall into three broad categories. I label them as:

- Eager beavers — Willing to try a different approach
- Fence sitters — Want to wait and see some progress
- Mules — Resist change all the way

In an ideal situation, a manager would like all of his or her employees to be eager beavers, but usually that is not the case. The objective here should be to have the eager beavers work with management in an effort to encourage the fence sitters to become eager beavers. Occasionally, the fence sitters will switch over to the mule category. Within a few weeks, the mules will be readily identifiable. Some typical samples of statements you might hear from them include:

"We have always done it this way; why change things?"
Real message: "Don't rock the boat."

"It'll never work"
Real message: "I don't want to do it."

"Changing the way we do business could chase our customers away!"
Real message: "I'm trying to scare you into going back to the "old" ways."

Sooner or later (preferably sooner), the CEO or owner of the organization will have to make a decision: "Am I running a business or a soup kitchen?" Employees should understand that while the organization is responsible for treating them fairly and providing them with a pleasant, challenging, and safe workplace, they have a responsibility too. Their responsibility is to help the organization achieve its mission! If this is not acceptable to someone, he or she should be counseled accordingly. If the person is still not willing to pitch in with the rest of the team, then it is time to let him or her go. This is not an easy thing to do, but if the person is allowed to stay, it would not be fair to the other employees and would certainly be detrimental to their morale. It would send the wrong message to the *good* people.

The following example illustrates how the lack of a mission statement coupled with a rigid departmental mind-set can be detrimental to an organization's health and well-being.

Example

Some years ago, Dr. Doe, a veterinarian, invited me to make suggestions on how he could improve his practice. I asked him the first question I ask any prospective client: "What do you perceive the problem to be?"

"Well," he answered, "I can't get the clients in and out fast enough. Some of them get quite mad about having to wait so long."

For several years, Dr. Doe had been attending seminars on veterinary practice management. He had also invested in books and video courses. Most of the instructions revolved around the "charge more, sell more" philosophy. Dr. Doe knew that was not the answer; intuitively, he knew that he had to do a better job of managing his practice. He just didn't know the route he should take, so he decided to ask for help from someone who had no preconceived ideas about the veterinary business.

The first time I was invited to a "management" meeting at the clinic, I walked into the room and saw eight people at the conference table: Dr. Doe, his two associate veterinarians, and five staff members. The staff members consisted of the office manager, an accounting administrator, and the supervisors of the receptionists, technicians, and boarding kennel. Right then, I knew that something was awry. For a clinic that employed 17 people (including the associate veterinarians), a management meeting attended by 8 just seemed a bit top-heavy.

One of the topics on the meeting agenda was timeliness of service to the clients. When Dr. Doe asked for ways in which this could be improved, the office manager promptly said that they were short of people. Every supervisor supported this view. After the meeting was over, I asked one of the senior members of the staff to walk me through the process of a typical client visit. Briefly, this is what I learned.

When a client comes in, the patient's file is located and the purpose of the visit is noted. The client and patient are escorted to an examination room (the pet is weighed along the way), and the file is placed in a pigeonhole for the next available technician. The technician then visits with the client, takes necessary samples (blood, stool) from the patient, and leaves to perform the appropriate tests. Once the tests have been completed, the technician notifies the doctor that the patient is ready for examination. Upon completion of the examination, the doctor notes in the file what was done and the technician escorts the client to the receptionist, who completes the paperwork, restores the file to its proper place, and invoices the client.

The key point in this whole scenario is that at every step, when responsibility for the client and patient shifted from one "department" to the next, the client was unattended and had to wait. More than half the time that the client was at the clinic was spent *waiting* for someone (receptionist, technician, doctor) to notice and pick up the file and to perform his or her portion of the "job."

It was quite clear that, over the years, departmentalizing had caused the staff to believe that they belonged to independent fiefdoms. While each employee worked very diligently to accomplish his or her department's objectives, nobody was tending to the clinic's objectives as a whole. In fact, the clinic's objectives had not even been properly and formally imparted to the staff. Dr. Doe firmly believed that *every* individual working there was a representative of the clinic and was there to serve the client and provide excellent veterinary care for the patient, but he had not conveyed this message to the staff. He assumed that they should intuitively know this.

When it was time for me to report my findings to Dr. Doe, I explained to him how the departmental mind-set had directed the employees' focus to their jobs instead of to the customers. He then agreed to go ahead with my recommendations for changes at the clinic. My recommendations focused on the following topics:

- Mission
- Organization (abolish departments and create teams)
- Improved communication
- Simplify internal processes
- Improved computer usage
- Cross-training and education
- Improved hiring practice
- Pay plans and a profit-sharing program
- Importance of continuous improvement

Just one year after embarking on this journey, the results posted by the clinic were astounding. Figure 2.1 shows the cumulative gross income before and after the changes were implemented. The difference is due to a 5% increase

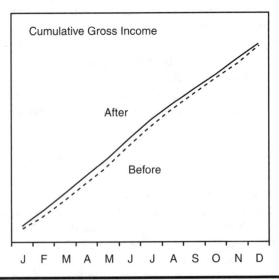

Figure 2.1 Cumulative Gross Income[3]

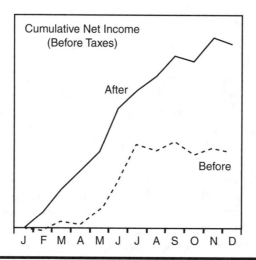

Cumulative Net Income
(Before Taxes)

After

Before

J F M A M J J A S O N D

Figure 2.2   Cumulative Net Income[3]

in fees. Figure 2.2 shows the cumulative net income comparison. The net income *doubled!* A major part of the savings came from a reduced payroll. They were doing more after the changes were implemented, with about two-thirds of the workforce of the previous year. This is not to say that a third of the employees were terminated. Just two employees had to be terminated because they fell in the "mule" category and nothing was going to change their minds. After several unsuccessful attempts to counsel them, in an effort to help them get on board, they were finally terminated. The others left as a result of normal attrition (starting a family, relocating to another city, etc.) or because they did not wish to participate in the new approach. With the cross-training program and streamlined processes, there was no need to replace these people. This shows the dramatic improvements that can be achieved, if only we do the *right* things.

MOTIVATION

"We need to come up with a way to motivate our workforce to work harder." At best, this statement arises from a snobbish and presumptuous attitude on the part of management. The fixed mind-set is that people, especially those in lower echelons of an organization, somehow need to be prodded to do a good job. Most people *want* to do a good job. No one comes to work thinking, "Today, I'm going to do a lousy job."

The Stick and Carrot

Yet managers continue to devise ways to get more work out of people — very often by presenting them with a stick and a carrot! It works with animals, so why shouldn't it work with people? Peter Scholtes writes eloquently on this subject in *The Leader's Handbook*. Referring to B.F. Skinner's philosophy, he says: "Essentially, Skinner regards human behavior as a set of responses that can be conditioned. Just as owners of pets train their animals to behave in certain ways with combinations of rewards and punishments, so too must human behavior be formed through such conditioned responses. People are not much different from Pavlov's dogs or the proverbial jackass whose movement is governed by the carrot and the stick. [As noted in Chapter 2], the carrot and stick approach is used to move a jackass and, as far as we know, its effectiveness is limited to that species."*

One major difference between humans and animals is that we have been bestowed with the ability to *reason*. When other humans try to treat us like animals, we find it demeaning and are resentful. Yet, we find ourselves using this approach all the same. Perhaps it is because the stick and carrot philosophy has been ingrained in us from childhood. If a child is well behaved, he or she is given candy or some other reward. If a child is not well behaved, he or she could be grounded for a few days or given some other punishment. Even the precepts of most religions adopt this approach: if you live well, you will go to heaven; if you do not, you will go to hell. This is an example of the stick and carrot philosophy that many of us were raised on, and we accept it — perhaps more out of fear than anything else.

I am no theologian by any stretch of the imagination. I am using religion as an example to point out that the stick and carrot philosophy has been so ingrained in our moral fiber that it seems like the natural approach to motivating people at work too.

I firmly believe that we cannot use external forces to motivate people, at least not for any significant length of time. People motivate themselves! However, external forces can very easily *demotivate* people. Traditionally, Western organizations try to hire exceptionally qualified people, then place them in a poor environment, usually rife with nonvalue-added processes and a departmental mind-set, and expect them to do a good job. Instead, the aim should be to *simplify* the processes, eliminate those that do not add value to products or

---

* From Peter R. Scholtes, *The Leader's Handbook: A Guide to Inspiring Your People and Managing the Daily Workflow*, McGraw-Hill, New York, 1998, p. 296. Reproduced with permission of The McGraw-Hill Companies.

services, and knock down the imaginary walls and tar pits that serve to demotivate the workforce.

Dr. Deming professed that we should not try to change the people, but rather we should change the processes; he called it *systems thinking*. More often than not, we place highly qualified people in impossible situations, effectively tying their hands behind their backs, and then expect them to perform well.

A Pictorial Depiction

Think of any organization with its prevalent processes and policies as a black box. Qualified individuals are hired and placed in the black box and are expected to meet certain goals and objectives. However, when the individuals enter the box, they feel like they are in a never-ending maze (Figure 2.3), full of imaginary walls and dead-end streets, each one serving as a hindrance to progress. This causes confusion, frustration, and dissatisfaction, which in turn result in finger pointing, lack of teamwork and the "not my job" syndrome. Who do you think suffers as a result of this? The one entity that everyone should be trying to please — the customer. And in the long run, everyone loses!

Management's job should be to knock down these walls and pave a clear, straightforward path for the workforce (Figure 2.4) so that people have a better chance of doing a good job. This can only be achieved by proper organization,

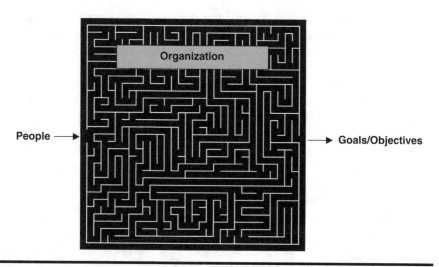

Figure 2.3   Inside View of the Organization

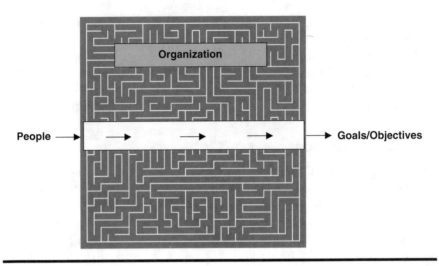

People ——→   →   →   →→ Goals/Objectives

Figure 2.4   A Clear Path

simplification of work processes, mutual trust within the entire workforce, and education.

Motivational Speeches

Perhaps these should be called inspirational speeches since they are meant to inspire thought, confidence, and belief in oneself. Regardless of what one calls them, the way that many organizations have chosen to use them is cause for concern.

When management senses lethargy or frustration creeping into the organization, the tendency is to schedule motivational meetings. Sometimes these are conducted in-house, but often they are held off-site, which costs the company a bundle of money in the form of speakers' fees, travel expenses, and room and board. The hope is that the workforce will get all fired up and return to work ready to set the world ablaze. While this may happen, it usually lasts only a short time. All it takes to douse the excitement is for the employees to realize that *nothing* has changed at their place of work, and in spite of getting all excited at the "motivational meeting," the same frustrations that they experienced before still exist. This, in turn, causes more frustration to develop. After a few such meetings, the workforce begins to treat them as off-site boondoggles and people look forward to them only as an opportunity to get away from the workplace. At best, the process has a counterproductive end result. The only ones who come out ahead are the motivational speakers.

Incentives and Intracompany Competition

Just as the basic objective of any business is to make money, the same is true for the employees. People work for a company to make money. In order to treat them fairly, they must be paid fair, competitive wages. Almost anyone who works for a fixed salary would like to make more money. Usually, the only avenue available to hourly employees is to work overtime. It is not unusual for an employee to request overtime work just because he or she needs more money to pay bills. This is equivalent to putting the cart before the horse. The employee's manager or supervisor should request overtime *only* when such work is justified.

Quite often, corporate management establishes bonus plans that reward individual performance. Usually, such plans are offered to a select group of individuals, invariably salespeople. While such plans benefit the salespeople, in the long run they can be a detriment to the organization. Such plans create competition within the company and have an adverse effect on employee morale. Intracompany competition is unhealthy for any organization, and when coupled with a departmental mind-set, it makes matters worse. Instead, management must create a culture that helps employees understand that the true competition lies outside the walls of the company and not within.

One way to provide a financial incentive while improving a company's profitability without creating an atmosphere of competition is to include the entire workforce in a profit-sharing program. Corporate management could offer to share a percentage of net profits based on certain guidelines. With such a program, the basic message to the employees is: "You can make more money if you help the company make more money." Depending on the size of the organization, profit-sharing programs can vary in flavor. One large organization I worked for offered profit sharing with an upper limit of 15% of an employee's income. The owner of a business that I consulted with offered to share 10% of his net profits with the employees. This plan had no upper limit. If the company's net income was $100,000, he would share $10,000 with the employees, and if the net income was $250,000, he would share $25,000. At the end of the first year, after the business went through significant changes in the way of improvements, the amount the employees received from profit sharing exceeded what they would have made from overtime. Such a program can provide the entire workforce with a true sense of ownership and help to keep the employees from looking for greener pastures elsewhere.

Some owners of small companies are reluctant to offer such incentives. They do not feel comfortable disclosing income-related information to the employees. My observation is that this is partly due to lack of trust in the employees.

Some CEOs are reluctant to implement a profit-sharing program because they do not want to reward nonperformers. My question to them has always been: "Why do you have them on your payroll?"

Other avenues for employees to progress financially are:

- **Cost-of-living increase**: If there is a true increase in the cost of living, employees should be compensated accordingly.
- **Merit increase**: This must be *earned!* The beginning of a new year does not automatically entitle employees to a merit increase.
- **Promotion**: Pay must be commensurate with added responsibilities.

PERFORMANCE EVALUATIONS

Few would argue that performance evaluations are not an effective way for managers and supervisors to let their direct reports know how they are fairing. Yet we find that most organizations continue to practice this ritual. Over the years, performance appraisals have proved to be a waste of time in general and a source of frustration in particular.

In an effort to arrive at a quantifiable method to rate the performance of employees, most organizations begin with measures that are subjective at best. Often, the conclusion of a performance evaluation cycle is established first, and the data are then manipulated to support it. Whether this is done consciously or not is a secondary issue. In fact, in many organizations, the objective of performance evaluations has shifted from rating performance to creating a paper trail to protect against lawsuits. How sad.

Some organizations continue with performance evaluations just because they are unaware of other means of rating employees and establishing monetary rewards. While Dr. Deming was one of the pioneers who preached against performance appraisals, when asked what to do instead, he has been quoted to say, "Whatever Peter Scholtes says." I suggest that you take a look at *The Leader's Handbook* by Mr. Scholtes.[4]

FEAR

The single biggest culprit that can stifle an organization is fear. Primarily, it is fear of the unknown and the possibility of failure that keeps most employees from making suggestions for improvement.

To make matters worse, when the first reaction of management during a downturn in the market is to trim the workforce, it is unrealistic to expect allegiance from people. Fear causes employees to crawl into their shells and hide. Their concern for the goals and objectives of the organization plays second fiddle to concern for their own security and livelihood.

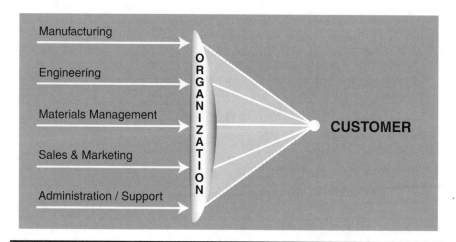

Figure 2.5   Customer Focus

It is management's responsibility to establish a culture of openness, honesty, and trust among the employees. This must start with the CEO of the organization. People must feel relaxed and secure in their jobs before they can be expected to stick their necks out. Honesty and openness are key requirements to encourage a healthy exchange of ideas among employees. Without such a culture, communication via the grapevine and water-cooler meetings will be the norm.

Failure should not be punished, but rather treated with empathy, in order to encourage the workforce to keep trying new ideas and concepts.

THE REAL OBJECTIVE

As a closing note, I must emphasize that the real objective of any business is to make money.[5] The best way to achieve this is to satisfy the customers. As an analogy, if you think of the organization as a lens, every discipline within the organization must work together to focus on the customer. Figure 2.5 drives this message home.

NOTES

1. Laurie Beth Jones, *The Path,* Hyperion, New York, 1996.
2. Definition of a "team player" from *Webster's New World Dictionary, Third College Edition.*

3. S.J. Engineer, Veterinary practice management: a different approach, *Texas Veterinarian,* 63(2), 22–23, 2001.
4. Peter R. Scholtes, *The Leader's Handbook: A Guide to Inspiring Your People and Managing the Daily Workflow,* McGraw-Hill, New York, 1998, p. 296.
5. Eliyahu M. Goldratt and Jeff Cox, *The Goal: A Process of Ongoing Improvement,* North River Press, Great Barrington, MA, 1986.

This book has free materials available for download from the Web Added Value™ Resource Center at www.jrosspub.com.

3

MY FIVE Cs

If you don't have passion, change.

Lauren Hutton

Regardless of magnitude, in order for any project to be successful, there is no substitute for proper planning, organization, and implementation from the very start. This requires a significant amount of passion, discipline, and TLC. In fact, it requires TLC[5] — tender loving *care, comprehension, commitment, communication,* and *common sense*. Ignore any one of these attributes and the project is doomed to extensive delays and untold confusion, if not failure.

For some people, addressing the technical aspects of the work at hand takes precedence over these attributes. Passion, discipline, caring, commitment, communication, and common sense are traits often relegated to the category of "soft stuff." They are not easily quantifiable, and it is hard to play "touchy-feely" with them — they are almost holistic in nature. As a result, while people recognize the importance of these attributes to the success of any project, they do little to promote them in the workplace; it is assumed that employees possess these attributes and utilize them.

I believe the five Cs are important enough to merit a chapter of their own. I am not suggesting that conquering the five Cs will ensure nirvana. Far from it! But I firmly believe that they are vital to the success of any project, whether landing a person on the moon or simply driving to work each day.

CARE

It is obvious that if we want to succeed at anything, we must care about the activity and the outcome. We must give a damn, because if we do not, the whole thing is meaningless to begin with, in which case we may as well not embark on that activity. Furthermore, we must care about the people who are going to help us achieve success — the people with whom we work. But to leave it at that would not be doing justice to the act of caring.

Caring About Work

Most people care about what they do. We all want to do a good job at work and we care about that. Nobody comes to work intentionally wanting to do a poor job — that would be sabotage.

When a group of people works on any given project, the various individuals within the group could direct their caring toward different things. This is true at work as well as in one's personal life. Take a family of four spending a Saturday at the beach, for instance. Mom and dad may have planned the outing to help the family bond. Little Sue and her teenage brother, John, although they are going along with their parents' wishes, have a different agenda. Sue is thrilled because she likes the ice cream that a particular store sells at the beach, and John is looking forward to showing off his six-pack abs to the girls he hopes to meet.

Likewise, certain members of a group, although they care about the success of the project, could have their own hidden agendas. Some may care more about what their peers or boss will think about them if they speak contrary to the party line. These people care more about holding on to their jobs and prefer to keep a low profile. They will go along with what the "boss" says. Others may care more about not getting home too late, instead of occasionally going the extra mile. I use the word "occasionally" because many managers assume that their subordinates do not have a life outside of work and expect them to work long hours consistently — a bad assumption that results in counterproductive stress at work and at home. In spite of this, for an employee to experience an occasional gut-wrenching feeling or sleepless night when things are not going according to plan is a healthy sign. It shows that the person does care about what he or she is working on.

In any group or team, there will be a few individuals who care passionately about the outcome of the project and will want to do whatever it takes to see the project through to a successful completion. These individuals will voice their opinions, recommend a change of course for the project if they believe that is the right thing to do, and also assist other members of the group in order to ensure success. These are the individuals who take pride in a job well done and should be encouraged. This is the type of caring to which I refer.

One must care enough to think things through at the outset of any project. This is a vital ingredient for arriving at an achievable plan of implementation, without which any project will flounder in uncertainty. The old cliché is true: We never have time to do something right the first time, but we always have time to do it over. We must do our best to anticipate and stave off any problems that we can foresee. But in order to be able to foresee problems, we must first be willing to spend the time to look for them. We must fast-forward the imaginary videotape to see what outcomes could result from decisions we make — or, in some cases, decisions we choose *not* to make. Based on what we see, we can then make the proper adjustments at the front end. This takes a special kind of caring, and it also requires us to change the way we think about and approach our work or "job."

Example 1

Invariably, because of time limitations but sometimes due to sheer laziness, we take the path of least resistance. Such was the case with a design engineer, Jim Atkins. Jim was responsible for designing, documenting, and building the first prototype of a brand new product. Once the design was finalized, production would be split between two suppliers, one in the United States and the other in Europe. On the day that the prototype had to be delivered to the customer, Jim realized that he was missing a canvas strap needed to hold a chair in place while the product was in transit. During his lunch break, he drove down to the local sporting goods store and found a strap that would serve the purpose. He installed the strap and shipped the unit to the customer. A job well done! Jim took the initiative to take time from his lunch break to find the strap.

At the company where Jim was employed, the accepted method for documenting commercially available items such as the canvas strap was to specify the name of the manufacturer along with the manufacturer's part number. That way, when a buyer gets a signal to purchase canvas straps, he or she knows *exactly* what to buy. The strap Jim found, however, did not have this information, so instead of trying to find the proper information for the strap, Jim took a shortcut. In the computer record, where the manufacturer's name would normally be specified, he entered "See Jim Atkins." The result was confusion, delays, and a number of international telephone calls — all over a ten-dollar canvas strap.

Example 2

An assembler at a client's facility stopped me while I was walking through the shop one day. He showed me a bracket that he had received from the warehouse to complete a work order. The design of the bracket had been modified several weeks before, but he received one that was built to the old design and it would not fit. He mentioned that he had received the corrected bracket in the past, but once in a while an incorrect part would show up, as it did in this instance. The first thing that came to my mind was to check the stock. There were seven brackets in inventory, four of which were built to the obsolete design and three others that were good parts. Yet they were all stocked in the same bin, under the same part number. When I asked the engineer what happened, he said, "Oh yeah! I changed the drawing a few weeks ago and I had told the buyer to scrap the old brackets. He screwed up again! I always make it a point to tell them when I change the design of a part, but they don't always remember to scrap or rework the old parts." When I asked him why he had not changed the part number of the redesigned bracket, he said that it was used in several products, and it would take too much time to change all the pertinent documentation. This is an example of a person who cared enough to know that he should inform someone of the consequences of his actions, but he did not care enough to implement the change correctly or to anticipate the disruptions that could occur if the person he informed "screwed up." That was not *his* problem. He had done his job and his desk was clear.

These are just two examples that highlight how in the proverbial "heat of battle" we take shortcuts which actually *create* opportunities for things to go wrong down the road. In both cases, the "correct" approach would have been to go through the proper steps for documenting the strap and the bracket, so that any opportunity for confusion would be eliminated. The problem lies with the temptation to minimize one's own workload, even if it is at the expense of introducing confusion and additional work for the people downstream.

Caring About People

"People are our greatest asset." Although this phrase is touted by many companies, when these same companies experience a downturn, the people are usually the first to go. They are treated like a commodity, not an asset. The workforce is not stupid! People see that management's actions speak louder than their words. In spite of this, many companies continue to operate in this manner. The first time a manager is asked to cut costs, he or she looks at the workforce. For many organizations, this is a never-ending drama. During times of boom, they go crazy hiring people, and during downturns, they let them go. Of course, the "economy" is always held responsible. The *care* that is exhibited here is not directed to the people within the organization. It is directed toward the company's bottom line, the price of the company's shares, or the hope of a favorable opinion from market analysts on Wall Street — often at the *expense* of the workforce.

So, what *should* these companies be doing to break this never-ending cycle? Somewhere along the way, preferably during a downturn, they should take a good, hard look inward. What they will find is that the excessive hiring and firing is due to bureaucratic organization structures, archaic processes that are blindly being followed, and in some cases "dead wood" within the organization. They should:

- Streamline and flatten the organization
- Eliminate those processes that are no longer needed and simplify the rest
- Keep the good people and let the others go
- Educate and cross-train the workforce

"Dead wood" is a term familiar to most of us. Dr. Deming liked to quiz managers about it, as cited by Rob Lebow and William L. Simon in *Lasting Change: The Shared Values Process That Makes Companies Great.* They state: "When the great management guru W. Edwards Deming met with a group of executives, he would often ask, 'How many of you have dead wood on your staff?' Most or all the hands would go up. Deming would then *shout* at the group, 'Did you hire them that way, or did you kill them?'"*

Dr. Deming made an excellent point. If dead wood was hired into the organization, then the *hiring* process needs to be changed. If perfectly good people were hired and then turned into dead wood, then the *management* process must change. Either way, it is the responsibility of management to ensure that such people do not creep into the organization.

One Way to Show That You Care

Some years ago, I walked into the office of the manufacturing manager of a multinational organization and found him talking on the telephone to some of his staff in France. I noticed that it was about 3:30 p.m. central time and wondered why he was calling them so late in the day (France is seven hours ahead of central time). When he got off the phone, he saw the puzzled look on my face and explained the reason for his call.

He told me that the major supplier in France was approximately 4.5 hours from the city where his group had its office. It took that long whether one flew, took the train, or drove. There was no quick and easy route between the office and the supplier. After trying different modes of transportation, it was decided that driving was the least painful alternative.

Having participated in several such trips, he was well aware of how things worked. The engineer and planner would leave for the supplier's facility one morning with all good intentions of returning the next afternoon. That way, they

---

* Copyright ©1997 John Wiley & Sons. This material is used by permission of John Wiley & Sons, Inc.

would get home at a decent hour, but that never happened. More often than not, they would end up leaving the supplier's facility late in the evening, about 7:00, and start the long trip home. Most times when he was present, he was able to convince them to spend the night in a hotel and head home the next morning, the safe thing to do. But they were eager to get home and sleep in their own beds, and he knew that when he was stateside, they would head home regardless of when they left the supplier, which concerned him.

When he was at the office in the United States and knew they were on their way home, he would call them on the cell phone. He was trying to make sure that they were awake and semi-entertained, so he would ask how they were doing and they would crack a few jokes. This was *his* way of helping to break the monotony of their drive home and reduce the risk of the driver dozing off at the wheel.

We must care enough to *want* to anticipate potential havoc that could occur downstream as a result of seemingly benign decisions we make. Here, I use the words "want to anticipate" instead of just "anticipate," because the *want* part of it can only come from caring. The *ability* to anticipate, however, requires adequate knowledge to enable someone to understand what *could* go wrong. It requires comprehension.

COMPREHENSION

Without a doubt, it always helps to understand *why* we do the things we do, and the consequences of our actions (or inaction). Very often though, the *real* answers to why we perform certain tasks are not intuitively obvious. It is in such cases that we must dig deep to get to the root cause. A reasonably well-advertised approach that has been attributed to the Toyota Production System and has worked well in my experience is called the *five whys*. Experience has shown that by the time you ask "Why?" five times, you have a good chance of knowing the *real* answer to your original question.

Example

While studying the existing processes at a client's facility, I ran into something that I later dubbed "photocopy mania." The business was a heavy-duty truck dealership. The controller, sales manager, and manager of finance and insurance each kept a full set of photocopies of every document pertaining to the sale of a vehicle.

I asked the manager of finance and insurance why he kept photocopies of sales documents and customers' checks. "Because we are supposed to keep hard copies of all documents," he replied.

"And why do *you* personally have to keep them in your office?" (the second "Why?")

"So that down the road, if I get a call from the customer, the financing institution, or the insurance company, I can answer their questions."

"Why and how often do you get such calls after a sale is completed?" (the third "Why?")

"Very seldom. For additional information."

"Why don't you look for this information in the computer system?" (the fourth "Why?")

"Because it's easier for me to reach into the filing cabinet in my office since I still haven't figured out how to get the information from the system."

Aha, I thought to myself. Now we're getting somewhere.

"The controller mentioned that he too keeps a hard copy of the same documents. His office is located just a few steps down the hall from you. Why can't you use the copies filed in accounting?" (the fifth "Why?")

"They don't like us to get into their files; on a couple of occasions when they couldn't find their copies, all hell broke loose and I caught a lot of grief because of that."

Bingo! Two issues were apparent here:

- The manager of finance and insurance did not know how to retrieve information from the computer system.
- A mutual lack of trust had developed between him and the controller.

He would rather spend time making his "own" photocopies than risk losing the accounting copies and "catch more grief." Self-preservation in action!

When I quizzed the sales manager, his responses were very similar to those of the manager of finance and insurance. However, my talk with Sam, the controller, took a slightly different path.

"Sam, why do you keep hard copies of all these documents?"

"Because our auditors require us to do so," he replied.

"But Sam, with today's advances in technology, why can't these records be retrieved from the computer system?"

"Most of the information can be retrieved from the computer system, but not photocopies of the customers' checks, and there is no way to show the customer's signature on a sales contract."

"Instead of photocopying the checks, why can't you scan and archive them in the computer system? There is a scanner in the accounting office. And instead of having the customers sign paper copies, why can't you use electronic signature pads?"

"I don't know how to do that. I guess we could call the software company's help desk, but they will label our request as 'customization of existing software' and charge us for it. Besides, it's anybody's guess when they'll get around to implementing it. I think we're better off doing it the way we've been doing it — but that's a good idea!"

My session with Sam took just four "Whys?" to know that he really did not want to change things.

The sad part of all this was that the other two managers were trying to justify hiring a clerk each, because there was so much manual photocopying and filing that they had to do in order to protect the interests of the business! The controller had already collected a bevy of clerks over the past few years.

Fortunately, the owner was able to see what was going on, and additional clerks were not hired. In fact, after the process was simplified, a couple of the controller's clerks were reassigned to perform tasks that were more productive for the dealership.

It is easy for any organization to become complacent, especially when a company is making money. During periods of boom, the fact that changing a few things could help a company make a lot more money does not seem appealing to most. It is only during periods of downturn that the age-old saying "We must learn to work smarter, not harder!" starts showing up and the sawdust begins to hit the fan. Unfortunately, once the business experiences the next upswing, people are only too quick to go back to the "old" practices.

People are truly the most flexible resource that any organization has, but people tend to link themselves to the "job" that they were hired to do. Employees sometimes try to turn themselves into "specialists," with a false sense of being indispensable to the organization. The risk here is that once someone is pegged a specialist best qualified to perform a particular job, that person goes where the job goes — sometimes out the door! The inherent message that management often conveys, more by actions than words is "Your job is to do such and such; if the need for this activity is eliminated, you might be too." In order for people to function at their full potential, first and foremost, they have to be put at ease. They must *know* and feel confident that they are valued and that if the business hits a downturn, management will look for ways to utilize their expertise in other areas instead of looking for ways to prevent lawsuits. The absence of such confidence causes discomfort any time someone's "job" is questioned. When questioned, people are prone to be resentful and allow defensiveness to overcome objectivity.

Employees must periodically question why they do what they do and why they take a certain approach to doing it. Invariably, the *real* reason why people perform certain tasks the way they do is that's what they were told to do or that's how it has always been done. Sometimes it is a result of apathy, but very often it is due to lack of knowledge, understanding, or information.

Ignorance can be corrected by proper communication, education, and training. Colloquially, training is often confused with education. Education pertains to increasing awareness and knowledge, enabling someone to follow a logical thought process to arrive at a logical conclusion. Training conjures up images of a circus or the execution of a rote process. Where people are concerned, education is truly the name of the game, though in some cases, such as learning to use a newly installed computer system, a bit of training is required to learn the new screens and inherent idiosyncrasies that invariably come with a new system.

As for cross-training, my guess is we use this phrase instead of cross-educating only because it rolls off the tongue more easily. Regardless of which terminology is used, encouraging and helping people to learn new skills is one of the best investments any company can make. Education and knowledge provide people with a broader view of the organization and increase their awareness and comprehension of how the other side lives. Knowledge, whether gained through education, experience, or cross-training, provides people with a wider set of skills, greater self-esteem, and confidence. This in turn makes individuals more valuable to an organization and during downturns allows for greater mobility within the organization — as opposed to mobility out the door.

COMMITMENT

Perhaps two of the most misused and misinterpreted statements are "I'll try" and "I'll do my best." Of course, "I'll try my best" covers it all. We use these terms not just in our business lives but in our personal lives, too. Before you are tempted to call me an insensitive, unrealistic hard-head, let me explain.

In certain situations, the goal or objective is not always readily achievable. This also applies to the route one may have to take to achieve such an objective. Take, for example, sending a person to the moon. When President Kennedy presented his vision of putting a person on the moon in the 1960s, it would have been foolish for anyone to have responded "Sure, boss, consider it done!" Yet the engineers at NASA took it as a challenge and *tried* to meet it — and they did.

Let's face it. No task we encounter in business even comes close in complexity to landing a person on the moon. Yet, there are people who view some of the simplest tasks as though the earth should stop turning while they *try* to work on them! If they are successful, they are heroes. If not, well, they tried their best.

This is a sign of lack of commitment to the job, the team, and the organization. The point that is missed is that employees take on tasks so that they will be successfully completed, not so that people can *try* to work on them or do their best. You are kidding yourself when you say you will do your *best*. You don't even know for a fact what your "best" is. Varying situations influence the level of your effort and output. Some tasks may be simple enough to not require you to do your best. Other tasks may require you to burn the midnight oil. For still other tasks, your "best" simply may not be good enough; these tasks may require additional information, equipment, or resources for successful implementation. That is when you are obliged to raise the flag and lay out the requirements.

Think about it. Suppose you were on a flight and heard the pilot announce "Folks, we're about to land, so please fasten your seat belts. I want to thank you for flying our airline, and I assure you that I will try my best to land the aircraft safely." The first thought that probably would come to mind is "What's this business about trying his best? He'd better land safely. I want to live."

An Analogy

One of the more daunting tasks for most organizations is keeping an accurate count of inventory. Some organizations brag about being on the leading edge of technology, but they can't tell you for sure what's in their warehouse. Why is that? I believe it is because of a lack of commitment and discipline. For some strange reason, even though companies spend mega-bucks to purchase inventory, they do not see inventory as money sitting in the warehouse.

Take banks, for example. They are nothing more than warehouses for money. They work with just one part, which is currency, but they have several stocking locations for it — the various accounts. Imagine what you would think if your banker were to tell you "We will try our very best to keep your account accurate." Your first reaction would probably be "What do you mean by *try*?"

You *expect* a bank not to make errors while keeping track of your money. Managing parts inventory must require the same degree of discipline and commitment as managing bank accounts. Yet, we condone inaccuracies in inventory counts, often excusing them as "the cost of doing business." We *allow* a lack of discipline and commitment. And what we allow is what we teach.[1] If management continues to allow inaccuracies in inventory counts, the message that is being sent to the organization is that it is okay. The workforce in turn will be less committed to keeping an accurate account of the inventory, and the self-fulfilling prophecy comes true.

People tend to become nonchalant about certain aspects of their work, and the longer they permit themselves to continue in this manner, the greater the likelihood of apathy creeping into the organization. When apathy begins to set in, the worst thing one can do is to ignore it. (I suppose encouraging it would be worse, but who would do that?) Allowing apathy to exist is the first step toward creating fresh dead wood (an oxymoron?).

There is always a reason behind an employee or a group of employees not being totally committed to the work at hand. It could be a situation at work or at home or even an illness. It is the responsibility of the manager or supervisor to talk with the employee, understand the reason, and help employee snap out of it. This is easier said than done. Many managers and supervisors cringe at the prospect of having a "heart-to-heart" chat with people who report to them. They find such talks to be too confrontational. As a result, they try to rationalize the behavior by thinking, "I'll wait a while and see if he comes around" or "Performance evaluations are just three months away; I'll bring up the subject with her at that time," or even "I shouldn't have to tell him that he is not committed to the work; he is not a kid and should know better." While patience (and at times the art of stalling) has several virtues, simply delaying the talk to avoid confrontation shows a lack of commitment on the part of the manager or supervisor. This is discussed further in the section on communication later in this chapter.

As the saying goes, anything worth doing is worth doing well. Tackling tasks in a halfhearted manner does not help the organization — at least not for very long. For instance, companies often tout their commitment to provide their workforce with a safe environment, but a bit of digging into the safety-related processes of some companies reveals that their commitment is really directed toward keeping OSHA off their backs.

Personal Experience

Before leaving the subject of commitment, I would like to share a personal experience. Several years ago, I volunteered to attend a presentation by a visiting consultant at the place where I worked. The subject of the presentation was the importance of quality.

The consultant began his talk with how the "customer" will refuse to accept anything short of perfect quality and that any reasons, however legitimate, for less than perfect quality are just excuses. "The customer wants perfect quality, not excuses. If we cannot provide perfect quality, we have no one but ourselves to blame," he said. While listening, I was casually leafing through the notebook that the consultant had handed out to the class. It contained copies of his slides. When I noticed that some of the pages in the notebook were filed upside down, I said to myself, "Hmm. I wonder if he looked at the notebooks before handing them out?" I guessed he had not. Suddenly, I noticed that every slide in the book included the name of the company I was working for — *and it was spelled incorrectly!* This was inexcusable, especially from a person who preached customer expectations of perfect quality. Some of the attendees also noticed the errors and just shook their heads.

I knew this consultant from prior professional meetings that we had attended together. During a break, I took him aside and showed him the incorrectly filed pages and gave him the correct spelling of the name of my company. In response to the misspelled name, he said, "My word processor doesn't have a spell checker," and his reason for the upside-down pages was, "That damned secretary of mine! I'm going to have to talk to her." How committed was he? How much credibility did he have with the class?

Frank Layden, president of the Utah Jazz and a man with a super sense of humor, talked about a former player: "I told him, 'Son, what is it with you? Is it ignorance or apathy?' He said, 'Coach, I don't know and I don't care.'"

COMMUNICATION

In the 1980s, when I was working for a fairly large company, I had the privilege of attending a series of lectures by one of the masters of transactional analysis, Abe Wagner. The one thing that has stayed with me from those lectures is a cliché that Abe used: "Say it straight, or you'll show it crooked."[2]

This little cliché struck a chord in me, and I have used it in my dealings with people in my business life as well as in my personal life. How often are people reluctant to say what is really on their minds? Quite often. This is true at work and at home. Most people have worked for a manager who did not approve of the work habits of one of his or her direct reports, but did not feel comfortable having a talk with the individual. One manager may avoid the person, while another may resort to making snide comments. The employee senses that something is amiss and begins to feel uncomfortable. Pretty soon, the body language between the two is almost deafening, and rumors begin to fly. All this confusion and uncertainty just because the manager didn't "say it straight."

This approach must be tempered with some care and sensitivity. One could choose to tell the truth blatantly — and be honest to the point of being rude. That could result in hurt feelings, giving rise to a completely different set of problems. This is not the intent. Honest thoughts and opinions must be conveyed in a professional manner. In the medical profession, for example, this is what separates good doctors from good medical technicians — their bedside manner. On the home front, look at the number of marriages that end up in divorce because the husband and wife cannot effectively voice their thoughts and feelings.

In some cases, people say what they need to, but not very clearly. To avoid potential antigravity situations, clear and specific communication is a must. Take, for example, one of the most commonly used terms at work — ASAP! We tell our suppliers, "I need this as soon as possible," or your boss could ask you for a report "as soon as possible." Think about what this term *really* states. We are telling the supplier, "I need this soon, and I need you to send it to me as *soon* as it is possible — for *you*." The time frame that is *possible* for the *supplier* may not be *soon enough* for *us*. If we need something in a hurry, we must know *when* we absolutely, positively *must* have it and we must communicate that to the supplier.

The following conversation between a buyer and a supplier is quite typical.

Buyer: "Jim, I need an assembled power panel in a hurry. I am mailing the P.O. to you today." *(What does "in a hurry" mean?)*

Supplier: "Okay, Bob, I'll start working on it ASAP." *(When will Bob have the power panel? Who knows?)*

Later that day, Bob's boss comes by his office and asks, "Hey, Bob, have you ordered the power panel yet?"

"I sure did, boss. Jim said that he'll start working on it ASAP," Bob was quite happy to tell his boss.

"When did Jim say that we can have the panel?" the boss asks.

"He didn't," Bob replies.

"But Bob, we need it when we start work on Monday. We need the panel at our doorstep by 9:00 a.m. Did you explain that to Jim?" The boss is now moderately concerned.

"Uh, no, I didn't. But I did tell him we need it in a hurry. I trust Jim," says Bob, squirming a bit in his chair.

The boss, now visibly disturbed, says "Please call Jim and tell him we need the panel by 9:00 Monday morning. If he has other things that he is working on for us, reschedule them to make time for the panel. The priority on the panel is not ASAP, it's STP!"

Bob asks the obvious question: "What's STP?"

"Sooner than possible. We need to rearrange Jim's priorities."

ASAP is just one example of the vague terms we commonly use at work. Here are some others:

- "You will have this part next week, for sure." (Next week has five work days. *When* next week?)
- "I'll call you first thing tomorrow morning with a good estimate for the cost of the part" (When would that be? Some people start work at 9:00 and others start at 7:00.)
- "Boss, I'm about 90% done with this project. I just need a couple of weeks to wrap it up." (We say this even when we don't know what

constitutes 100% of the project. Ever wonder why the last 10% of many projects takes about 90% of the time?)

■ "I've got 90% of the cost figured." (Does this mean that I can just add another 10% and get the total dollars for the part? Hmm.)

This may seem like splitting hairs, but what is the real purpose of making such statements? The only purpose served is to get the immediate pressure off one's back or to buy more time to accomplish the task. Such statements shed absolutely no light on why a project slipped in the first place or what can be done to avoid such a slippage in the future. Furthermore, they do not really instill any degree of confidence in the recipient that the task will get done per the revised "promise." Yet, we continue to make such statements and recipients continue to accept them with a simple "Oh, okay."

Setting objectives is another activity where some people experience verbal diarrhea. How often does the verbiage used to report on the status of an objective exceed the number of words it took to formulate the objective? Invariably, the status does not really indicate where the objective stands and seldom sheds light on when it will actually be accomplished. Very often, the status report ends up being a list of reasons or excuses why the objective is not yet complete.

This results mainly from objectives that have not been stated properly. Many years ago, I learned that an objective must specify a "what" and a "when." Think of it as the crosshair on a gun. This is not to imply anything about the fate of someone who misses an objective. An objective must state very clearly *what* task needs to be accomplished and *when* it needs to be completed, so that when the target completion date is reached, the status of the objective is stated as a simple "Yes, the objective was met" or "No, the objective was not met." This constitutes clear communication.

This brings to mind a joke that applies to communication. A doctor calls his patient on the telephone: "Mr. Smith, I have received the results of the tests we performed on you. I have some good news and some bad news."

"Okay, doc, give me the good new first," the patient says.

"Mr. Smith, you have two days to live."

"Doc, if that's the good news, what's the bad news?"

"I forgot to call you yesterday!"

COMMON SENSE

The best piece of advice pertaining to common sense is to *use* it. Sometimes we get so wrapped up in what we are doing that we forget to check if the results we arrive at are reasonable. Time and time again, I have witnessed individuals using a mathematical formula, a forecasting algorithm, or a software package to help them solve problems and accept the answers as gospel. Answers must be checked for "reasonableness" — they must pass the "smell test."

Returning to the home front, let's say you decide to thaw salmon filets for dinner one night. Once the fish has thawed, if it smells bad, it is highly advisable to throw it out and change the menu — or plan a family outing to the emergency clinic. Similarly, if the results of a forecasting algorithm or software to plan material requirements do not fall within the realm of common sense, if they don't smell right, they must be questioned and altered. It could be that economic conditions have changed and the forecasting algorithm is insensitive to them. It could be that there is erroneous data in the inventory records of certain parts, which is causing the material planning system to make seemingly illogical suggestions.

In every organization, there are at least a few individuals who seem to be oblivious to common sense. These are intelligent individuals who make rational decisions in their personal lives, but somewhere on their way to work drain themselves of any power of rationalization that they may possess.

The personal experience related below, as ridiculous as it may sound, *actually happened!* It took place about 15 years ago, so the numbers may be a bit off, but the message still rings as clear as a bell.

Personal Experience

We were getting ready to embark on building the first prototype of a newly designed product. The design called for several complex electrical cables. The manufacturing manager, in trying to decide whether to build the cables in-house or to subcontract them, wanted a feel for the workload. The product had to be complete by late June or early July of that year, so in January he asked the manufacturing engineer responsible for the project to estimate by month the number of people that would be required to build the cables in-house.

The manufacturing engineer, using the prototype bill of material, back-scheduled the "need dates" of the cables from the target completion date of the finished product. It just so happened that a few cables were needed early on in the assembly cycle and a few more were needed at the tail end, during final assembly of the finished product. But the majority of the cables were needed in between, roughly a couple of weeks before the product was to be completed. The manufacturing engineer used the PC-based scheduling software that was available to us at the time and presented the manufacturing manager with the following labor requirements:

- 4 people in April
- 64 people in May
- 3 people in June

You will have to trust me when I say that the manufacturing engineer was a reasonably intelligent individual, but it never occurred to him that building the cables could be staggered so that the job could be accomplished with a relatively constant head count from one month to the next. The fact that the cable assemblies could be started in February instead of waiting until April totally escaped him. Common sense didn't have a chance!

CONCLUSION

Few individuals would dispute that the five Cs are essential to the success of any project. Yet we find that most organizations seldom devote enough time and energy to promote them. This is because, psychologically, these characteristics are treated as "soft" issues. They do not fit in with concrete, technical issues that we prefer to focus on, and they are subjective and difficult to measure.

It is my firm belief that if we don't interweave these soft issues into the corporate culture, the workforce simply goes through the motions with the technical issues.

NOTES

1. Rob Lebow and William L. Simon, *Lasting Change: The Shared Values Process That Makes Companies Great,* John Wiley & Sons, New York, 1997.
2. Abe Wagner, *Say It Straight or You'll Show It Crooked,* T.A. Communications, Denver, 1988.

This book has free materials available for download from the
Web Added Value™ Resource Center at www.jrosspub.com.

SECTION II: PRODUCTS AND SERVICES

*When the product is right,
you don't have to be a great marketer.*

Lee Iacocca

4

PRODUCT DESIGN

Intellectuals solve problems; geniuses prevent them.

Albert Einstein

Design engineering is the gateway for all the good things that any manufacturing organization hopes to achieve. An elegant design meets customer requirements and can be used to manufacture products of high quality, using readily available components, in a cost-effective and timely manner.

Design documentation usually consists of drawings, specifications, and bills of material. Drawings stem from the philosophy that a picture is worth a thousand words. Engineering specifications are documents used to convey additional requirements such as test specifications, calibration, and metal coating. A bill of material, in its simplest form, is a list of parts, along with their respective quantities, that are required to build the product.

Of these, the bill of material is the single most important document. It serves as the drumbeat for a host of activities downstream from the design stage. A properly structured bill of material is a powerful tool that an organization can utilize to smooth the flow of parts and subassemblies through the facility. It can also serve to improve productivity and to reduce costs.

Three significant factors that lend themselves to good customer service are low cost, good quality, and on-time delivery. A fourth factor that sometimes plays second fiddle to cost, quality, and on-time delivery is flexibility.

The design of a product has an impact on every one of these factors. Hard-to-get material and components can have an adverse effect on cost and delivery schedules. I call such items "un-obtainium."[1] Likewise, a complicated design can affect the quality of the finished product.

As much as possible, designers should steer clear of exotic components that fall in the "un-obtainium" category. For example, if a part can be made from steel, don't use titanium. Of course, we must be conscious of the environment in which a part will be used. That will have a lot to do with the selection of the raw material. If the environment is noncorrosive, then steel (with a few coats of paint) may be okay, but a corrosive environment may call for material that is more robust. The same applies to machined parts and assemblies. Remember the buzzwords of the 1980s: DFM (design for manufacturing) and DFA (design for assembly)? We don't hear much about them these days. Maybe that band-wagon ran out of gas or had a flat tire along the way. Regardless, these are important concepts. If a part can be assembled using mechanical fasteners or by welding several smaller parts together, then it should not be designed so that it calls for a solid block of metal to be milled. Once again, the application of the product and safety-related issues should be the guide. In some cases, such as wing sections for aircraft for instance, milling a part from a large chunk of metal may be the proper way to go.

Over the years, I have grown to believe that engineers and designers are sometimes prone to show little sympathy or consideration for manufacturers or even customers. Often, engineers fall in love with their design and forget why they designed the product in the first place. It's not so that they can hang it on a wall and say, "What a lovely work of art!" They design a product so that someone downstream from them (the manufacturer) can build the product and someone else farther downstream (the customer) can use it and maintain it.

Traditional mind-sets pertaining to the structuring and uses of bills of material have also kept many organizations from achieving their true potential for improvements in productivity. The objective must be to simplify downstream processes and to eliminate nonvalue-added work — not to blindly comply with tradition. Some of the methods presented in this chapter may seem to be unconventional, but sometimes that's just what it takes to break through barriers that hinder progress.

BILLS OF MATERIAL

In its simplest form, a bill of material is a list of parts, along with their respective quantities, that are required to build a product. Depending on the complexity of the product, the bill of material may be structured to reflect various milestones or subassemblies in the production process. For example, a given length of bar stock may be used to create a machined part, which could be a component of a weldment, which in turn is used in a subassembly, which will

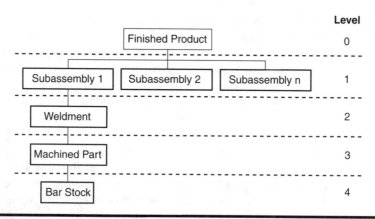

Figure 4.1 Levels of a Bill of Material

be used in the final assembly of the finished product. Each of these parts would appear at a different level on the bill of material of the finished product.

Usually, the uppermost level of the bill of material for a finished product is considered to be "Level 0." Consequently, the subassembly would appear at "Level 1" of the bill of material, the weldment at "Level 2," the machined part at "Level 3," and finally the bar stock at "Level 4." This is shown in Figure 4.1.

Just One Bill of Material, Please!

Many professionals in the field of manufacturing, particularly authors of books on material requirements planning (MRP), go into the definition of the different "types" of bills of material, such as:

- Final assembly bill
- Options bill
- Modular bill
- Phantom bill
- Planning bill

This only serves to complicate the job of defining how the various components of a product go together. Plus, the various *uses* of bills of material are often mistaken for "types" of bills. A bill of material is a bill of material is a bill of material. What is important is how it is used and not the name assigned to it.

Some professionals talk about manufacturing bills as being different from engineering bills because engineers are more concerned about how a product is designed than how it is actually built. These professionals simply accept this as a fact of life! Then, further into the discussion, they go on to preach the benefits of concurrent engineering and teamwork. You can't have both! While it is true that several decades ago the conceptual divide between engineering and manufacturing was accepted as standard operating procedure, and in many organizations this is *still* the case, it is the *wrong approach!* Traditionally, the position of engineering has been: "We will design the product and configure its bill of material, drawings, and specifications as we see fit. How you people in manufacturing choose to build the product is *your* problem." By the same token, the position taken by manufacturing is: "Those people in engineering! They sit in their ivory towers and have absolutely no idea what we have to go through to build to their design. More often than not, we build the product *in spite of* the documentation."

In the 1980s, with the hope of easing the working relationship between design engineers and manufacturing personnel, an interim group of individuals became a popular concept. These people were called manufacturing engineers, and their charter was to act as an interface between the design and manufacturing groups. While the concept behind creating the position of manufacturing engineer is a noble one, some organizations, like the one I was working for at the time, went overboard with it. They created three distinct groups of manufacturing engineers:

- *Advanced manufacturing engineers*, who were expected to work hand in hand with design engineers at the initial design stage of the product.
- *Manufacturing engineers*, whose job was to participate in "make" or "buy" decisions and to generate product routings, time estimates, and process instructions.
- *Sustaining manufacturing engineers*, who were required to "sustain" mature products. This involved participating in efforts to replace obsolete components and tweaking the manufacturing process. In reality, a large portion of their job was to clean up the mess that was handed down to them.

After a couple of years of operating in this manner, without noticing any significant benefits, these organizations were replaced by a single group of individuals renamed simply as manufacturing engineers, who also served as project leaders for specific product lines. Each manufacturing engineer worked as a liaison between engineering and manufacturing and led the effort to improve cost, quality, and delivery.

Any organization that hopes to survive in the 21st century must shed the archaic mind-set relating to the working relationship between engineering and manufacturing. It is imperative for engineering and manufacturing to work together in order to eliminate duplication of effort, confusion, and resultant ill feeling. Teamwork between the two groups has also been demonstrated as one of the better ways to achieve successful results in terms of cost, quality, and delivery. This is how it has to be, and it should not be open to negotiation. A strong, knowledgeable individual serving as a manufacturing engineer/project leader helps ease the way toward achieving this goal.

THE NEED FOR EDUCATION

How does one go about changing a culture that has been ingrained in people's minds for such a long time? My answer is by educating all those involved.

Engineers have to understand why they design a product in the first place. As mentioned before, it is *not* to create a work of art. It is to facilitate the manufacturing, usage, and maintenance of a product.

One way to achieve this is to have design engineers spend time with the planning and procurement groups, along with a short tour of duty on the shop floor, with the manufacturing engineer acting as a chaperone. Every engineer and designer should be required to spend from three to six months, cycling through the various manufacturing disciplines. This approach would give the engineer an excellent feel for how the design and documentation are actually used to plan production, procure parts, and assemble the final product. The engineer would experience the good and bad repercussions of the documentation downstream from the design phase. Armed with this knowledge and experience, he or she would recognize why the traditional approach of tossing the design over the proverbial fence to manufacturing is, at best, counterproductive. The first-hand experience that this approach can provide to the engineer cannot be taught in a classroom.

Manufacturing, on the other hand, must understand that not everything that goes awry on the shop floor is a result of engineering errors. Some of it may have to do with poor planning and/or improper execution of the plan. People in manufacturing also need to have more empathy for the engineers and designers. They need to understand why a design change that they requested yesterday has not been implemented by lunchtime today. Once again, the best way to increase their awareness of the world of engineering is to have them spend time with the engineers. In this case, the tour of duty does not need to be nearly as long as for the engineers in manufacturing. It just needs to be long enough for buyers, planners, manufacturing engineers, and shop supervisors to understand the process and sometimes the research that an engineer needs to go through to implement a seemingly simple change to the documentation. A week or two with the engineers and designers should serve as a good eye-opener for those in manufacturing.

And what should be done with the engineering and manufacturing managers and sometimes their managers who are quick to accept that "these groups are culturally different. They have never worked together and they probably never will"? More often than not, with managers, it is not so much a matter of education as it is a matter of pride. Someone higher up in the pecking order needs to explain some basic facts of organizational life to these individuals. If that does not work, more drastic action is called for.

STRUCTURING BILLS OF MATERIAL

Whatever route is taken to educate the people in engineering and manufacturing, it is critical that both groups learn and understand the role played by bills of material through the entire process, from the design stage all the way through to maintaining the product in the field.

To provide an initial explanation, I will use a recipe from a cookbook. Figure 4.2 shows a recipe for "Spaghetti & Meatballs."[2]

Most cookbooks present recipes in a two-part format. The first part lists all the required ingredients along with their respective quantities. The second part tells you what to do with these ingredients. In its simplest form, a bill of material is the equivalent of the first part of a recipe.

One way to reflect the list of ingredients as a bill of material would be to list each ingredient as a direct component of the finished product, "Spaghetti & Meatballs," as shown in Figure 4.3.[3] In the lingo of bills of material, the ingredients are listed as single-level components of "Spaghetti & Meatballs." This is a typical parts list — a simple list of ingredients required to make the finished product. It really does not tell us anything about how, when, or where each ingredient is used in the manufacturing process.

A more meaningful representation would involve grouping the ingredients logically, as and where they are used. In our example, the bill of material for the finished dish could be structured to reflect three distinct and logical paths, all leading up to "Spaghetti & Meatballs": one for the tomato sauce, one for the meatballs, and one for the spaghetti. The end product of each of these paths will be labeled "Cooked Tomato Sauce," "Cooked Meatballs," and "Cooked Spaghetti," respectively. Each of these items or subassemblies will be a single-level component of the finished product, "Spaghetti & Meatballs."

Spaghetti & Meatballs

1/2 cup bread crumbs	1 tbsp brown sugar
1 egg	1 tbsp Worcestershire sauce
2 oz butter	1 medium sweet onion, chopped
1/2 cup olive oil	14 1/2-oz can diced tomatoes
red pepper flakes, pinch	2 stalks celery, finely chopped
1/4 tsp ground cumin	3/4 lb ground beef
1/4 tsp ground coriander	1/2 cup beef broth
1 1/2 tsp Hungarian sweet paprika	salt and pepper to taste
1 tbsp dried oregano	6 qts water
1 1/2 tsp minced garlic	1/2 lb spaghetti
1 1/2 tsp fresh mint, chopped	fresh parsley sprigs, to garnish

Meatballs: Combine the ground beef, half the chopped onion, egg, cumin, coriander, garlic, chopped mint, and 1 1/2 teaspoons salt. Mix thoroughly while ensuring that you take the appropriate safety precautions for handling raw eggs and meat.

  Note: You may want to fry a small sample meatball to taste it for seasoning. Adjust seasoning, if necessary.

  Shape the mixture into 6 meatballs. Roll the meatballs in the bread crumbs. Heat the olive oil in a skillet and fry the meatballs until golden brown. Bake in oven at 350° for 20 minutes. Check that meatballs are done to taste.

Sauce: Melt the butter in a pan on medium-low heat. Add the celery and the remaining onion and cook until they are translucent. Add the tomatoes, oregano, paprika, red pepper flakes, Worcestershire sauce, salt, and pepper. Cook for 5 minutes. Add the beef broth. Simmer for 45 minutes, stirring occasionally. Stir in the brown sugar. Allow the sauce to cool, then blend until smooth.

Spaghetti: In a large saucepan (8–10 quarts capacity) bring 6 quarts of moderately salted water to a boil. Add the spaghetti, bring back to a boil. Cook until the spaghetti is al dente. Drain the water.

To serve: Warm sauce while the spaghetti is cooking. Serve meatballs with spaghetti and cover with sauce. Garnish with parsley sprigs.

Figure 4.2   A Typical Recipe

Let's begin with the tomato sauce. Based on the instructions in the recipe, we begin by cooking the flour in some butter, followed by the beef stock, tomatoes, tomato paste, sugar, and tarragon. This concoction is then seasoned with salt and pepper and allowed to simmer. The end result is the subassembly, "Cooked Tomato Sauce." Since there are no logical subassemblies under "Cooked Tomato Sauce," its bill of material is a simple list of each required ingredient, with its associated quantity (Figure 4.4).

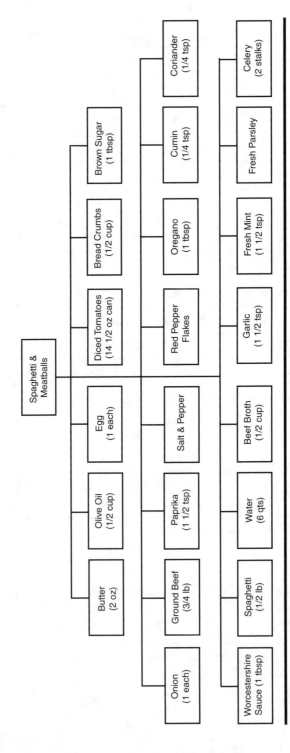

Figure 4.3 A Single-Level Bill of Material for "Spaghetti & Meatballs"

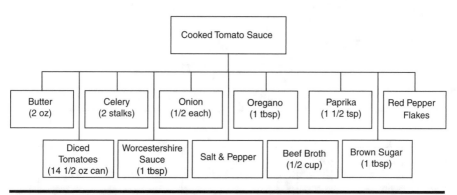

Figure 4.4 Bill of Material for "Cooked Tomato Sauce"

Moving on to the meatballs, per the instructions in the recipe, the ground beef is mixed with several ingredients. The mixture is shaped into meatballs, which are then rolled in bread crumbs, browned in oil, and baked, resulting in "Cooked Meatballs." Each of these steps can be viewed as a milestone or a subassembly, and the bill of material for "Cooked Meatballs" could be structured as shown in Figure 4.5.

Finally, the third path, for the "Cooked Spaghetti," could be structured as shown in Figure 4.6.

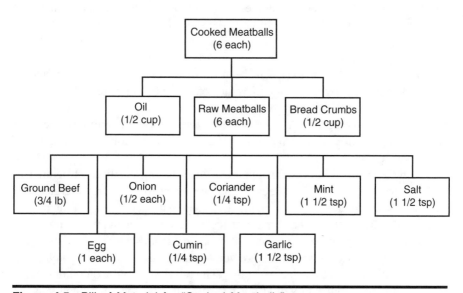

Figure 4.5 Bill of Material for "Cooked Meatballs"

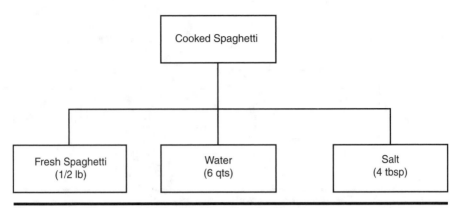

Figure 4.6 Bill of Material for "Cooked Spaghetti"

The bill of material of the finished product, "Spaghetti & Meatballs," incorporating these subassemblies, is shown in Figure 4.7.[4]

By structuring the bill of material in this manner, several options become available. For example, you may choose to make the "Raw Meatballs" and the "Cooked Tomato Sauce" ahead of time and freeze them in portions that are enough for one family meal. Now that each one is identified as a separate subassembly, it can be "stocked" under its own part number. On days when you want to serve "Spaghetti & Meatballs" for dinner, you could thaw the meatballs and sauce and do just the final cooking (or final assembly) before serving with spaghetti. Just before serving dinner, you could roll the meatballs in bread crumbs and brown and bake them while the sauce is warming and the spaghetti is cooking. The total time to prepare the dinner for this evening would be reduced significantly.

Viewing the bill of material in the form of a tree diagram, as depicted in Figure 4.7, makes it easy to identify the total number of levels (four in this case), along with the different levels at which the various ingredients are used. However, for ongoing use, a more portable format is the commonly accepted *indented bill of material,* which provides the same information in a tabular form, as shown in Figure 4.8.

Another benefit that becomes apparent once the bill has been structured in a logical form is that you can decide what you want to make from scratch and what you would prefer to buy premade. Let's say that after looking at the recipe, you decide that making the tomato sauce is just too much work. You may choose to buy prepared sauce instead of making it from scratch. The equivalent in the production world would require you to change the "make" or "buy" code for the "Cooked Tomato Sauce" to "buy." The bill of material would not change as a result of this, but you would not need to purchase the components of the

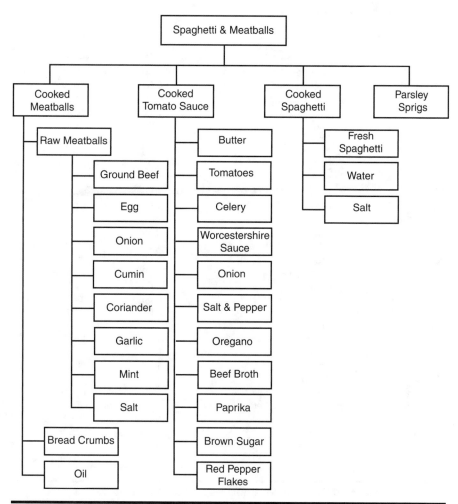

Figure 4.7 Structured Bill of Material for "Spaghetti & Meatballs"

sauce. The material planning system would recommend a planned purchase order for the "Cooked Tomato Sauce" instead of a planned work order.

ACCURACY OF BILLS OF MATERIAL

Many authors and professionals in the field of production and inventory management recommend that bills of material be "at least 98% (or some number close to it) accurate" to enable proper planning. Forget it! That's like being

Level	Component	Quantity	Unit of Measure
0	Spaghetti and meatballs	1.00	each
.1	Cooked meatballs	6.00	each
..2	Raw meatballs	6.00	each
...3	Ground beef	0.75	pound
...3	Egg	1.00	each
...3	Onion	0.50	each
...3	Cumin	0.25	tsp
...3	Coriander	0.25	tsp
...3	Garlic	1.50	tsp
...3	Mint	1.50	tsp
...3	Salt	1.50	tsp
..2	Bread crumbs	0.50	cup
..2	Oil	0.50	cup
.1	Cooked tomato sauce	1.00	each
..2	Butter	2.00	ounces
..2	Diced tomatoes	14.50	ounces
..2	Celery	2.00	stalks
..2	Worcestershire sauce	1.00	tbsp
..2	Onion	0.50	each
..2	Salt and pepper	1.00	tsp
..2	Oregano	1.00	tbsp
..2	Beef broth	0.50	cup
..2	Paprika	1.50	tsp
..2	Brown sugar	1.00	tbsp
..2	Red pepper flakes		pinch
.1	Cooked spaghetti	1.00	each
..2	Spaghetti	0.50	pound
..2	Water	6.00	quarts
..2	Salt	4.00	tbsp
.1	Parsley		garnish

Figure 4.8   Indented Bill of Material for "Spaghetti and Meatballs"

slightly pregnant. Bills of material are either accurate or they are not. They need to be accurate. It is not that hard. It is understandable that the bills of material may be "iffy" while the product is being designed and the first few prototypes are being built, but once a problem with the bill of material has been identified, there is no justifiable reason why it should not be corrected promptly. Lack of time is often the excuse given for not correcting a bill of material. It is just that — an excuse. The real reason is usually either not understanding the implications of *not* making prompt corrections or that changes to bills of material require corresponding changes to drawings and the resources to do that are not available. The second reason is a result of yet another mental paradigm, which

I will address in more detail later in this chapter in the section titled "Changes and Corrections to Bills of Material."

STRUCTURING BILLS OF MATERIAL: IS FLATTER BETTER?

Yes, when it applies to organizational structures, but not necessarily where bills of material are concerned. Unfortunately, in practice, the reverse has happened. Engineers and production planners have attempted to "flatten" bills of material, and managers have justified reasons for adding levels to the organization. Often enough, people even brag about these accomplishments! The reason why engineers and planners prefer flat bills of material is because they help reduce their workload. Fewer levels require fewer unique part numbers and drawings to be created and updated when changes are implemented. This is a good thing for engineering. For production planning, fewer levels translate into fewer work orders and less paperwork. In fact, planners have been known to change the coding of certain "make" parts to "phantom" (explained at the end of this chapter) parts, to flatten the bill even further than engineering did. This method of structuring bills is the brainchild of the "flat bill society."

This tendency results from each group, engineering and production planning, looking at just its portion of the entire process and trying to "optimize" it. Sure, flattening bills does reduce the workload for engineers and production planners. But what about the buyers and shop floor assemblers? Who is looking out for them? They have no means of tweaking bills to their advantage. And who is looking to optimize the entire process as a whole? Very often, no one!

While the concept of phantom parts, if used correctly, can be used to benefit the manufacturing process, getting carried away with it can be harmful to the process.

DOING WHAT'S RIGHT

What's right is what helps to optimize the entire process — from the design stage to maintaining the product in the field.

How we choose to structure and use bills of material determines the degree of pain we wish to inflict upon ourselves as an organization. One option is to rigidly adhere to the "old school of thought" and continue to let engineers structure bills of material (and to let production planners "tweak" them) as they deem fit, without paying much attention to downstream activities. The other is to educate and familiarize all concerned with the production process and to work with them during the definition stage of the bill of material. The latter must be the method of choice. The bill of material for any product is the single most important document relating to the design of the product. It serves as the drumbeat for a host of activities downstream from the design stage. Such activities include:

- Manufacturing and assembly process
- Planning material requirements
- Inventory management
- Ordering spare parts
- Computing product cost
- Addressing cost reductions
- Outsourcing

If used with an open mind (to be explained later in the section titled "Streamlining the Procurement Effort"), a properly structured bill of material can be an extremely powerful tool that an organization can utilize to smooth the flow of parts and subassemblies through the facility. It can also help eliminate a significant amount of nonvalue-added work in the production, planning, and procurement processes, thereby serving to improve productivity and reduce costs. Some methods and concepts that fly in the face of traditional lore but have worked very effectively will be presented.

It should be obvious by now that defining subassemblies can allow stocking parts at different levels in case the decision is made to build certain parts ahead of when they are needed to avoid conflicting capacity requirements or to satisfy demand for spares. Sublevels also give the flexibility to decide whether to make the part or subassembly in-house or purchase it from a supplier. The logical question, then, is how many subassemblies should be configured into the product's bill of material. And the logical answer is as many as are needed to enable achieving the objectives pertaining to cost reduction, quality improvement, adherence to delivery schedules, process simplification, and elimination of nonvalue-added work.

One way to build any product is to provide the assemblers with all the required parts and ask them to have the finished product ready to ship to the customer on a certain date. If the product is relatively simple, such as a ballpoint pen, this approach could work well. However, for a more complicated product, such as a fire engine or an aircraft, chances are that the finished product will not be ready on the target date and it will not be possible to capture the true cost of building it. Also, the process would most certainly force reliance on final inspection to ensure that the various systems in the product (electrical, hydraulic, etc.) operate per their specifications. While this may be a bit of an exaggeration, it is not too far off the mark if the "flat bill society" were to have its way.

Another way, which is a more suitable alternative in my opinion, is to break the work down into discrete subassemblies. This requires the design engineer, manufacturing engineer, and production planner to work with the assemblers, trace the steps in the production process, identify logical subassemblies, and reflect them in the bill of material. Doing so would ensure that each subassembly would be released to the shop floor under a separate work order. The work order would call out just those parts required for that specific subassembly, and the need for searching and sorting through a large pile of parts would be totally eliminated. The process of breaking the work down into smaller segments is called work breakdown structure.[5]

WORK BREAKDOWN STRUCTURE

Work breakdown structure originated with the U.S. government as a project-tracking tool. It is a method for estimating, quoting, and tracking the cost of any project, and a Department of Defense handbook, MIL-HDBK-881, is dedicated to applicable definitions and procedures. It is widely used by the Department of Defense and the aerospace industry.

Work breakdown structure involves breaking a project down into smaller, finite, manageable, controllable tasks that can be easily assigned and tracked. This concept has also worked very well in helping to establish a logical sequence within a production process. Keep in mind that one of the key objectives must be to first *know* the cost of producing a product and then attempt to drive it down — *continuously.* Finite tasks, lasting between 4 hours to 16 hours each, are far more easily tracked than long-running tasks, which result from "flattening" bills of material. The work involved in performing finite tasks is easier to analyze, and areas for potential improvement are readily identified. Furthermore, with a bill of material structured in this manner, key milestones during the production process can be designated for performing in-process inspections. For example, the electrical or hydraulic system on a subassembly of a fire engine can be checked far more easily than the electrical or hydraulic system on the completed fire engine. The network of cabling on a subassembly would be far less complicated than the potential "spider web" on the finished product.

The bottom line is that work breakdown structure is not just for project management anymore. It has a legitimate place in production and bill of material structuring. As a matter of fact, I have witnessed time and again that regardless of how flat the structure of a bill of material is, when the assemblers actually perform the work, they go through a mental work breakdown anyway.

Let's say that using the traditional approach, the engineer and planner will have "flattened" the bill of material for a major assembly, involving more than 100 discrete parts. If these parts are stored in a centralized warehouse, as they usually are, the components required for the work order to build the assembly would have to be picked and delivered to the assemblers on the shop floor, probably on three or four pallets (maybe more, depending on the size of the individual components). Furthermore, the parts would probably not be grouped on the pallets in any logical order. About the only method in the madness would perhaps be to minimize the number of pallets used, which could result in parts being stacked on top of one another. Sound familiar? Once the assemblers receive the pallets of parts, they will:

1. Check the pallets to make sure that they have all the parts they need.
2. Group the parts based on the sequence in which they will be preassembled (or subassembled).
3. Perform the work.

In step 2 above, the assemblers "mentally" break the work down into logical groups. They know from experience that certain subassemblies must be performed before other subassemblies, so they will look for the parts they need for the initial subassembly, pull them from the pallets, and perform the work. Once the initial subassembly is completed, they will follow the same process for the next one, the one after it, and so on, until the job is completed.

This is like sending the assemblers on an Easter egg hunt every time a work order is released. In addition to the fact that several pallets of parts can clutter up a work area and potentially make it unsafe for the workers, this is unproductive work. It is a waste of time and money! Every time a part is touched, its cost increases! Initially, the people responsible for pulling the parts from the warehouse picked the parts, arranged them on pallets, and moved them to the shop floor. Then, for each logical subassembly, the assembler had to do the same thing: look for the parts on the pallets, pull the ones needed first, and set them aside. How much value was added to the finished product? How about zero! And how much cost was added to the overall operation? Your guess is probably as good as mine.

Recall that the engineer and production planner went through a concerted effort to "flatten" the bill of material. The assembler now has to ferret through a pile of parts in order to group them logically and organize the assembly work as it actually happens. The assembler is just following the logical order of things. However large the work order may be (as a result of flattening the bill), the component parts can only be assembled in small groups. The amount of time "saved" by the engineer and production planner is totally negated by the amount of time spent by the assembler just searching and sorting through the pile of parts.

While it is more work for the design and manufacturing engineers, it is work that they would perform *just once*, as opposed to the assemblers having to cherry-pick and trip over components *every time* a massive work order is released.

USES OF BILLS OF MATERIAL

Earlier in this chapter, I mentioned that certain authors confuse uses of bills of material with types, such as:

- Final assembly bill
- Options bill
- Modular bill
- Phantom bill
- Planning bill

It is unnecessary to rehash these concepts. Almost any book on MRP or production and inventory control worth its salt does a good job of explaining these uses. Just keep in mind that that is *all* they are — *uses* of bills of material. The discussion of usage of bills of material here will focus on areas where they have not gained enough popularity.

Streamlining the Procurement Effort

Earlier in this chapter, I stated that "If used with an open mind, a properly structured bill of material can be an extremely powerful tool." Now get ready to open your mind, because the following approach has made many a design engineer cringe.

Let's say that a particular assembly requires six brackets that are similar, but not identical. As a result, each bracket will have its own unique part number. Let's also assume that all six brackets are purchased from a single supplier.

Following the traditional, tried-and-true method of structuring bills of material, the assembly would call out each bracket as a single-level component. This would require each individual bracket to be stocked under its own unique part number, in its own unique stocking location. Furthermore, each time a requirement crops up for the brackets, six line items would have to be specified on the purchase order. When they are received, six receiving transactions would have to be performed, and when a work order is released for the parent assembly, each bracket would have to be pulled from stock and issued separately to the work order.

A preferable alternative to this approach is to "kit" the brackets under one part number, which would be coded as a purchased part. Using a kit in place of the individual brackets would require just one line item to be specified on the purchase order. Also, just one receiving transaction would need to be performed, just one line item for the kit would have to be issued to the parent work order, and the six stocking locations would be reduced to one.

The key to using this concept successfully is to ensure that the kit is never scavenged. Suppliers of such kits need to be provided with packaging instructions, so that the parts are delivered as a kit. Favorite questions from people who have been reluctant to take this approach are "What if we receive a customer order for just one of the brackets?" and "What if someone takes a single bracket from the kit? How good is an incomplete kit?" The answers are quite straightforward. If there is independent demand for a single bracket, it can still be ordered, received, stocked in a temporary location, and then shipped. After all, each bracket still has its own unique part number. Furthermore, once the bracket has been shipped, its stocking location can be used for another part. Pilfering, on the other hand, is a result of a lack of education and discipline. Employees must be taught the importance of maintaining the integrity of a kit, and the proper discipline must be enforced.

Taking It a Step Further

A slightly more involved example relates to purchased components that are similar, but not necessarily used on the same assembly. Let's suppose that there are 45 unique hydraulic hoses that are purchased from a single supplier. Fifteen of these hoses are used on assembly A, 20 on assembly B, and 10 on assembly C. With the traditional approach, each hose would be specified as a single-level component on the bill of material of its parent assembly. How else is an assembler to know where each hose is used? The following five-step approach works like a charm:

1. Kit all the hoses under one part number.
2. Code this part number as a purchased part.
3. Call out the kit under the subassembly that is the first to require any of the hoses in the kit. For example, if assembly B is the first one to be worked based on the manufacturing process, place the entire kit under the bill of material for assembly B.

4. With the traditional approach, all three assemblies would have their respective hoses configured under them as "hard call-outs." With the revised approach, while the assemblies should still include their respective hoses, the hoses should be configured as "referenced items." Coding a bill of material component as a referenced item ensures that MRP and work-order pick lists will ignore it. It also ensures that the assemblers will know which hoses are required on a particular subassembly. Most decent bill of material software packages will allow for this.

5. Include a note on the drawing pertaining to each assembly, to point the assemblers to the part number of the kit (so that they know that the hoses are called out under the kit) and the part numbers of the referenced items (so that they know which hoses are used on which assembly).

In this example, 45 unique hoses were grouped under one part number, the one for the kit. If the hoses are not kitted, 45 unique part numbers must be ordered, 45 receiving transactions must be performed, and the hoses must be stocked in 45 unique locations. Another alternative would be to create three kits of hoses: one for each of the assemblies (A, B, and C) on which they are used. Even that would be a great improvement over not kitting them at all. It is not difficult to see the gains in productivity by incorporating kits in bills of material.

Very often, people think that such an approach is too far off the beaten path. I am a firm believer in persistently questioning the beaten path, and if there is a logical, common-sense approach to achieve the same objective more elegantly, resulting in a lower total cost of operations, then that is a sword on which I would willingly fall. In fact, the common engineering reaction to such methods is, "This does not conform to our engineering documentation standards." My response is simple: "Let's change the standards!"

The concept of using kits was not my idea. One of my colleagues and a good friend, George Cox, who has since passed on, suggested it to me. I tried it, it worked, and since then I have become one of its biggest proponents. Of course, it took a significant amount of browbeating with my friends in the design group to get the ball rolling.

Let's Take It Just One Step Further

At one company where I was employed, the practice of kitting components worked so well that we decided to take it still one step further. This time, it had to do with components of electrical cables and harnesses that were built in-house. The end product required about 70 cables and harnesses during the various stages of assembly. While some of the cables were quite simple, with a connector, strain relief, and a back shell at each end of a long, insulated, multiconductor wire, many called for multiple branches and connectors. We called them octopus cables.

Each time a set of cables had to be built, the assemblers would go to the inventory bin (the components were stocked on the shop floor) and pull individual connectors, contact pins, back shells, and other pieces of hardware that were required. This took a lot of time.

It just seemed logical to store the parts required for each cable in a sealed plastic bag. Each time a cable had to be built, the assembler would pull the appropriate bag of parts and use the bill of material to measure out and cut the required amount of wire, shielding, and insulation. The time required to go through a detailed work order pick list and cherry-pick individual pieces of hardware was totally eliminated.

A couple of meetings with the supplier of the electrical hardware and the engineering group did the trick. The engineers reconfigured the bills of material to call out a hardware kit with a unique part number, as a single-level component of the finished cable. The wire and shielding also were called out as single-level components of the finished cable. While components such as tie wraps, anchors, and sealants were called out on the bill of material, they were not carried in inventory; they were treated as shop supplies and were available at each assembler's workstation. The supplier agreed to "kit" the hardware and to stock the kits in the appropriate inventory locations on the shop floor. Of course, the supplier charged a small fee for that service, but it was a much smaller price to pay compared to what the cherry-picking efforts cost.

This is just one more example of improving productivity by defying tradition.

CAN BILLS OF MATERIAL HELP WITH OUTSOURCING THE FINISHED PRODUCT?

You bet! There are two key areas where a bill of material can help with outsourcing finished products:

- Establishing a "statement of work" for each supplier
- Managing "free-issued" components to suppliers

Before going into the details of each of these areas, it will be helpful to set the stage using a product and a company with which I am intimately familiar. After several years of building a highly engineered and customized truck in-house, XYZ, Inc., which also uses the trucks to provide special services to its customers, decided to concentrate on its core business and stop building trucks in-house altogether.

A thorough search conducted by XYZ, Inc. for a qualified supplier led to the selection of Company A as its primary (first-level) supplier. The core expertise of Company A was building major assemblies along with minor fabrication and machining work. Company A did not have the capability to build the elaborate electrical cables and control panels required on the trucks, nor could it fabricate a customized body for the trucks. For these components, XYZ, Inc. decided to stay with its long-time suppliers, Company B, for the electrical components and Company C for the bodies. A small group of people at XYZ, Inc. were responsible for planning and procurement. In order to avoid the material markup that Company A would charge, they decided to purchase these components from the two suppliers and "free-issue" them to Company A.

Along with the electrical components and bodies, XYZ, Inc. also decided to free-issue expensive purchased components such as the truck chassis and hydraulic equipment. This made sense, because during its in-house manufacturing days, the company had already gone through the negotiations and specifications with the chassis manufacturer and the distributor of hydraulic components. Why pay Company A a 15% markup to simply place a purchase order for these components when XYZ, Inc. could do the same with its existing workforce? XYZ, Inc. had also developed a proprietary computerized data collection system, which it would continue to install, once the finished truck was received from Supplier A.

Now that the stage is set, let's look at how a bill of material can help with outsourcing.

Establishing a "Statement of Work" for Each Supplier

Given that the end product consisted of several hundred subassemblies, some of which were to be built by different suppliers, it was imperative to have a document that identified every supplier's scope of work. XYZ, Inc. decided to represent the bill of material of the truck as a tree diagram, with each box uniquely coded to highlight the responsible supplier.

The tree diagram was created with the help of the major suppliers involved with the project, and they were all given a copy for their records. The advantages of having such a document were quite obvious. All major suppliers were aware of the scope of work for the entire project, along with their share of it. Any potential guesswork was eliminated. Figure 4.9 shows a sample of such a tree diagram, which has been simplified by excluding multiple levels that are not pertinent to the current discussion and limiting the number of suppliers to three. Although the actual version was far more involved, it helped eliminate ambiguity and get the job done!

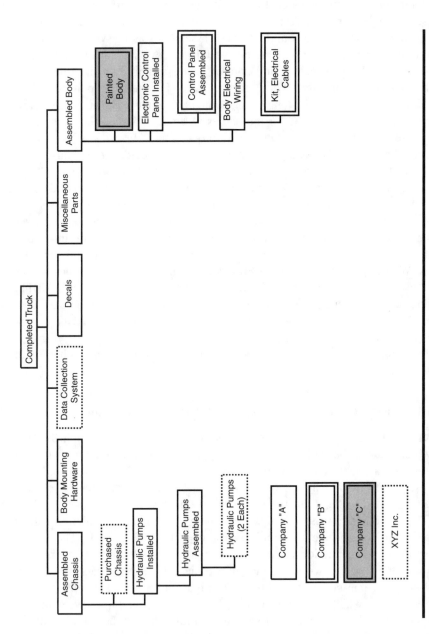

Figure 4.9 Tree Diagram Showing Responsibility of Each Supplier

Managing "Free-Issued" Components to Suppliers

This presented an interesting challenge at XYZ, Inc. Had the truck been sub-contracted to Supplier A on a "turnkey" basis, Supplier A would have been responsible for providing the "Completed Truck" along with every component on its bill of material, and XYZ, Inc. would simply change the "make" or "buy" code for the "Completed Truck" to "buy." But this was not the case. While Supplier A was responsible for a major portion of the truck, bits and pieces within the bill of material were "free-issued" components, which XYZ, Inc. had opted to provide. Replenishments for these components had to be planned using the existing MRP system, and the total cost of the truck had to be readily computable.

XYZ, Inc. used a commercially available MRP system for planning component replenishments. The software was also capable of performing cost rollups to compute the cost of the finished product.

If XYZ, Inc. could only structure the bill of material of the truck to reflect the current outsourced configuration, the "system" could then take over and recommend replenishment orders for the "free-issue" components and roll up the cost of the "Completed Truck."

With a little bit of creative configuring of the bill of material, all of the above conditions were met. What is even more important is that the original bill of material of the finished truck was not compromised.

XYZ, Inc. decided to:

■ Create another part number which was identical to the part number of the "Completed Truck" as designed by engineering, but with an additional alpha prefix. For example, if the part number of the "Completed Truck" was 123456, the newly created part number would be A123456.

■ Code A123456 as a "make" part.

■ Create a routing for A123456 that reflects the labor hours required by XYZ, Inc. to install the data collection system and perform an operational test.

■ Include every "free-issue" component as a single-level component of A123456.

■ Code the completed truck, 123456, as a "buy" part and include it as a single-level component of A123456.

■ Assign a cost to 123456 that represents the amount of money paid to Supplier A for its portion of the work.

The resulting bill of material is shown in Figure 4.10.

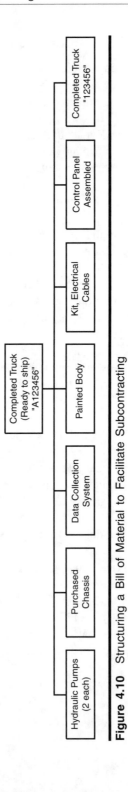

Figure 4.10   Structuring a Bill of Material to Facilitate Subcontracting

By structuring the bill of material in this manner, the following benefits were realized:

■ Since A123456 is coded as a "make" part, it was included in the master schedule and MRP planned replenishment orders for every one of its single-level components — the "free-issue" parts, along with the truck as it is purchased from Company A. This enabled every supplier to be on the "same page" as far as delivery commitments were concerned.

■ The purchase cost of every single-level component of A123456 was known, and the final cost of A123456 could be rolled up without manual intervention or the use of spreadsheets. The cost pertaining to the installation of the data collection system and operational testing was captured by means of the routing for A123456, during the cost rollup.

■ The integrity of the bill of material of the completed truck, 123456, was not sacrificed. The bill of material still represented how the components went together.

■ The planner/buyer had complete autonomy to change the bill of material of A123456 any time a "free-issue" item was added or deleted. He or she could do this without affecting the main bill of material for 123456 and its related documentation.

The only aspect of this exercise that may appear to be not quite kosher is that the cost assigned to 123456 is just what is paid to Supplier A and is not what one might expect the total cost of the completed truck to be. Yet, it reflects reality.

The key to this whole exercise is that *everyone* in the organization must understand what is being done and why it is being done. The people in accounting and customer service in particular must know that even though 123456 is the part number of the completed truck, it is not what is sold to the customer. Instead, A123456 is the product that will be sold.

Sometimes companies modify the main bill of material of the finished product based on how the product is outsourced. This sacrifices the integrity of the bill of material and creates havoc with the documentation each time "free-issue" components are added or deleted. Furthermore, engineering does not need to be involved with making changes to the bill or documentation each time the planner/buyer decides to change the "free-issue" items.

When I first presented this approach to our team, I was accused of "bastardizing" the system. But after everyone agreed to try it out on one product as a "test case," no one wanted to change back. Every future product was configured in this manner. So much for traditionally acceptable engineering standards.

CHANGES AND CORRECTIONS TO BILLS OF MATERIAL

Bills of material and drawings are often referred to as the "documentation package" for a product. Certain changes to a bill of material require a corresponding change to be made to the drawing and vice versa. Bills of material are generally easy to change, while drawings are not. It is those changes to a bill of material that require the drawing to be changed that designers are sometimes reluctant to address with any degree of promptness. This is particularly true when a massive documentation effort is underway or when the design group is short of people.

Any designer worth his or her salt knows that a bill of material cannot always be changed by itself. If the drawing is affected, then it must also be changed. The designer's workload coupled with the effort required to change the drawing usually puts these changes on the back burner. The truth is, there will always be some design-related activity that will *keep* those pending changes on the back burner. In the meantime, production personnel modify the bills of material at the work-order level and make do with redlined drawings. It is in these situations that another concept that is a bit off the beaten path can work.

Traditionally, the "documentation package" pertaining to a product refers to bills of material, drawings, and specifications. Also traditionally, design engineers are reluctant to release these documents to the production floor until all the i's are dotted and t's are crossed. As a result, in an effort to do a thorough job of documentation, production staff have to make do with manual updates to work-order bills of material and with redlined drawings with notes attached to them, a process which is prone to errors.

Some years ago, it occurred to me that if production has to work with sketchy documentation anyway, why not formalize it? With new technology such as document scanners, it would be a simple task to scan a redlined drawing along with any associated notes and store them as formal documents in the computer. A revision level could even be assigned to the documents. This way, the redlined drawings could be easily reproduced and send to suppliers via e-mail if necessary. Later, when the designers had the time, the redlined drawing could be replaced with the corrected version. This was a simple compromise that everyone could live with.

There was, however, no compromising on the accuracy of the bills of material. With this approach, the designers were able to reflect the changes on the bill of material and write in the corresponding changes on the drawing. I like to call this "adequate documentation." It is just enough documentation to get the job done accurately and repeatedly. The procedure worked well, but it took a significant amount of "friendly persuasion" to convince the designers to be a bit less puristic. I even had ISO standards thrown in my face by the engineering group as a reason why this method would not work. Once the process was documented and explained to the auditors, however, they were satisfied.

Once the designers accepted this concept, they in turn took it a step further. In situations where assembly drawings were nonexistent, they suggested taking digital photographs of an actual assembly and filing them in the system with appropriate revision levels.

A True Story

On the first day of a class that I was teaching on production and inventory management, I asked the students to introduce themselves and to briefly explain their job functions. One of the students said, "I am the RTS coordinator at Micro, Inc."

Quite puzzled, I asked him what that meant.

"Oh, I'm the return-to-stock coordinator."

Of course, I couldn't resist asking, "Why do you need to return anything to stock?"

"Well, our bills of material are a bit questionable, and for some components, the planners issue more than what's called out on the bill, just to keep the assemblers from hollering at them. When the product is finally built, my group collects all the 'extras' and returns them to stock."

"Your *group?* How many people are in your group?"

"Including myself, four."

"Have you folks considered correcting the bills?"

"Yeah, but the people in engineering are really busy designing the next-generation product, and they don't have time for this."

I didn't want to hold up the entire class, so I waited for a break to talk to him some more. "So tell me, how does the 'return-to-stock' process work?"

"Well, my group goes through all the components that are left over and tries to identify them. That's the hardest part. We keep telling the assemblers not to throw away the bar-coded labels with the part number and description, but they don't listen. Sometimes we just have to guess at the part number. If the part is incorrectly coded, we catch it while restocking; we compare the part to the ones that are in stock, just to make sure."

"What does your accounting group have to say about this?"

"Not much. It's our department manager who gives us a lot of grief."

"How so?"

"He wants to see a spreadsheet listing the parts along with their respective quantities and costs. If the extended cost of the returns exceeds $1000, he needs justification before he will sign off on it. Needless to say, this keeps us pretty busy."

"You know, I can't believe that *someone* in the organization isn't trying to stop this."

"Actually, our department manager is pretty sick of it too, so he has created a task force to come up with a solution."

"How long has the task force been working on this?"

"About three months."

This individual did not work for a mom-and-pop operation. He worked for a high-tech Fortune 500 company that boasts about being on the leading edge of technology and certified to ISO 9001 standards. Instead of solving the *real* problem, which was incorrect quantities on the bills of material, the symptom was attacked — and the process of returning "extra" components to stock was institutionalized. To make matters worse, the department manager threw good money after bad, by creating a task force to analyze the problem. This is not a problem worth analyzing; it should be a no-brainer to tell the engineering group to correct the bills of material.

PHANTOM PARTS

A phantom part is one that has components that do not necessarily exist in an assembled form. As an example, consider a nut, bolt, and washer. While all three components would be required to fasten two parts together, they would seldom exist as an assembly. However, in the interest of convenience, the three components could be grouped under a "pseudo" part number called a hardware kit, which could be coded as a phantom part. APICS defines a phantom as "a bill-of-material coding and structuring technique used primarily for transient (non-stocked) subassemblies."[6]

Phantom parts differ from conventionally coded manufactured or purchased parts in the way that MRP treats them. If MRP encounters a need for a phantom, it will not recommend planned orders to build it. Instead, it will "blow through" the part and recommend orders for its immediate components. This has the effect of flattening the bill of material.

Coding parts as phantom has proven to be a convenient tool for design engineers and production planners. Suppose a particular combination of a nut, bolt, and washer is used in several subassemblies. If they were configured under a hardware kit, the design engineer would simply add the hardware kit as a component under each of those subassemblies. If they were left as individual components, the engineer would have to add each individual component to every subassembly.

Production planners sometimes code minor subassemblies as phantom. This way, when a work order is released for a parent assembly, the components of the subassembly would be included on the work-order pick list. The subassembly would be made as a part of the parent assembly's work order. This is a time-saving approach for planners because it reduces the number of work orders they have to create.

Caution must be exercised when coding parts as phantom; it is easy to get carried away with this concept. While it is true that it eases the workload for engineers and planners, too much flattening of a bill of material can cause several problems for assemblers, as described earlier in this chapter. The objective should be to optimize the entire manufacturing process and not just bits and pieces of it.

NOTES

1. Many thanks to my friend Sean McPartland for teaching me this term.
2. This is a recipe that I have cobbled together as a sample to explain bill of material structuring; it has little value in culinary terms.
3. I have not specified the quantities of ingredients in cases where they are subjective (to taste, pinch, sprig). Such items can be thought of as "shop supplied" in production terms.
4. Component quantities are not shown in the interest of clarity of presentation.
5. I thank Dr. James E. Ashton and Richard L. Fagan for teaching me this technique, along with several others that I have been able to utilize very effectively.
6. APICS — Online Dictionary

This book has free materials available for download from the
Web Added Value™ Resource Center at www.jrosspub.com.

5

INVENTORY

*One accurate measurement
is worth a thousand expert opinions.*
Admiral Grace Hopper

A simple but important fact that seems to elude many people is that inventory is *money*. It is money invested in raw materials and components required for building and selling finished goods, in order to help the organization make more money.

While in the accounting world inventory is treated as an asset, in the production and inventory management world it can be a liability. The more inventory, the greater the investment required to account for it and to store it in an organized manner, and the greater the chance that it may be lost or damaged or that some of it may have to be scrapped due to obsolescence. To make matters worse, certain components have a limited shelf life. If they are not used in time, they have to be trashed — and that's money down the drain!

HOW MUCH IS ENOUGH?

The eternal question that plagues most manufacturers and assemblers is how much inventory to carry in order to meet production requirements resulting from customer demands. To help answer this question, one must first understand the different types of inventory and the reasons why companies feel obliged to carry inventory. This discussion will address only parts that are components of the finished product. Parts such as shop rags, safety glasses, gloves, and the like, which are usually referred to as "shop supply," are not included. While such parts are used in the production process, they are not components of the finished product.

TYPES OF INVENTORY

Broadly speaking, there are three types of inventory. They have been defined by accounting rules to help differentiate between purchased parts and value-added parts.

- **Raw material**: Includes true raw material such as sheet metal and bar stock, along with purchased components.
- **Work in process**: Typically includes all parts that are being worked on in the shop. All components that have been issued to open work orders would fall in this category.
- **Finished goods**: Any value-added item (labor has been applied) that can be sold. Once a work order has been completed, the part or assembly for which the work order was created is placed in stock under this category.

There are other classifications of inventory, such as safety stock, buffer, distribution, pipeline, hedge, and anticipation inventory, but they are either offshoots or special cases of the three main categories described above. Some of them will be addressed in the discussion of reasons for carrying extra inventory.

WHY CARRY INVENTORY?

One reason to carry inventory is to support production. The other is to support the demand for spare parts.

At home, you need to have the necessary ingredients to cook and serve meals to your family. People often make a trip to the grocery store on the weekend to shop for a week's worth of ingredients based on what they plan to eat during the course of the following week. These ingredients constitute inventory that will be used to make the final dishes. Most of this inventory is made up of purchased ingredients. You may choose to cook the final dish or major components of it and freeze them for use when you lack the time, energy, and inclination to cook. This would constitute an inventory of subassemblies and finished products. Once the dishes have been made and the ingredients have been depleted, the procurement cycle is repeated.

Conceptually, this is no different from manufacturing and assembling products to sell to customers. Parts are needed to build products. What makes this significantly more challenging than planning meals and procuring ingredients to support the following week's menu is that:

- The demand for the finished product and spare parts may not be stable and companies have little control over it.
- The volume and variety of components are much larger. This requires a team of buyers and planners to procure the parts and plan for production.
- Based on sheer volume and the fact that some components may be very expensive, the financial outlay is much higher.
- Components are procured from several suppliers, instead of just one or two.
- Components may not always be available just when they are needed. Invariably, they take longer to procure than most ingredients needed for cooking a meal. If you forget to buy a certain ingredient during a weekend shopping trip, you can always make a special trip to the store at the last minute. This flexibility is often lacking for many components required for production.

In an effort to address these challenges and uncertainties, the general trend in the production world has been to carry more inventory. In fact, the single biggest culprit that causes companies to carry more inventory than needed for current production is *uncertainty* — fear of the unknown! The basic hope is that if a company carries enough inventory, it will be able to meet most demands for the parts. This is subjective, at best.

Other causes for increased inventory levels fall in the "not too smart" category — such as trying to optimize the use of shop resources (people and machines), building components in large lots to spread setup times, purchasing components in large lots to secure a good price, accepting long lead times as a way of life, continuing to operate with poor processes, and tolerating incorrect data.

Ideally, a company should bring in just what it needs, when it needs it, use it up, and begin the cycle over again. However, reality may feel like juggling in a gravity-free environment because life seldom offers ideal situations. Let's address the reasons why companies tend to carry extra inventory and arrive at an approach to reduce it.

Compensating for Uncertainty

Uncertain Demand

We seldom know our customers' true needs, and the picture becomes even more blurred as we try to look into the future. This is particularly true for organizations that build products in anticipation of future customer demand. Customer demand, often referred to as independent demand, is stochastic. It follows the laws of probability and, as such, cannot be computed. As a result, we try to forecast or guess what our customers are going to require from us in the way of finished products and spare parts.

Several techniques are available to forecast such demand, but when all is said and done, we must remember that the end result is still a forecast. I always chuckle when inventory managers are told to arrive at an "accurate" forecast. I do not believe that there is such a thing as an accurate forecast. If by chance the forecast happens to match reality, then I would sooner call it a "lucky forecast."

What I find amazing and dangerous is the number of organizations that use very simple (and often simplistic) forecasting techniques, such as a six-month moving average (assuming that the trend from the previous six months will continue to hold true), and treat the results as gospel. According to an old adage, there are lies, damned lies, and then there are statistics. The results of any forecasting technique must be studied and tempered with a good dose of common sense. It could be that a six-month moving average worked in the past, but economic conditions have now changed, resulting in a significant change in actual demand.

Several extrinsic factors such as economic conditions, new competitors, or a threat of war could affect actual demand. If the forecasting model used is insensitive to such factors, it must be changed or the results must be adjusted manually.

To protect against potential stockouts in case the actual demand in a certain period exceeds the forecast, most organizations carry extra inventory, which acts as buffer stock. This is called *safety stock* and is computed by applying a multiplier to the average variation of actual demand from the forecast. The multiplier, called the *safety factor,* represents the degree of certainty at which the parts are needed in stock. This degree of certainty is called the *service level* and is usually expressed as a percentage. A 90% service level means that nine times out of ten when a part is needed, it will be available. The higher the service level, the larger the safety factor, resulting in a larger quantity of safety stock. This is a universally accepted practice, and it works well if used correctly. There is a danger in using this concept blindly. When the forecast is way out in left field, it is sometimes accepted as a fact of life and the same formula continues to be applied. This is a very effective and speedy way to raise the amount of safety stock and, consequently, inventory levels. Often, we tend to use inappropriate forecasting techniques, which provide unrealistic forecasts, resulting in large quantities of safety stock. Instead of changing the forecasting technique, we switch the forecasting exercise to autopilot and continue to react by changing the level of safety stock. This is *so* wrong! If the forecast is significantly different from the actual demand pattern, we must question why and make appropriate adjustments to the forecast.

Sometimes we become so enamored with the thought of using statistics or other mathematical formulae that we let common sense and good judgment fly out the window. We must review the results of the forecasting algorithm used and, if necessary, alter the forecast and safety stock, using sound judgment and basic common sense.

In some cases, instead of going through fancy calculations for safety stock, the empirical approach can be quite effective. A simple review of the variations between the forecast and actual demand can provide a reasonably good estimate of the amount of safety stock required. My advice is to be stingy. Pick a small quantity for safety stock to begin with, and then review the resultant service level for the next few periods. If the safety stock quantity that was selected was low, then raise it; if it was high, lower it. There is no substitute for periodic reviews of the consequences of one's decisions. Based on the findings from such reviews, appropriate adjustments must be made. We must pay attention to detail. Simply adopting a mathematical formula and letting it run amok is the wrong approach; doing so will offer less than a snowball's chance in hell of making *any* improvements, let alone reducing inventory levels.

Uncertain Scrap Rate

Scrap rate refers specifically to components that are scrapped during the manufacture of a parent part. Some components are more susceptible than others to being scrapped during a manufacturing process. Sometimes it is because of the process involved, and occasionally it is because the components themselves are fragile.

In either case, we must first review the process and attempt to improve it. The objective should be to minimize, if not totally eliminate, scrap. Do not simply accept a poor process and compensate for it by carrying extra inventory.

Traditional teachings suggest assigning a number representing the scrap percentage on the bill of material record where the component is used. The intent is that when material requirements planning (MRP) calculates the component quantity required for production, it would increase the quantity by this percentage to accommodate for the scrapped amount. And oh, by the way, it will do so every time it generates requirements for such components, whether or not they actually are scrapped.

While the logic is quite sound, in practice this is not the most elegant approach. It can be confusing and introduce unnecessary "nervousness" in the system.

Keep in mind that the scrap factor, which is what the above percentage is usually called, is an estimate. It is a guess based on experience with a particular component when it is subjected to a particular process. We do not *know* for a fact that *any* of the components will be scrapped the next time they are used. All we know is that some *might* be scrapped, and we feel obliged to keep a few extra on hand, just in case.

Suppose, for instance, that fewer parts than estimated are scrapped on a particular work order. A few extra components would be left over at the work-station. The correct approach would be to return those components to stock — extra nonvalue-added work! Chances are good, however, that the assembler will throw them in his or her toolbox, just in case they are needed down the road. Now we have an informal stocking location, the toolbox, and no record of the number of components in it.

The point is that the scrap rate, just like independent demand, is stochastic; it follows the laws of probability. If carrying safety stock works for easing the effects of fluctuating independent demand, it should work equally well to compensate for scrap. And it does! Am I suggesting carrying safety stock for a dependent demand item? Am I violating one of the Ten Commandments of MRP? At face value, yes! But it is no different than carrying safety stock for a dependent demand item, which also experiences independent demand, in the way of spare parts requirements. The scrap rate represents a form of stochastic independent demand.

The bill of material should be left alone. If a few components happen to be ruined during the manufacturing process, the safety stock can be used. When the on-hand balance for the component dips below the safety stock, MRP will do its thing by recommending replenishment the next time the program is launched. This is a far more elegant approach than including scrap factors in bills of material.

Uncertain Yield Percentage

It is important to differentiate between yield and scrap. As mentioned above, scrap pertains to a *component*, which could be trashed while manufacturing its parent. Yield, on the other hand, pertains to the *parent*. For example, a 90%

yield suggests that if a work order for a parent part is for 10 units, we should expect to end up with 9 good parts.

Once again, traditional practice has been to include a yield percentage on the inventory record of the part, so that MRP can increase the quantity of the planned order accordingly. In the grand scheme of things, yield is no different from scrap. It, too, is stochastic, and carrying an appropriate amount of safety stock to compensate for it is the way to go.

Of course, the process must first be reviewed and, if economically feasible, modified to raise the yield to 100%.

Optimizing Shop Resources

The traditional mind-set is that shop personnel and machines must be kept busy at all times. In many companies, it is not uncommon to hear statements like "We have the machines in our facility and the people in our employ; since we're paying for both, we must get the most out of them. They must continue to build parts and products." To highlight just how absurd this mind-set is, let's visit the home front again.

When you buy a house, it is quite common (in the United States) to take out a 30-year mortgage. The price of the house usually includes a stove. For all practical purposes, you finance the stove for 30 years and pay for it every month as part of the mortgage payment. So why don't people keep the stove blazing away, cooking their favorite dishes around the clock? Why don't they try to get the most out of their investment? They don't because it makes sense not to. They have no need for all that food, don't have enough space to store it, and couldn't possibly consume it before it goes bad. The reason why people have a stove is so that they can cook their meals whenever they *need* to.

Yet, at work, this minor tidbit of common sense seems to escape us. The reason why we have people and machines in our employ, very simply, is so they can build parts and products *when the parts and products are needed.* They are a means to an end, to enable us to make and sell products that our customers want.

Occasional periods of low activity in the shop are not a cause for alarm. In fact, they can be a blessing in disguise. Periods of low activity are perfect for improving outdated processes and educating the workforce in new skills. This way, during periods of boom, we stand a better chance of filling our customers' needs without excessive hiring. If, however, periods of low activity are the norm, then we have a different problem on our hands. It could be a result of poor resource management, the introduction of stiff competition, or a lengthy downturn in the market, just to name a few. In such cases, we must address the real problem and not the symptom.

Another downside of trying to keep the shop's resources busy is that it can cause confusion in the workplace. I have personally witnessed such situations, one of which I will share.

Example

At one facility, the production level was set to meet the customer requirements. Parts were scheduled to arrive when they were needed, and appropriate work orders were scheduled in time to build the finished products. However, based on the level of customer demand, there was not enough work for all the assemblers. Some of the assemblers were asked to help out with "indirect" activities, such as reorganizing the layout of portions of the shop and performing cycle counts.

During a conversation with the shop supervisor, the general manager made some remarks about the excessive amount of "nonproductive" time that was being reported. Feeling the heat, the supervisor decided to take two courses of action.

First, he approached the production planner and asked him to release work orders for certain electrical control panels in lots of five instead of one at a time. The planner, who wanted to remain on good terms with the supervisor, obliged by releasing work orders for the control panels in lots of five.

A few key components of the panels were not scheduled to come in until much later, when they were really needed, and the released work orders were short parts. The supervisor promptly went to the general manager and told him, "How can I keep my people busy if I don't have the necessary parts to work with?" The general manager met with the planner and buyers and told them to expedite the components with their suppliers.

The components that were being expedited were not very common and could not be expedited at the drop of a hat. As a result, the planner and buyers were frustrated, the suppliers were chasing their tails, and the assemblers were upset with the planner and buyers because the parts were not there. The supervisor continued to report nonproductive time at about the same level, but this time he had a valid excuse: "waiting for parts."

Second, he asked three of the assemblers who did not have any work to help two others who were already working on a major assembly. These assemblers reported their time against the work order that they were "assisting" on. Needless to say, the actual time reported on the work order was more than three times what it should have been. The law of diminishing marginal returns kicked in, and instead of being of assistance to the two main assemblers, the three "assistants" got in their way. *But* they were charging their time to a work order instead of a nonproductive activity.

This company relied heavily on its actual costs to justify price increases with its customers. This is a textbook case of how easily confusion and bad blood can set in among the employees while management tries to keep the workforce busy.

Lot Sizing

I was tempted to dedicate a separate chapter to lot-sizing techniques and write "This page intentionally left blank." But, I need to get this off my chest — so here goes.

For the past several decades, the simple knee-jerk reaction to spreading high setup costs in the manufacturing world has been to build components in large lots. This also applies to purchasing. The message many suppliers convey to potential buyers is: "The larger the quantity you purchase, the lower the unit cost."

With this noble cause taking hold of our thought process, we are sometimes prone to ignore asking certain elementary questions, such as "Do we really need so many components? Are we going to use them in the foreseeable future?" "Do we have the space to store the parts?" "Can we strike a different deal with our suppliers?" "What can we do to reduce the setup costs?" Instead, we have asked: "Given that we have high setup costs, what quantity of this component should we order to help balance the cost of ordering with the cost of carrying inventory?"

This gives rise to several lot-sizing techniques and algorithms. Many of them originated in academia, and I believe that is where they should remain, because most of these algorithms are theoretical and hold very little practical value. Let's take the economic order quantity (EOQ) formula as one example.

The EOQ formula attempts to strike a balance between what it costs to order a component and what it costs to carry it in inventory, given that the demand for that component is uniform and known. For the resultant quantity computed via this formula to be "correct" and meaningful, the following assumptions must hold true:

- The demand for the component must be uniform and known. (*It is not.*)
- The cost to place an order is known. (*It is not.*)
- The cost to carry the component in inventory is known. (*It is not.*)
- The entire order quantity is received at the same time. (*Sometimes it is.*)

Think about it. Three out of four assumptions are guesstimates at best. We lull ourselves into believing that after we have guessed at the demand, the ordering cost, and the carrying cost, we can use this formula to arrive at the "true and correct" order quantity. If we are going to guess at all these variables anyway, why don't we just make an educated guess at the order quantity and skip the ritual?

To further emphasize my point regarding the EOQ approach, let's assume that we know the ordering cost for purchased parts in a hypothetical organization. Traditionally, the ordering cost includes activities such as purchase requisition approval, order placement, expediting, receiving, and receiving inspection. As a result, it is safe to assume that these costs pertain to individual line items on purchase orders. Based on this assumption, let's say that the total annual ordering cost is $100,000. Let's also assume that, based on the annual demand, we expect to place 20,000 purchase order line items during the course of a year. This would translate to an ordering cost of $5 per line item.

Now, let's go back to Chapter 4, where I laid out the benefits of grouping similar purchased components procured from a single supplier, such as hydraulic hoses, into kits. In the example, 45 hoses were grouped as a kit under one part number. Let's also assume that the annual demand for each hose is 50 units. If we were to kit the hoses, we would order 50 kits or 50 line items. If we do not kit the hoses, we would order 45 times 50 hoses or 2250 line items. Thus, by configuring the hoses as a kit, we can reduce the total number of line items ordered by 2200 — a substantial improvement.

Now, instead of ordering 20,000 line items, we will order 17,800 line items. Keep in mind that the employees whose costs are included in the computation of the ordering cost are still employed. Therefore, the total ordering cost of $100,000 does not change. What does change is the cost of ordering each line item. The new cost per line item becomes ($100,000)/(17,800) = $5.62. The line item ordering cost just went up from $5 to $5.62! Is that bad? Should we recompute the EOQ? Given the fixed cost of $100,000 for ordering, should we instead increase the number of line items ordered, just to be able to show a lower ordering cost per line item? Isn't that the approach we take to spread setup costs? Should we lay off some of the people who constitute the fixed cost of $100,000? Should we chastise the employees responsible for creating the kit of hoses and tell them not to let it happen again? I hope you get my drift.

In the Shop

Lot sizing, using any algorithm, just for the sake of spreading setup costs is yet another textbook case of attacking the symptom instead of the real problem. The symptom is that parts need to be built in large lots to spread high setup costs. The real problem is high setup costs. Finding ways to minimize setup times, if not completely eliminate them, is where we should be spending our time and energy. Once we are able to achieve this, lot sizing becomes a nonissue.

Some organizations, probably more so in Japan than anywhere else, take the correct approach. They work hard to reduce their setup costs. They create dedicated setups and sometimes customize the machine that is used to build a part.[1] However, in order to justify this approach, adequate demand must exist for the part. In his book *Non-Stock Production: The Shingo System for Continuous Improvement*, Shigeo Shingo talks about SMED (single-minute exchange of die), where setups that once took four hours can be accomplished in three minutes. Other options that can help reduce setups are simplification of the design of a part and the process used to create it. There are several ways by which setup times can be reduced — but we must first *want* to look for them. We need to take the time and spend the effort to find ways to minimize setups, if not totally eliminate them. Sticking one's head in the sand and accepting that long setups are a necessary evil is not the right answer.

With Suppliers

It is in the suppliers' best interest to encourage buying components in large quantities by offering tempting discounts. The more they sell, the more money they make — it's that simple. It is not unusual for a zealous buyer to accept such special "deals" in an effort to lower the unit cost of each component. Sometimes such deals work in a company's favor, but often enough they do not. If there is not a need for the volume of parts a supplier is offering, then it does not make sense to blindly accept the offer. That would be like a joke I once heard. Jane comes home all excited and tells her husband, John: "Honey, I got a terrific deal at the store today. I bought a hundred pounds of cat food for just ten bucks!" "But sweetheart, we don't own a cat," John reminds her. "Yeah, I know. Now we can get one!"

Several avenues are available to help lower the cost of purchased items while offering suppliers a good chunk of our business. The one that is most effective in many respects involves reducing the supplier base. In many instances, what prevents this is the popular objective of minimizing vendor cost. This objective forces buyers to shop around each time a part needs to be ordered. General practice seems to be to get three quotes and pick the supplier that offers the lowest unit cost. There are two distinct disadvantages associated with this approach. It requires a significant amount of overhead to perform the quoting exercise every time a part is ordered, and it does very little to promote a long-term working relationship with suppliers, resulting in a lack of allegiance from them.

Attempting to minimize vendor cost is a result of a false mind-set that if every component of the total cost of the product (or project) is minimized, then the total cost will also be minimized. This philosophy seldom holds true. The objective should be to minimize the total cost. In this effort, certain components of the total cost, such as vendor cost, may be suboptimized, which is okay. This will be discussed further in Chapter 7.

A good alternative is to reduce the number of suppliers and purchase larger groups of components that are similar or fall within the same commodity from the selected suppliers. For example, all electrical components, such as connectors and back-shells, can be consolidated with two or three qualified suppliers. The suppliers should be made to understand that purchases will be consolidated with them, and in return they are expected to price the components competitively. It is important to understand that for some components, the selected suppliers' prices may be higher than others, and for some, they may be lower. However, the total cost of doing business would be lower. Such an approach would also go a long way in establishing a good working relationship and allegiance with the selected suppliers. Furthermore, it would help minimize the personnel and associated overhead required to obtain multiple quotes.

In such a relationship, it is important not to betray the trust and faith of the suppliers. The old adage applies: "Fool me once, shame on you. Fool me twice, shame on me." Suppliers are not naïve. In turn, they must also understand that the relationship is a two-way street.

Long Lead Times

Suffice it to say that long lead times are a hindrance to flexibility and an organization's ability to respond promptly to the needs of its customers. In an effort to compensate for long lead times, organizations are prone to carrying extra inventory, just in case. This topic is covered in detail in Chapter 6.

Inefficient Processes

These generally lead to high degrees of scrap and rework. The more scrap, the more inventory a company is likely to carry; misery loves company. Inefficient processes often involve nonvalue-added work and result in longer lead times. Scrap and nonvalue-added work have an adverse effect on any company's bottom line. The only correct answer to this problem is to improve the processes. In his classic book *Out of the Crisis*, Dr. W. Edwards Deming clearly explains the causes of variation in systems and processes. If you have not read this book, I urge you to do so.

Erroneous Data

The words of Rob Lebow and William L. Simon come to mind: "What we allow, we teach."[2] If we condone errors and inaccuracies in our data, the message that we are sending is that it is okay. Well, it is not okay. When errors are detected, they must be corrected promptly. But stopping there is not enough. We must identify and solve the problems that caused the errors so that they do not recur. The approach to problem solving should be to "seek and destroy" problems.

The following are a few typical reasons why errors creep into work:

Incorrect Bills of Material

The repercussions of incorrect bills of material are fairly obvious. In addition to last-minute surprises, incorrect parts and/or quantities called out on bills of material can result in carrying more inventory.

Incorrect or incomplete bills of material can only be justified when new product prototypes are being designed and built. Once the design has been established, errors and omissions in bills of material must be rectified promptly.

Incorrect or Missing Inventory Locations

This can only result from sheer carelessness. Some production planners close work orders without ensuring that the parts being stocked have assigned bin locations. Their excuse is that they are in a rush and do not have the time.

This is a typical case where vagueness is introduced instead of eliminated, thereby creating problems. How can anyone be expected to find the parts when they are needed? In fact, if the parts cannot be found, additional orders will have to be placed and rushed through the shop.

Sometimes a part has an assigned bin location, but due to lack of space, the person responsible for physically stocking the part selects another location and "forgets" to change the location in the computer. There is no excuse for such sloppiness.

Incorrect Inventory Counts

This can occur if the parts are not identified correctly or if the proper transactions are not performed. Every part must be uniquely and correctly identified with its own part number. When a part is physically removed from or placed in stock, the appropriate transaction must be recorded in the computer system. Likewise, if a receipt or an issue is recorded in the computer system, it must be followed by the appropriate physical action. This is not hard to do; it just requires the proper discipline.

Several years ago, George W. Plossl presented an analogy between inventory management and financial banking. Banks are nothing more than warehouses for money. They work with just one part, which is currency, but they have several stocking locations for it — the various accounts. What would you say if your banker were to tell you: "We will try our very best to keep your accounts accurate"? Your first reaction would probably be "Huh? What do you mean by *try*?"

We expect a bank not to make errors while keeping track of our money. Managing parts inventory must require the same degree of discipline and commitment as managing bank accounts.

DAILY CYCLE COUNTS

In the "real world," things may go awry and errors can creep in, but this should be the exception and not the norm. However, to keep things honest, it is good practice to conduct frequent inventory audits. An effective method is to count a few parts each day to verify that the on-hand balance in the computer system matches the physical count. This procedure is normally referred to as cycle counting. If the physical counts match the quantity in the computer, great. If not, the discrepancy must be resolved. Once again, the problem that caused the discrepancy must be identified and corrected.

Cycle counting differs significantly from an annual physical inventory, which is performed more for financial reasons, to verify that the total inventory value recorded in the computer system matches reality. An annual physical inventory does nothing to ensure accuracy at the individual component level on an on-going basis. In this respect, with the implementation of a proper cycle counting system, the ritual of the annual physical inventory can be discontinued. Of course, the external auditors would have to be convinced of the effectiveness of the cycle counts. The ultimate objective should be to carefully manage and account for inventory, because it *is* money.

NOTES

1. R.J. Schonberger, *Japanese Manufacturing Techniques,* The Free Press, New York, 1982.
2. Rob Lebow and William L. Simon, *Lasting Change: The Shared Values Process That Makes Companies Great,* John Wiley & Sons, New York, 1997.

Web Added Value™

This book has free materials available for download from the Web Added Value™ Resource Center at www.jrosspub.com.

6

LEAD TIMES

*Do not squander time
for that is the stuff that life is made of.*
Ben Franklin

The lead time for any activity is the time it takes to perform that activity. In production and inventory management jargon, lead time is typically the time it takes to purchase or manufacture a part. If a part is manufactured in-house, the lead time is referred to as the manufacturing lead time, and if it is purchased, it is called the purchasing lead time. Typically, these times reflect the number of days from when an order is placed to when the part is received. While it utilizes a definite start and finish date, this approach sometimes understates the amount of time that it takes to build or buy a part. Lead time should include the time interval between the time it is determined that a part needs to be ordered and the time the part is expected to be available for use. This includes certain administrative activities, which are performed *before* the order is placed. I will refer to the time taken to perform these activities as *administrative lead time*.

In fact, the definition[1] provided by APICS says just that:

1. A span of time required to perform a process (or series of operations).
2. In a logistics context, *the time between recognition of the need for an order and the receipt of goods.* Individual components of lead time can include order preparation time, queue time, processing time, move or transportation time, and receiving and inspection time.

In the APICS definition, what I refer to as the administrative lead time is called *order preparation time.*

Before getting into the components of administrative lead time, let's look at the "traditionally accepted" components of lead time.

COMPONENTS OF LEAD TIME

Purchasing Lead Time

This is quite straightforward. Purchasing lead time is usually the number of days that a supplier would need to furnish a part. It would normally include time for shipping the part.

Manufacturing Lead Time

This is a bit more involved. Traditionally, manufacturing lead time is comprised of five components or activities. They are:

- **Queue**: Time waiting for work to begin
- **Setup**: Time required to set up equipment
- **Run**: Time required to work on the part
- **Wait**: Time waiting for the part to be moved to the next operation
- **Move**: Time taken to move the part to the next operation

By recognizing just these elements of lead time, the tendency is to understate the overall lead time for any part. This is because the inherent assumption is that the work order to build the part has already hit the shop floor or that a purchase order has already been issued to a supplier. However, there are several administrative activities that have to occur either before the order (work order or purchase order) is actually placed or after the parts are received but before they are available for use.

Now let's look at the components of administrative lead time.

Administrative Lead Time

- Compile a "job packet" (work order)
- Pull and issue components from stock (work order)
- Obtain approvals on purchase requisitions (purchase order)
- Receive quotes on price and delivery from suppliers (purchase order)
- Inspect finished/received parts (work order and purchase order)
- Stock parts (work order and purchase order)

Some organizations may include a few of these activities in their lead time calculations, but few recognize all of them.

Let's investigate each of these activities individually.

Job Packet

The job packet consists of documents required to build the product. It usually contains:

- The work order, which specifies the part number, revision level, quantity, and due date
- A routing that specifies the sequence of operations that need to be performed, along with associated times and work centers
- Process instructions detailing specific procedures that must be followed
- A single-level bill of material that lists the components of the part to be built (also referred to as a pick list)
- Engineering drawings and related specifications
- A list of special tooling, fixtures, and/or programs (for programmable machines)

Invariably, the production planner or dispatcher compiles the job packet, and the activity usually takes a few days.

Pull and Issue Components from Stock

Most organizations carry component inventory in a central warehouse. When the production planner releases a work order for a parent part, the warehouse is signaled to pull components from stock by the printing of a pick list. The parts also need to be issued to the work order (in the computer system) for which they are being pulled. Depending on the size of the bill of material, pulling and issuing can take from a few minutes to several hours. Invariably, this time is rounded off into days. Allowing from one to three days for warehouse personnel to pull components from stock, issue them to the respective work orders, and deliver them to the shop floor is not unusual.

Purchase Requisition Approval

Many organizations follow a hierarchy for assigning signature authority to individuals. For example, a buyer may have a signature limit of $1000, while the purchasing manager could have $5000, and so on up the chain. This is especially true while building prototypes, when purchases are made outside the mainstream manufacturing planning system. Depending on the value of the purchase order and the signature limits for the various levels of management, this activity could easily take several days and sometimes weeks.

Receiving Quotes from Suppliers

In an effort to minimize vendor costs, several organizations require their buyers to request three quotes for any part that is to be purchased. Invariably, the supplier with the lowest bid gets the order. This can take several days and is seldom included in the calculation of the lead time of a part.

Quality Inspection

This "ritual" was very popular several years ago. Actually, it was more than popular — it was required. This mind-set is still prevalent in many shops today. Conceptually, it is a policing function designed to ensure that people build parts to specification (in-process inspection/final inspection) and that suppliers ship the correct parts (receiving inspection). This activity usually involves an individual (or a group of individuals) who acts as an unbiased inspector of parts. It is not unusual for the inspection step to take several hours. For machined or fabricated parts, many shops include this as a discrete step in the part routing, along with an estimate of the time required to perform it. This is not commonly practiced for assembly work. Assembly shops generally do not perform quality checks at the subassembly level; they tend to rely more heavily on final inspection of the finished product.

Stocking Parts and Finished Goods

This falls into the same category as pulling parts from stock. While the computer transactions are performed either by the receiving person (for purchased parts) or the production planner (for manufactured parts), the physical act of stocking the components in inventory is performed by warehouse personnel.

Once again, each task does not take much time to perform, but given the fact that these tasks are performed by a centralized group of people (receiving and warehouse), a certain amount of "waiting" time should be expected.

In some shops, the task of moving manufactured parts to stock is included as the last operation in the routing. It is obvious that if these activities and their associated times are not included in the calculation of lead time, the result could be understated by days and sometimes weeks. Realistic time estimates must be included for these activities in the lead time for the part, in order to be able to plan its requirements without ugly surprises. Yet, more often than not, many of them are ignored.

pletely subcontracted with one supplier. As a result, each potential purchase order for a quantity of five or six of the end product would easily add up to several hundred thousand dollars, which was very close to the signature authority of the local vice president. When the individual purchase orders for the drop-ship parts were added in, the vice president's signature limit was easily exceeded. Keep in mind that once a requisition for the end product was approved, the procurement of the drop-ship parts was a necessity. Therefore, it would make sense to combine all the requisitions into one big requisition for the end product and drop-ship parts, thereby simplifying everyone's life in general and the planner/buyer's life in particular. Sadly, we were not able to sway the vice president's opinion on this. The amount would definitely exceed his signature limit, requiring the requisition to be sent higher up to the corporate office.

This required our group to submit several requisitions with the same end product requirement as justification. Just the act of writing the requisitions was quite time consuming. Add to that several telephone discussions with individuals higher up in the organization, reminding them to approve the requisition and verbally explaining the written justification, and a couple of weeks would fly by in a hurry. Oftentimes, we found ourselves within the lead time of the end product and the requisition would still be sitting on someone's desk.

The informal system that took over was that the purchase orders were placed while the requisitions were going through the approval chain. Never once was a requisition turned down. How effective was this procedure? We were just going through the motions and creating busy work.

Receiving Quotes from Suppliers

Several organizations exhibit a penchant for minimizing vendor costs. In this seemingly noble effort, buyers are required to get quotes from different suppliers (usually three), and the lowest bidder usually gets the purchase order.

Anyone who has witnessed or participated in this activity will tell you that at best it is painful! The greater the number of components that a buyer is responsible for, the higher the level of pain. Pretty soon, the buyers end up requesting clerical help to accomplish the task. Before you know it, a small army of people could be working toward minimizing vendor cost. This is how things were at one of the companies where I worked. There were purchasing clerks, buyers, senior buyers, and purchasing agents, all marching toward the objective of minimizing vendor cost. It did not require fancy multivariate analysis to figure out why overhead was as high as it was. As a result, the product cost also began to soar. This is equivalent to stepping over dollars to pick up pennies or, as the British say, being penny-wise and pound-foolish.

The objective of minimizing vendor cost is wrong. A far more meaningful objective is to minimize the *total cost* of the finished product (or project cost), thereby optimizing the cost of the entire operation. With regard to material cost (or vendor cost), this can be achieved by:

- Consolidating the supplier base into a small, select group of suppliers that are willing to meet the requirements for cost, quality, and timely deliveries
- Contracting with these suppliers to provide certain types of components (e.g., hydraulic, electrical, hardware, etc.) based on their capability

The point to keep in mind is that while no supplier may offer the lowest price on *every* component, the overall cost of doing business would be optimized, because with fewer suppliers, fewer people would be needed in the procurement group. This also clears the path for writing multiline purchase orders for parts purchased from the same supplier, thereby reducing the number of purchase orders that have to be written. Of course, each supplier should know that you reserve the right to test the waters periodically to ensure that you are getting a fair deal. Once such relationships have been established, the need to obtain quotes each time a purchase order has to be placed is eliminated.

What would you do if you moved into a new neighborhood? You would probably try out the different grocery stores nearby. After a few shopping trips, once you have a good feel for the quality, variety, and prices at the different stores, you would probably decide on one or two select stores where you plan to do most of your shopping for groceries. Imagine how painful it would be if you shopped at one store for onions, another for potatoes, and so on.

Quality Inspection

Some organizations still believe that they need someone to check other people's work. They are convinced that this is the only way to go. The short answer to that is, it is not! It is just another good way to add unnecessary overhead.

For purchased parts, suppliers must be made responsible and held accountable for ensuring that what was ordered is what they deliver and that it works. This becomes much easier once the supplier base has been consolidated, assuming, of course, that the right suppliers were selected.

For work performed in-house, the responsibility and accountability must lie with the shop workers (machinists, fabricators, and assemblers). In-process quality checks should be performed by the shop workers, not by a cop! To keep from getting carried away with this, the complete production process must be reviewed and key milestones identified for inspection. Several organizations skip the in-process inspections and rely heavily on final inspection of the finished product. For these organizations, a successful final test provides a warm, fuzzy feeling and ensures that the product works like it is supposed to. My question to them is "How would you perform final inspection if you were building torpedoes?" Enough said.

Do you perform in-process quality checks when you cook for your family? Sure you do. It is only natural to taste the food as you are cooking it and to adjust the seasoning. You probably also check the meat to make sure it is done the way you know your family likes it.

A story about Sally and Jerry illustrates that inspection can help only up to a point. Sally does most of the cooking for her family and usually does a very good job of it. However, on a few occasions, Sally has been known to burn something. Stuck very prominently on the door of the microwave oven is a placard that her husband, Jerry, gave her. It reads: "Dinner will be ready when the smoke alarm goes off." This is a classic example where final inspection cannot help you correct the problem.

Stocking Parts

Given the fact that this activity traditionally is performed by a specific group of individuals (warehouse and receiving personnel), a certain amount of waiting time is to be expected. Toss in the other traditional mind-set of stocking parts in a centralized warehouse (usually some distance from the shop), and the time to stock parts can be quite significant. Once again, zero value is added when parts are moved from the shop (or receiving station) to the centralized warehouse, only to be moved back to the shop floor at a later date.

The earlier suggestion to carry parts at their point of use works very well to virtually eliminate the time required to stock parts. What becomes important here is the assignment of responsibility to move the parts to their respective points of use. For purchased parts, when possible, the supplier must be made responsible for delivering the part where it is to be stocked. However, in many cases, suppliers ship parts by a common carrier and this option is not feasible. In such cases, the person(s) responsible for performing the receiving transactions must be the responsible entity. For manufactured parts, the assembler, fabricator, or machinist who completes the part must be made responsible to deliver the part to its point of use. Once again, depending on the size and weight of the part, some assistance may need to be provided to this individual.

A special case arises when a part (purchased or manufactured) experiences independent demand. In this case, the part must be moved from its "normal" stocking location on the shop floor to the next logical point of use (the shipping area) for packaging and shipping to the customer. The responsibility for the move can lie with either the assembler responsible for the stocking location on the shop floor or a person working in the shipping area.

In all of the above cases, the computer transactions must be performed either by the receiving person (for purchased parts), the production planner (for manufactured parts), or the customer service person (for parts moved to shipping).

What is presented in the preceding paragraphs is a different way to approach traditional processes and procedures that often seem to be taken for granted. Perhaps the traditional methods were legitimate at an earlier point in time, but they must continually be questioned to determine if they still make sense. If an elegant alternative is available, then it must at least be given a fighting chance instead of assuming that it will not work or that there is no need to change the way something has always been done.

MINIMIZING TRADITIONALLY ACCEPTED COMPONENTS OF LEAD TIMES

Now let's examine ways to reduce the more traditionally known elements of lead time: queue, setup, wait, move, run, and vendor (or purchasing) times.

One can hardly pick up a book on inventory management and not read about the evils of queue time, setup time, waiting time, and move time. Not one of these elements serves to add an iota of "value" to a part. Experience has also shown that they can comprise anywhere from 60 to 80% of the total manufacturing time for a part. It only makes sense to investigate ways to minimize if not totally eliminate them.

Let's look at these nonproductive elements to understand them and see what we can do to reduce them if not totally eliminate them.

Queue Time

What is a queue? What causes queues to exist? Very simply, a queue is a waiting line. In our personal lives, we stand in queues for all sorts of things. We stand in queues at the post office, at an ice cream parlor, at a bus stop, and at an airport boarding gate. We queue up to obtain a product or service. The reason why we have to stand in line is because the number of people wanting the product or service exceeds the number of people providing it. As a result, we have to wait our turn.

How does this pertain to manufacturing? Why does a part have to wait in queue to be worked on? Three reasons come to mind:

1. The work order for a part or assembly is sent to the shop before its time. We knew that we did not have the resource to work on the order, but we sent it on anyway.

   I cannot think of a single good reason why people do this. Could this be the origin of what some gurus call the "*push* system"?

2. The work order for a part is sent to the shop at the proper time, but the machine or assembly station has fallen behind, and the part has to wait in line. This could also happen if a machine breaks down unexpectedly or an assembler does not show up for work.

   We must understand why the machine or assembly station fell behind in the first place and then try to keep it from happening in the future. Asking employees to submit requests for vacation time and adhering to a preventive maintenance schedule for machines will also help minimize surprises. Of course, as in all walks of life, things tend to go bump in the night on the production floor too. These occurrences should be few and far between and must be handled individually. It is all part and parcel of juggling without gravity!

3. The work order is for a large batch of parts, and while each part is being worked on, the rest have to wait in line.

   This one merits more paper and ink than the first two. I could be glib and say "Change your lot size to one." But then you probably wouldn't read another page of this book. Shigeo Shingo calls the delays in the first two scenarios above *process delays* and the third *lot delays*.

Let's examine *why* the work order is for a large batch of parts. For purposes of discussion, let's assume that the batch size is ten parts, although realistically, ten would represent a tiny batch in many production facilities.

Is there a short-term demand for ten parts? If all ten are built now, will they be used in the next few days or weeks? If ten are built, will other parts that are also needed be delayed because the machine or assembler is busy building ten instead of two, which is what is really needed right now? If the answers to these questions are "yes," "yes," and "no," respectively, then by all means build ten. However, if other critical parts are going to be delayed, then build just the two that are needed right now.

Any time the decision is made to build components in lot sizes other than one, some additional factors must also be considered. For instance, is the design of the part mature? Is the process that is used to build the part stable? If the answer to either question is "no," then there is a risk of making nonstandard parts which may require rework or may even be scrapped. In such instances, it is best to stick to a lot size of one or what is needed immediately.

Returning to the question of short-term demand for a part, if it does not exist, we have to question what "inspired" the selection of a lot size of ten. There are all kinds of reasons: "We have this expensive five-axis mill and we can't let it sit idle." "The setup involved with this component is quite elaborate, and spreading the setup cost over ten parts is cost efficient; besides, we hope to use these parts some time during the course of the year." "Based on how much it costs to place an order and the cost to carry the part in inventory, ten is the *computed, most economic* lot size." Sound familiar? These are more examples of rigid, archaic mind-sets. We simply *accept* as a fact that the setup times are high and we increase lot sizes to spread the setup time over several parts. Very little thought is directed toward reducing the setup times.

Setup Time

As the term suggests, this is the time it takes to set up a machine, workstation, or fixture so that a part can be manufactured. Several companies in the Western world, regardless of their size, treat long setup times as a way of life and a necessary evil. They pay little or no attention to shortening setups or eliminating them. They assume that since their setup times are high, they have to build parts in large batches; that way, the setup time is spread over several parts, resulting in a lower part cost and a lower operating cost for the company. Instead, they should address the *real* problem. They must question why the setup times are high and find ways to reduce them if not totally eliminate them. Some organizations do this, but many do not.

Wait Time

Once again, we must question why a part has to wait. One reason is that the part is being manufactured in large lots, and by definition, the first part made would have to wait for the remainder of the lot to be completed. In this case, the earlier discussion under queue time applies.

Another reason for a part to wait could be that the shop has a centralized dispatching function, a group of material movers whose responsibility is to move parts from one machine or assembly station to the next. This is no different from the centralized warehouse scenario and can also act as a bottleneck. In most cases, requiring the machinist, fabricator, or assembler to move the parts works very well. In cases where the size or weight of the part requires the use of a forklift, this person may require some assistance.

Move Time

Any time a part needs to have multiple operations performed on it, a certain amount of time will be required to move the part. Traditionally, move times associated with parts that require machining and/or fabrication have been lengthy. There are two reasons for this:

1. **Shop layout**: Several machining and fabrication shops are organized functionally. Milling machines are usually located in the "milling department," lathes in the "lathe department," and so on. Depending on the number of operations to be performed on a part, such a shop layout forces the need for the part to be moved several times and often over long distances. In such instances, lengthy move times are preordained. The seemingly simple solution would be to change the layout of the shop so that the machines are arranged to reflect the most common processes followed in the shop. I said seemingly simple because it would really depend on the volume of production, the uniformity of demand, and the number of available machines. Smaller shops with sporadic demand patterns may not be able to afford this luxury, but then again, smaller shops would not have their machines spread out over a large area.

2. **Method used to move parts**: Depending on their size and the volume of production, different organizations use different methods to move parts and products through the shop. Major manufacturers of automobiles, for example, use a moving assembly line for the automobile, with conveyor systems to deliver components to the line, while some large-scale machine shops utilize Automatic Guided Vehicles (AGVs). In contrast, smaller shops with relatively low production volumes utilize manual methods such as forklifts or pallet jacks.

   In some special cases, such as large commercial aircraft, it is not feasible to move the product through the shop during the various stages of assembly. For such products, it is much easier to move people to the product instead of moving the product to the people. This also makes sense for other relatively large products such as fire engines, where the relatively low volume of production does not justify an automated, moving assembly line.

It is obvious that reducing the number of nonproductive activities does not require a rocket scientist. The hard part is that it requires patience, perseverance, and the right attitude.

Run Time

While run time is traditionally not considered to be time spent performing a nonvalue-added activity, there is much to be gained by reviewing and revising the manufacturing process and sometimes the design of the part. This is particularly true in the case of assembly and fabrication operations, as opposed to machining operations where machine speeds and feed rates are relatively constant for a specific type of material and component.

While most gurus in the field of manufacturing preach the importance of reducing nonproductive components of lead time (queue, move, etc.), very few address ways in which run time can be reduced. Furthermore, many manufacturers fall into a psychological rut, thinking that it takes what it takes to build a particular part (or assembly), and there is not much that can be done to reduce the time short of buying fancy, expensive equipment or asking people to work faster. I once was part of such an environment, but I found that with a bit of care, understanding, and effort, significant headway can be made toward reducing run time without spending a lot on capital equipment or placing unreasonable demands on the workers. This is particularly true for fabrications and assemblies.

Two broad factors play a major role in the effort to reduce run time for a part or an assembly: the psychological and technical aspects of performing the work.

Psychological

The psychological aspects fall into the "soft" or holistic category. A vital psychological element on which all potential improvements depend is the zeal and passion with which one wants to make improvements. Without passion, the majority of such efforts are reduced to an exercise in futility and doomed to fail. Management must really want to look for ways to improve. Most improvements are a result of hard work and perseverance. They do not fall on us like manna from heaven. Very few companies pursue their improvement goals with such passion. Most find it easier to resign themselves to the way things are: "We tried that, but our business is different, so it didn't work for us."

Another simple fact of life is that people do not like to run out of work. As a result, running low on work on the shop floor is usually seen as a prelude to potential layoffs. Several work orders waiting their turn on the shop floor is usually a pleasant sight for most assemblers. This tells them that there is enough work (even if it will only last another week or two) and there is no reason to worry about losing their jobs. Once the queue of orders starts to dry up, there could be cause for concern, and basic human nature is to drag out the order that is currently being built, resulting in longer run times. Very simply, it is bad practice to release a large number of orders and send them to the shop floor prematurely just to provide the assemblers with a sense of job security. Yet the psychological aspect must also be recognized and addressed.

One way of addressing the psychological aspect is to give the assemblers a preview of orders in the pipeline without physically pulling the parts and staging future orders on the shop floor. A chalkboard with future jobs listed by start date can be a very useful tool for achieving this. This procedure was implemented at one of the facilities where I worked. It took a few weeks for the "system" to be accepted by the assemblers — we had to first earn their trust! In fact, I took it upon myself to update the information on the board. On occasion, due to a critical part coming in late, an order would be delayed by a day or two. Such exceptions were also duly noted on the board. Once the assemblers were satisfied that they could rely on this information, they felt more secure. It also worked wonders in keeping inventory levels down.

Technical

Technical improvements hinge mainly on the design of a part or product and the process used to build it. Of the ones discussed below, some are intuitively obvious, while others are not.

Jigs and fixtures: In many cases, making use of fixtures eases the job of building a part. This is particularly true for parts that require a lot of welding, but can be quite effective for certain assembly operations too. More often than not, simple fixtures dedicated to a particular part can be made quite cheaply. Simplifying the welding or assembly job results in a lower run time to build the part. An added benefit of using fixtures is that they help produce repeatedly consistent parts.

Documentation: In some cases, not enough documentation is created to build a part or product. One of the reasons (or excuses) why this happens is the lack of importance placed on documentation: "We will only build two or three, and that does not justify spending time on detailed documentation." Another reason could be a false sense of security that the assemblers are experienced and should be able to build the part or product without much handholding in the way of documentation.

It is perfectly legitimate and understandable to have sketchy documentation while the first few prototypes are being built. However, once the prototypes have been completed and the design criteria have been established, there is no excuse for continuing to build more parts without proper documentation. Not creating adequate documentation sets the stage for building the first prototype over and over again every time the part or product is built. This is equivalent to reinventing the wheel.

Consider an electrical harness that is to be assembled and routed through a subassembly of the finished product. Adequate documentation for the harness requires specifying every component along with its quantity. This includes the length of every wire that is used to build the harness. Furthermore, adequate documentation for the subassembly on which the harness is used must show how the harness is routed through the subassembly. This is the bare minimum of information required in order for any assembler who is capable of such work to be able to build the harness and route it on a consistent, repeatable basis. Without such information, the assembler would be required to measure the various lengths of wire physically on the subassembly *every time* the harness is built. To make matters worse, without proper documentation, different assemblers may route the harness differently through the same subassembly. This is not efficient, nor does it resemble professional production work; it is too much like artisan work and results in building the first prototype over and over again.

It is amazing that companies do this. Their rationale is that they save a lot of engineering time by trusting their "experienced" assemblers to do the work without complete documentation. With this approach, a lot is left to guesswork and subjective decision making by the assembler, and the job takes longer to perform.

Process change: Certain assembly jobs are better suited to be performed at a workbench, while others are better suited for assembly on a preexisting major assembly on the shop floor. It is imperative to analyze the job at hand to decide on the most efficient way to perform it. The following example illustrates this point.

Example: Suppose a certain product, a fire engine for example, utilizes several electrical components that are connected to a source of power by means of cables. In the interest of safety and to protect the components from burning out due to potential power surges, the electrical circuit includes a breaker box with 50 circuit breakers. Each cable that is used to provide power to the electrical components has a connector at one end which plugs into the component and a pigtail at the other, to be inserted into the corresponding circuit breaker. Each pigtail has ferrules crimped on it to protect the bare wire.

While building the first prototype, it would be normal to follow the steps listed below:

- Leave the wires on each cable a few inches longer than what the final length of the cable is expected to be.
- Connect each cable to the component to which it is meant to provide power.
- Route each cable through the product.
- Trim any extra length of wire for each cable.
- Crimp ferrules on the circuit breaker end of each cable.
- Insert the ferrule end of each cable into the corresponding circuit breaker.

Performing these steps would be necessary to establish the "fit" and "form" for each cable. However, once the fit and form have been established and the final length of each cable is known, there is an easier, less time-consuming way to perform this work in production. Crimping ferrules on bare wire is a task that is far easier to perform while sitting at a workbench than while standing in a potentially cramped area of the product through which the cable is routed. In many cases, even the task of inserting the ferrules into their respective circuit breakers is easier to do while sitting at a workbench. As a result, during the production phase of the finished product, the assembly and installation process for the cables should be different from what was used during prototyping.

Oddly enough, instead of simplifying the work for the assemblers, many establishments choose to continue with the procedure used during prototyping. Their justification is usually something like: "It worked fine the first time, so why shouldn't we continue to do it in the same manner in production? Besides, the amount of time saved would not justify the amount of time required to produce the necessary documentation." You decide what makes sense.

Design change: Another justification for the above example is: "If we were to completely assemble the breaker box with the pigtails on a bench, we would have to route the cables to the various components. The design of the cable troughs will not permit threading the connector end of the cables through them." This indicates that the assembly and installation process was not completely thought through before the design was established. In such situations, the design of the cable troughs should be revised to allow for easier installation.

The above are but a few examples of how work can be simplified once entering the production phase of any product. Oftentimes, people tend to accept long lead times as a way of life. Then they go through a variety of analyses on how to become more flexible in reacting to changing customer demand. The *real* problem is long lead times, and that is what needs to be addressed. Take a very close look at lead times in your own applications and do whatever is financially feasible to reduce them.

CAVALIER TREATMENT OF LEAD TIMES

Often, people tend to take shortcuts. This is particularly true during the implementation of a new material planning system. One shortcut that comes back to bite them is making broad-brush assumptions such as: "We should be able to buy any C item[2] within a month; let's update the lead times for all C items to 30 days." As a result, they tell the programming staff to make the necessary updates, saving the buyers the trouble of having to update lead times manually. Talk about fudging lead times!

By definition, under the theory of A-B-C part classification, C items are cheap and readily available. Most of them should be available within a week, if not a couple of days. If a mass update of lead times must be done, we should be aggressive and use a number that reflects reality. Then, as orders are placed for the individual components, the default time should be changed to reflect the real time it takes to procure each individual part.

The problem is that in our zeal to get the "new system" implemented, we make some decisions across the board which at best can only be described as dumb. More often than not, these decisions result from a round table discussion among some resident "experts." These are times when a reality check is merited.

Does it really take a month to buy nuts, bolts, or washers? When I ask this question of buyers, the answer is quite predictable: "Oh, that's just the *system default*. I can have the parts here within a day." The buyer is an instant hero! If we know something to be true, then the truth must be reflected in the computer system. Traditionally, once a new system is implemented, we tend to switch to an "autopilot" mode. We take recommendations from the system as gospel and diligently obey them. Later, when inventory builds up or stock-outs occur, it is always the inanimate "system" that is to blame. What can we expect the "system" to do for us if we lie to it in the first place?

The above scenario depicts how people can be overly pessimistic about lead times. The one below shows how management can sometimes be overly aggressive.

One newly appointed materials manager decided that the lead times specified in the computer system were inflated. He asked the programming staff to programmatically cut all lead times by half! He also sent a memo to all buyers and planners informing them of his decision and telling them that they "should" be able to procure the parts within the revised lead times. How did he know that? The turmoil that this caused with some of the major suppliers could have filled a term paper on how *not* to manipulate lead times.

Before moving on to the next chapter, one more term pertaining to lead times warrants explanation.

CUMULATIVE LEAD TIME

Over the years, this has come to be known by several names: cumulative lead time, cumulative manufacturing lead time, gross manufacturing lead time, and critical path lead time. A layperson's definition of cumulative lead time for any product is the amount of time it would take to build a product if one were to start with zero inventory of its components.

The definition offered by APICS is "The longest planned length of time to accomplish the activity in question. For any item planned through MRP, it is found by reviewing the lead time for each bill of material path below the item; whichever path adds up to the greatest number defines cumulative lead time."[3]

The best way to clearly explain cumulative lead time is with a sample bill of material, as shown in Figure 6.1. In this example, A and B are assemblies, and D is a machined part made from a purchased casting, G. Parts C, E, and F are purchased components. The lead time associated with each component is shown next to it.

Let's rotate this bill clockwise by 90° and, along the time scale shown, extend each leg of the bill of material in proportion to the lead time of every component on that leg (Figure 6.2). The result of adding the individual lead times for the parts along each leg is shown in Table 6.1. The cumulative lead time for part A is determined by the path that adds up to the longest lead time.

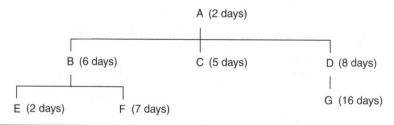

Figure 6.1 A Sample Bill of Material

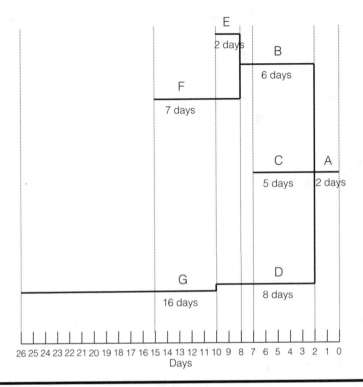

Figure 6.2   Cumulative Lead Time Explained

In this example, it is 26 days, along the path A-D-G. This means that if we were to start with zero inventory, it would take 26 days to procure the necessary components and to build part A — a worst-case scenario.

This information is important because it helps provide customers with reasonable delivery dates. If an organization's manufacturing philosophy is to build finished goods only after receiving a firm order, then in this example the

Table 6.1   Total Lead Time Along Each Path of the Sample Bill of Material

Bill of Material Path	Individual Lead Time (Days)	Path Lead Time (Days)
A-B-E	2 + 6 + 2	10
A-B-F	2 + 6 + 7	15
A-C	2 + 5	7
A-D-G	2 + 8 + 16	26

customer should expect to wait 26 days before part A can be delivered. If, however, the philosophy is to carry inventory in anticipation of receiving customer orders, the information in Table 6.1 can be used to decide which components should be kept in stock to effectively reduce the cumulative lead time for part A. This is discussed further in the section on master schedule in Chapter 10.

NOTES

1. APICS — Online Dictionary.
2. In the context of A-B-C classification of parts.
3. APICS — Online Dictionary.

This book has free materials available for download from the Web Added Value™ Resource Center at www.jrosspub.com.

7

PRODUCT COST

We do not what we ought;
What we ought not, we do;
And lean upon the thought
That chance will bring us through.

Matthew Arnold

Product cost is a key contributor to a company's bottom line. It is also a vital factor that determines whether or not an organization is competitive in the marketplace. Given this, it makes sense for each organization to establish the costs of its products, understand the various components of the costs, and then strive to reduce them. Very often, companies pay less attention to the first two steps and tend to concentrate on cost reduction. This can result in frustration for the organization, but more so for the suppliers of purchased components. What is even scarier is the general lack of awareness about the basic ingredients of product cost among the employees of many organizations. This is true at all levels of the organization. What is very disconcerting is the type of response heard from individuals who have a direct impact on product cost. Very often the response is: "I don't know anything about product costing. You should talk to the controller about that." This is not to suggest that every individual in the organization should know the nitty-gritty details of how to compute product costs, but it is crucial for everyone to have at least a basic knowledge of what goes into the cost of manufactured products. This information helps elevate the employees' level of awareness of the impact of their actions (or inaction) on product cost.

Before getting into product costing too deeply, let's establish a simple definition.

DEFINITION

The cost of any product is the sum total of all expenses incurred while building or procuring that product. This includes what suppliers are paid, the amount of in-house labor that goes into building the product, and the overhead associated with conducting the business.

It is important to establish this definition at the outset, because of the confusion that exists. It is not uncommon for many individuals to confuse "cost" with "price." In fact, some people even use the two words interchangeably, which leads to unnecessary confusion. In several parts of the world, the term used to represent "cost" is "cost price," and the term used to represent "price" is "selling price." This can be confusing, because it is very difficult to differentiate between the two in conversations. The resulting confusion is due to the use of the word "price" in both terms. Very simply, "cost" is what it costs to build and provide a product to customers, and "price" is what customers are charged for that product.

COSTING METHODS

Generally accepted methods for computing product costs include standard costing, average costing, and actual costing. Another procedure that gained some steam in the 1980s but seems to have sprung a few leaks along the way is activity-based costing.

Regardless of the method used, the basic premise of product costing lies in identifying the total cost of material and labor used to produce parts and products. The first three methods listed include overhead costs that are spread across the material and labor content as an arithmetic average. In activity-based costing, the overhead costs are weighted for different products based on the amount of activity required to produce them.

Standard Costing

The traditional and perhaps most common method used by organizations is standard costing. With this approach, the most current costs associated with products are "frozen" at the start of the company's fiscal year and treated as a standard against which performance for the remainder of the year is measured. (We will assume that the fiscal year begins on January 1.) Given the fact that costs can change during the course of a year for a variety of reasons, by definition there will be variances. A variance is nothing more than a deviation of the current cost from the frozen standard. If the current cost exceeds the standard, an unfavorable variance occurs, and if the current cost is lower than the standard, the variance is favorable. At the end of the year, the cumulative total of all such variances reflects either favorably or unfavorably on an organization's bottom line. One of the more unenviable aspects of a manufacturing project manager's job is to explain these variances periodically. More often than not, this is done during a monthly spending review.

Average Costing

As the name suggests, the basic premise of this method is to maintain a running average of the prior cost and the last actual cost. In order to compute a representative average, the quantity associated with each cost must be considered. As an example, let's say that the most recent average unit cost of a component is $10. The next purchase order received is for a quantity of 50 of the same component, but at $9 per part. Let's also assume that there are 45 parts already in inventory. As a result, the extended cost of the items in stock will be 45 units × $10, or $450. The total cost of the components on the latest purchase order is 50 units × $9, also $450. Once the parts are received, the new average cost per component will be ($450 + $450)/95 or $9.47.

Actual Costing

In this method, the last actual cost is considered to be the cost of the product. In the case of purchased components, it would be the unit cost of the component as reflected on the last purchase order. For manufactured parts, it would include the actual cost of all materials used, along with the actual labor and/or machine costs (including the appropriate overhead costs) required to build the parts.

This method is applicable where a company makes one-of-a-kind or a small number of products based on a customer's design and specification. It is the method with perhaps the lowest risk for an organization to lose money because of cost fluctuations.

Activity-Based Costing

In a nutshell, this method differs from the others in the way in which overhead costs are allocated. It stands to reason that certain products require a greater amount of indirect labor than others. This is especially true for new products that are being introduced into the production cycle. Such products usually require more attention from the engineering group than mature products. As a result, a larger percentage of the overhead costs is allocated to the newer products than to mature products. With activity-based costing, the resultant product costs are more accurate than those computed by the other methods.

A word of caution: Even though there is a certain degree of "science" involved in the allocation of overhead costs, keep in mind that they are still *estimates*. It is easy to get carried away with algorithms to allocate overhead expenses. In many cases, it can result in too much pomp for the circumstances.

COST ELEMENTS

The three broad elements of cost mentioned earlier in the definition merit some explanation.

Supplier Cost

This is what is paid to suppliers for parts and services they provide. Other commonly used terms for supplier cost are vendor cost and material cost. If the cost pertains strictly to a service that is purchased from a supplier, it is referred to as outside processing cost. Examples of this would be galvanizing, anodizing, and painting.

Labor Cost

Also referred to as direct labor cost, this is computed by multiplying the labor rate by the number of hours spent making the product. The labor rate is usually the average hourly rate paid to employees in a particular work center.

Overhead Cost

Broadly speaking, this is the cost of doing business. A percentage of this cost is allocated to the material and labor content of the product cost, in an effort to recover all the overhead expenses incurred over a fixed period of time (usually a year). Typically, overhead costs cover the expenses incurred for the facility (land, building, etc.), utilities (electricity, water, etc.), support staff (engineers, buyers, planners, administrative employees, management, etc.), and miscellaneous expenses (equipment, stationery, furniture, etc.). A special case would be an organization that "engineers to order." The custom engineering and design effort would normally be charged to the customer separately, and the engineering group would be excluded from the overhead pool.

More often than not, the way in which the overhead expenses are allocated to product cost is arbitrary at best and does not resemble an "exact science." Approximate as it may be, several organizations use this method to compute the cost of their products, so it is important to be reasonably familiar with the concept.

Let's look at how the various cost elements come together to comprise the costs of purchased and manufactured parts.

COST OF PURCHASED COMPONENTS

The most critical element of the cost of purchased items is what suppliers are paid, the material cost. It is also the element that is truly known. If you pay $5 to purchase a certain component, then its material cost is $5. But other costs associated with buying parts must also be considered. These are the costs associated with negotiating contracts, placing purchase orders, receiving, inspecting, and warehousing. As a result, the costs associated with these activities, along with an appropriate allocation for facility, utilities, and miscellaneous expenses, are spread over the aggregate material cost of all expected purchases during the course of a year. Some organizations also include an estimate of freight charges associated with the expected purchases as part of the overhead expense.

Example

Let's assume that during a given year, an organization expects to purchase $5 million worth of components. Let's also suppose that the total annual cost of maintaining the purchasing, receiving, receiving inspection, and warehouse departments is $250,000. The theory is that it takes $250,000 worth of overhead to purchase $5 million worth of parts. In order to spread the overhead expense evenly over the total purchases, the $250,000 is divided by $5 million to arrive at 5% as the overhead cost allocated to purchased parts. Add to this an estimate for freight charges (around 3% of material cost), and the total purchasing overhead is 8% of material cost. As a result, the *total cost* of a part for which the supplier is paid $5 is $5.40, of which $5 is the material cost and $0.40 is the material overhead.

If in fact exactly $5 million worth of components are purchased, then the associated purchasing overhead cost would be "fully absorbed." However, if customer demand falls during the course of the year and only $3 million worth of parts are purchased, 5% (purchasing overhead without freight) of $3 million, or $150,000, would be absorbed. The remaining $100,000 would be treated as unabsorbed overhead, and the bottom line would reflect it as a loss. This is assuming that there are no personnel layoffs as a result of the decrease in demand. The freight percentage remains unchanged.

Similarly, if more than $5 million worth of parts are purchased during the year without hiring more personnel or expanding the warehouse, the difference would be overabsorbed overhead and would be reflected as profit.

COST OF MANUFACTURED COMPONENTS

Along with the material and purchasing overhead costs associated with purchased components, the total cost of manufactured parts includes a labor cost and an overhead content associated with the labor cost. The labor cost is usually referred to as direct labor because it reflects the hours expended by the shop floor workers during the course of manufacturing components and products.

The overhead cost associated with labor is computed by summing all the overhead expenses (excluding those associated with the purchasing overhead) for the year and dividing by the total estimated labor hours the organization expects to work during the year. It is often represented as a percentage of the hourly labor rate.

Example

Assume that the hourly labor rate is $10 and that the direct labor workforce will be paid for a total of 10,000 hours during the course of the fiscal year. If the total overhead expenses (excluding overhead associated with purchasing) for the year are expected to be $200,000, then the hourly overhead rate for that year will be ($200,000)/(10,000 hours) or $20. Often, this would be expressed as a percentage of the hourly labor rate, in this case 200%.

What does this mean in plain English? It means that for every hour spent on production work, the labor cost will be $10 and the associated overhead cost will be $20, resulting in a "fully burdened" labor and overhead cost of $30 per hour.

Assume that a particular component takes one hour of labor to build. If the total vendor cost of components used for making this part is $15 and the associated purchasing overhead including freight is 8%, then the total cost of this component will be $15 (material) + $1.20 (8% overhead on material) + $10 (labor) + $20 (200% overhead on labor), or $46.20. More often than not, the total cost of components is stored in computer systems in their elemental form, and the term used to describe the form is true material, labor, and overhead or true M-L-O. For the component in the current example, the true M-L-O cost would be:

$$\begin{aligned}
\text{Material} &= \$15.00 \\
\text{Labor} &= \$10.00 \\
\text{Overhead} &= \$21.20 \\
\text{Total} &= \$46.20
\end{aligned}$$

The common term used to describe the computation of higher level product cost is *cost rollup*. This term gets its name from the procedure used to compute the costs of finished goods. The procedure requires starting with the costs of purchased components at the lowest level of each leg of a bill of material and working up. The costs of purchased parts are added up and "rolled" into the cost of the next higher assembly with its labor and overhead costs and so on, until the cost of the finished product has been totaled. A detailed example of a cost rollup is provided in Appendix A.

Now that we have a general, working knowledge of the various components of cost and the popular methods used to compute it, what should we do with it? Two objectives that pertain to product costs are important. Once computed, we must use them and continually work toward reducing them. The primary use of product costs is to set prices.

PRODUCT PRICING

The primary objective of any business is to make money.[1] The way in which this is commonly achieved is by charging customers for products and services. The price set for any product should be dependent on two things: the cost of the item and what a company believes the market will bear. Logically, the price of any product must exceed what it costs to build it. However, in some cases, in order to promote sales of other products, a company may decide to take a loss on a particular product. The question that begs to be asked is how high the price should be. It should be as high as it can be set to still be able to sell the product on a continuing basis. In order to ensure a continuous revenue stream, a company must be competitive in the marketplace.

On occasion, especially when introducing a new product, the cost of the product may not be known. Yet the price needs to be established in order to market the product ahead of when it becomes available for sale. Most organizations will estimate the cost in order to set the price. This is usually done by comparing the new product to similar products with which a company has experience.

Another factor used to establish the price of a product is the quantity produced. This will be addressed in the section titled "Role of Improvement Curves in Pricing" later in this chapter.

The key issue here is that regardless of the maturity of a product, the cost must be known or estimated before the price is set. The following example shows how one company took the wrong approach.

Example

One morning, I met with John, the person responsible for spare parts sales at a client's facility. Part of John's job was to set the prices for spare parts. I asked him to explain the procedure that he used.

"Depending on the customer that orders the part, I use the appropriate markup," he began. "For example, we have an agreement with XYZ, Inc. to mark up the material cost by 15% and to price the labor at $35 per hour. So I look at the job ticket for the material and labor that were spent and go from there."

A week prior to this conversation, I had met with the controller and James, the general manager of the facility. The controller informed us that the overhead rates had been revised, and as a result, the fully burdened labor rate had been raised from $40 per hour to $42.

At yet a third meeting, which I had with the owner, he mentioned that all parts and products should be sold at a markup of 15% over cost. Can you guess where this ship was headed?

During my talk with John, I asked him if he knew about the revised labor rate. Actually, even the old labor rate ($40 per hour) was higher than the rate he was using to establish prices for XYZ, Inc.

His response was, "Those are cost numbers used by accounting. James (the general manager) gave me the numbers I'm using when I took this job."

"When did you take this job?" I asked John.

"A couple of years ago," he replied.

I was flabbergasted. In electrical engineering terms, this was an "open circuit." Some of the wires were broken, and there was no current (information) flowing through the circuit (organization). There was an obvious "disconnect" between the general manager and John. There was an even bigger disconnect between the owner, the controller, and the general manager, because the controller and general manager had not received the message about the 15% markup. I was the only link among the three, and I was an external consultant!

To put things in proper perspective, I met with James (the general manager) and told him what I saw going on. I used an example to explain the situation.

Let's say that a particular component that is built for XYZ, Inc. requires $200 of material and takes four hours to build. Based on the rates provided by the controller, applying a purchasing and freight overhead of 8% would result in a fully burdened material cost of $216. Also, at $42 per hour, the fully burdened labor cost would be $168, resulting in a total cost of $384. With a markup of 15% (based on the owner's wishes), the price *should* be $441.60 per part.

According to the algorithm that John is using, only the true material cost of $200 (the 8% burden is not included) is marked up by 15%, and the labor is "priced" at $35 per hour, resulting in a final price of ($200 × 1.15) + (4 hours × $35) = $370 per part.

Very simply, not only is the company not making a profit, it is *losing* $14 [$384 (cost) – $370 (price)] every time one of these components is sold to XYZ, Inc. And this was for just *one* of many such components.

James's response: "Damn!"

COST REDUCTION

Managers talk about cutting costs, but they do not always know where to begin. This is true in many organizations. More often than not, when it comes to reducing product costs, the money paid to suppliers of purchased components becomes the focus of attention.

As mentioned in Chapter 6, the popular method that many organizations gravitate toward is to obtain three quotes for any component that needs to be purchased. Invariably, the lowest bidder gets the purchase order. This holds true for commercial items (components available off-the-shelf), as well as manufactured parts and assemblies. While this approach works to serve the precise objective of reducing supplier costs, it requires the organization to spend additional time and money. The added time shows up in the basic act of placing a purchase order (waiting for quotes, negotiating, etc.). The added cost is reflected in the purchasing overhead as more people (buyers, purchasing clerks, etc.) are required for the quoting process. The other downside to this approach is that it hinders an organization from establishing a long-term working relationship with its suppliers. Such a relationship is a key factor in establishing clear expectations of product quality, adherence to delivery schedules, flexibility, and competitiveness (cost) with suppliers.

The real objective should be to reduce the *total* cost of the finished product — the sum total of supplier costs, purchasing and freight-related overhead, labor hours, and operating costs (other overhead). The common fallacy is that if every element of total cost is minimized, then the total cost will be minimized. At face value, this philosophy is hard to argue with, but in reality that is not how things pan out.

Another popular approach to reducing material costs that is adopted by many organizations is to conduct hard-nosed negotiations with their suppliers. "Beating up" suppliers is often tacitly expected of buyers. This may work for a short while, depending on how "hungry" a supplier is, and the buyer may appear to be a hero, but it invariably results in an unhealthy working relationship and is a form of exploitation. Very often, people resort to negotiations without really understanding the various contributors to a seemingly high cost. One such contributor is the design of a component or assembly. It is not unusual for an intricate design to require either exotic materials, an involved production process, or both. Instead of working with suppliers and soliciting their input to reduce the cost of the part, it is assumed that the part *must* be made per the design and negotiations commence. I call this approach "fish market negotiations." The negotiations may pertain to a highly technical component, but it is treated as so many pounds of catfish! The first step must be to understand the cost; only then can one legitimately look for ways to reduce it.

In most organizations, the manufacturing team must be the driving force behind cost reductions. The team should consist of representatives from purchasing, planning, design engineering, the shop floor, and a few key suppliers and should be led by the manufacturing engineer or project manager responsible for the product. The cost elements that are usually within the control of this team are the material cost and the hours (labor and/or machine hours) required for the various manufacturing processes. Overhead costs are normally not within the control of such a team; reducing overhead falls squarely in the lap of management.

A rarely used tool that can be of great help when addressing cost reductions is improvement curve theory, also known as learning curve theory.

IMPROVEMENT CURVE THEORY

Using improvement curve theory enables us to focus our efforts toward cost reduction and to set targets. It is used quite extensively in the aircraft industry. Although it can be used equally well for most types of products, it is particularly useful in the production of low-volume, custom-built technical products. A general lack of awareness of its potential benefits is why improvement curve theory is not popular with many organizations.

The basic premise of improvement curve theory is that repetition enables learning. Consequently, the amount of time taken to perform a task is expected to decrease as the number of repetitions increases.

I prefer to use the term improvement curves over learning curves, because the word learning triggers impressions of reduced times, simply by virtue of repetition, in some people.

Often, when I talk to people about improvement curves, their initial reaction is, "Oh, so if I do this assembly enough times, I should be able to do it in no time at all!" That is not the case. For one thing, the improvement curve is a logarithmic function which never reaches zero.

An analogy about learning how to knot a necktie is quite effective in distinguishing between learning and overall improvement.

An Analogy

The very first time most people try to knot a necktie, the result is often disastrous. However, with practice, the task becomes easier and takes less time to perform. Sooner or later, you reach a stage where it is second nature, and you can knot a tie without conscious effort. For all practical purposes, you have reached the bottom of the learning curve and should not expect to see any significant reduction in the time it takes to knot a tie.

Let's change the objective just slightly, from learning how to knot a tie to simply wearing a tie. This gives rise to a different set of possibilities. You no longer have to knot the tie in order to wear it. I know what my friends and I did as kids in school, where a tie was part of the uniform. Every evening after school, I would loosen the loop just enough to slip it over my head. Every morning, I would slip the tie back on and pull it snug around my neck. This was an *improvement* to the *process* pertaining to the objective of wearing a tie.

Another option is to consider *redesigning* the tie. The early 1960s brought the introduction of the clip-on tie, which is a snap (pardon the pun) to wear. This was an overall improvement achieved not just by repetition, but also by making improvements to the process *and* the design.

Improvement curve theory suggests that each time the number of repetitions doubles, a fixed percentage of reduction in time is experienced. The percentage of reduction depends on the slope of the improvement curve. The steeper the slope, the greater the reduction. Keep in mind that the reduction is not just a result of mere repetition, but also assumes improvements to the process and design.

Let's say that when the first prototype of an assembly was built, the task took 100 hours to perform. In the case of an 80% improvement curve, we should expect to see a reduction of 20% (1.00 − 0.80) from the first unit to the second. The second unit should take 80 hours to complete. Similarly, the fourth unit (the

Table 7.1 Unit Hours of an 80% Improvement Curve as the Number of Units Doubles

Unit #	1	2	4	8	16	32	64
Hours	100.00	80.00	64.00	51.20	40.96	32.77	26.21

number of units must double) is expected to take 80% of the time taken to build the second unit, the eighth unit will take 80% of the time required for the fourth unit, and so on. Table 7.1 displays the hours through unit number 64. The figure 80% represents the slope of the curve. The lower the percentage, the higher the degree of improvement and the steeper the slope of the curve.

It is important to note that while the percentage of reduction remains constant from one milestone to the next, the actual amount of the reduction is lower as the number of units increases. The reduction from the first unit to the second is 20 hours. From the 4th to the 8th is 16 hours, and from the 32nd to the 64th is only 6.56 hours. As the number of units increases, the hours per unit decrease at a decreasing rate. Figure 7.1 shows this in graphical form.[2]

What does all this have to do with cost reductions? Improvement curve theory helps project potential reductions in cost based on the anticipated volume of production. It also helps establish product pricing, which will be covered later in this chapter.

The example cited earlier (Table 7.1), definitely does not say that if 64 units were to be built, the 64th unit would take about a fourth of the time the first unit took, as a result of learning through simple repetition. The inherent assumption is that people actually *learn* from their experiences and past mistakes *and* that they *do something* with what they learn, to keep from repeating the same mistakes.

It is not unusual while building the first prototype of a newly designed component to experience several starts and stops and possibly some rework. If one has "learned" from this experience, then the second unit should encounter fewer disruptions, the third even fewer, and so on. Also, by the time the first two or three prototypes have been built, the need for special tooling and fixtures may become apparent. It may even make sense to switch some operations around to facilitate a more economic process or to modify the design of the component to make it easier to manufacture. These are all avenues available to help reduce product costs, and we must be willing to explore every one of them.

Different cost elements have been shown to follow different trends when it comes to the slope of the associated improvement curve. The following discussion pertaining to manufacturing, testing, and purchasing indicates the percent-

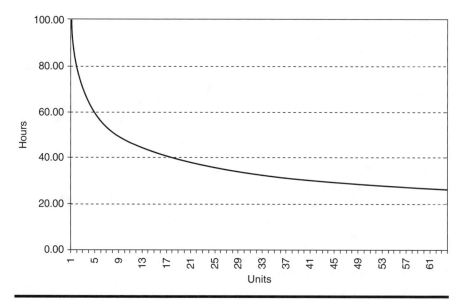

Figure 7.1   An 80% Unit Curve Plotted on Arithmetic Axes

age of learning that is applicable in each case. Note that these are the numbers that I experienced based on the type of product and the amount of effort that went into cost reduction. You may experience slightly different values based on your circumstances, but these numbers should help get you started.

Manufactured Components

It is important to differentiate between machine-intensive and labor-intensive operations.

Machine-Intensive Operations

For this type of work, the rate at which components are made depends heavily on speeds and feeds pertaining to the machine and material being used. Unless significant changes are made, either by replacing existing equipment, specifying different material, or drastically redesigning the component, not much reduction can be expected.

However, setups pertaining to such components are a different story altogether. Invariably, setups involve a significant amount of manual work that can be thought of as labor intensive. One can definitely expect to see some improvement in the setup times, but again, just a small portion of the improvement would be a result of repetition. The major chunk of the improvement should come from designing "quick" setups or, when economically justifiable, dedicated setups.

Keep in mind that when such components are made in batches, the improvement in the setup time can only be projected from one setup to the next and not from one component to the next.

In my experience, the finished product involved very few machine-intensive components. We did not go through a significant change in equipment, nor did we spend too much effort redesigning the components. We were not going to get a big enough bang for the buck. But we did work on reducing the setups. Overall, we experienced an improvement curve of about 95%, with both setup and run time combined.

Labor-Intensive Operations

This is a horse of a different color. Significant improvements can be achieved with labor-intensive operations. The degree of improvement (within reasonable limits) is proportional to the amount of "heart" put into the effort and the changes that can be implemented.

An 80 to 85% improvement curve has worked well for my applications, but it involved some serious teamwork among the various individuals on the project, and almost everything covered so far in this book played a significant part in the exercise.

Operational Testing

Depending on an organization's philosophy on testing, a significant amount of improvement can be realized. In my experience, a 70 to 75% improvement curve is a reasonable target. This does not imply performing the same tests repeatedly, only that much faster. The basic objective is to improve the manufacturing process *and* the design of the product so that the *number* and *frequency* of tests are reduced.

One way to build a product is to put everything together, then test it to death until it works. This is often referred to as final test and inspection and goes back to the analogy of manufacturing torpedoes in Chapter 6. Quality cannot be tested into a product. It must be designed and built into the product from the start. As long as an organization continues to rely solely on final testing, not much improvement should be expected.

Purchased Components

By definition, purchased components have a direct impact on material cost. I was once told that the best way to reduce material cost is to reduce the amount of material. Although this may sound a bit facetious, over the years, I have become a firm believer.

Let's suppose that we are dealing with an intricately designed product that consists of hundreds of different components, scattered over multiple levels of the bill of material. The question often asked is, "Where do we begin to reduce material costs?" A good place to start is by relying on Pareto's theory (commonly known as the 80/20 rule). In this case, we can assume that roughly 20% of the purchased components will account for roughly 80% of the total material cost.

We begin with a summarized bill of material. A summarized bill is sorted by part number. This way, multiple call-outs of the same part number in the bill of material will appear together. A simple spreadsheet can help with the remaining steps. Most bill of material listings include the make/buy code for each part. Using this code, only the purchased components would be selected, and the quantities of like parts would be consolidated, so that each part number appears just once with the total quantity used in the bill of material. Once the quantities have been extended by the material cost for each part, the entire list can be sorted in descending order of extended cost and a column for cumulative cost created. The point on the list where the cumulative cost is approximately 80% of the total material cost is where the proverbial line would be drawn. Chances are that the number of individual components above this line will equate to approximately 20% of the total components on the list. Logically, directing our efforts to this subset of components would provide the biggest bang for the buck. For the products with which I was associated, we used 95 to 98% improvement curves to project reductions in material costs.

So, where do we go, armed with this information? No, the supplier's doorstep is *not* the first place to visit.

Design

The design of a product in general and its components in particular should be scrutinized with the objective of simplifying them. It is not unusual for some designers to get carried away and design a fortress, when all the customer wanted was a lean-to. Anyone who has been involved with manufacturing has had experience with products that were "overdesigned." In some cases, it may be that too many fasteners are called out for a certain assembly, or it may be that a certain "un-obtainium" (see Chapter 4) is designed into the product when ordinary steel would work just fine. Designs must be reviewed by a team consisting of individuals from manufacturing and engineering, along with representatives from key suppliers.

One of the more drastic (more so psychologically than mechanically) design changes with which I was associated took place in the late 1980s. We were about to introduce a new version of a special-purpose heavy-duty truck with a total weight of approximately 50,000 pounds. The truck consisted of a chassis, on which a cabin was mounted. Rudimentary versions of the truck had been in operation for 20 years, and the design kept evolving as newer technology became available.

The basic structure of the cabin consisted of a frame made of welded steel tubing. The outer walls consisted of aluminum sheets that were attached to the steel tubing with pop rivets. The rivets were installed at intervals of 1.5 inches. Holes in the aluminum sheets for the pop rivets had to be punched on a numerically controlled machine to hold the close tolerances, and the holes in the steel tubing had to be drilled manually using templates.

While the design of major operational parts for the new truck had been upgraded, the method described above for attaching the aluminum skin to the frame was simply copied from an older design because we were in a hurry to build the prototypes. On the fifth unit, the method for attaching the skin was changed to a special two-sided adhesive tape and the pop rivets were eliminated. Doing so saved approximately $1000 on the cost of the skins. It was no longer necessary to punch holes in them. Close to another $1000 was saved by reducing the labor hours required to attach the skins. All the drilling required in the frame for the rivets, along with the labor to install the rivets, was now unnecessary.

The biggest hurdle was convincing some of the die-hards in the organization that the skins would not fly off when the trucks were driven on the freeway. Several tests were performed over a wide range of temperatures and the tape stayed put! Since then, every new truck design has incorporated the adhesive tape. A few years later, we were able to improve on that too. The frame and skin design was replaced with structural sandwich panels. That change helped reduce the cost even further.

None of these changes jeopardized the quality of the product. In fact, the quality was enhanced because the potential water leaks in the pop-rivet version were history. Plus the cabin looked much nicer.

It cannot be emphasized enough that design improvements have the greatest impact on lowering material costs.

Errors

It may seem trivial, but it is amazing how much design errors can cost in material, not to mention disruptions on the shop floor. It is not that difficult to transpose a couple of digits in a part number and call out a completely different part than what was originally intended. Incorrect quantities constitute another type of error on the bill of material. In dealing with a 200- to 300-page bill of material, it is not realistic to expect to find such errors just by flipping through the pages.

The validity of the bill of material must be proven while building the first few prototypes. Errors and discrepancies must be corrected as soon as they are identified.

Supplier

Once we have cleaned our own house, we can approach our suppliers and ask how they can help with additional reductions in material costs.

Continuity

The basic premise underlying the successful application of improvement curve theory is to maintain some semblance of continuity in the workforce and in production.

Workforce

Moving people frequently from job to job does not help the cause. It results in a break in continuity, and the anticipated "learning" cannot be realized. This is not to suggest making an operation totally dependent on a particular assembler or even a crew of production workers; that would be unhealthy for any organization. Time and money must be invested to cross-train the workforce so as to allow the organization greater flexibility.

Production

The same thought process that pertains to the workforce applies to production, even though production depends on demand. If the demand for a product is sporadic, it would seem logical for the production to follow suit, but it does not always have to be that way.

Let's say that a customer orders 15 units of a custom-engineered product. It could be tempting for an organization to build all of them in one batch or possibly three batches of five each. This goes back to philosophical differences between batch processing and flow processing. The danger in batch processing is that it allows for minimal improvement from one unit to the next. More often than not, any potential improvement in process or design that may be identified will have to wait for the next production batch. Learning through repetition virtually disappears due to potentially long intervals between customer orders, as frequent starts and stops are not conducive to learning. In addition, errors will probably be repeated on every unit of a given batch.

The key is to satisfy the customer's demand while maintaining a steady flow of production. This may require a certain amount of negotiation with the customer. If an order for 15 units is received, we could try to negotiate deliveries at a rate of 1 unit every 7 to 10 days. The timing of the first unit would depend on available capacity in the shop and the amount of time required to procure the necessary components. This approach has worked well with many customers. Even though an order for 15 units is placed, the customer seldom wants all 15 to be delivered at the same time. Invariably, the order is spread over a few months.

The greatest benefit of this approach is that, from one unit to the next, it enables having a dedicated crew of assemblers repeating the same operation every seven to ten days, thus providing the necessary continuity. It is like setting up a temporary production line for a few months. Of course, the work breakdown structure (see Chapter 4), along with process improvements, would play an important part in this effort.

ROLE OF IMPROVEMENT CURVES IN PRICING

One of the challenges faced when dealing with intricate products, where the unit cost can change significantly over the span of a number of units, is how to price them. One way of pricing is to mark up the cost for each unit and charge customers a different price every time they buy a unit. Most customers would not like that very much. They would prefer to pay a fixed price for all units. In the example in Table 7.1, if the hours represent the total time required to build the product, which number would be used to establish the labor cost if the customer ordered 64 units? Which number would be used if the customer ordered 16 units?

In such cases, it makes sense to use the average cost of the units, based on the total number ordered. Figure 7.2 shows the cumulative average curve plotted

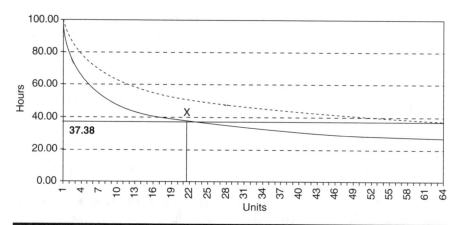

Figure 7.2   An 80% Unit Curve and Cumulative Average Curve Plotted on Arithmetic Axes

with the unit curve. Note that the unit curve is the same as the one in Figure 7.1. With the exception of unit #1, the average hours over "N" units will be higher than the unit hours for the Nth unit. For example, the average hours for the first two units (or the cumulative average hours for the second unit) will exceed the unit hours of the second unit. The cumulative average hours for the second unit are 90 hours [(100 + 80)/2], while the unit hours for the second unit are 80 hours.

From Figure 7.2, the cumulative average hours for 64 units are 37.38 hours. Very simply, this means that if 64 units were to be built, the average time per unit would be 37.38 hours. If an order for 64 units were to be received, the pricing on the labor content of the job would be based on 37.38 hours per unit. Combining a corresponding number from the material content of the job would allow us to set the total unit price.

There are usually two major concerns that most people express when presented with this approach:

1. *What if the customer cuts back on the number of units once we have quoted a price?* The contract must specify that the price is based on a certain number of units. One way to approach this is to agree with the customer that if the order quantity is reduced, the price will be recalculated. Another method would be to specify a range of prices up front, based on the number of units ordered.

2. *What if we don't achieve the improvements projected on the curve?* A simple fact of life is that the improvements will not be realized simply

because an improvement curve was plotted. We have to *make* them happen. The projections on the improvement curve should represent what we truly *believe* we can achieve and not a pipe dream.

A little known fact can simplify life a bit. Looking at Figure 7.2, notice that the cumulative average hours for the 64th unit are quite close to the unit hours for the 21st unit (represented by point X on the plot). Actually, the cumulative average hours for 64 units are 37.38 hours, and the unit hours for the 21st unit are 37.53 hours — scarily close! As a general rule of thumb, you can assume that the cumulative average hours for N units will be approximately the same as the unit hours of unit N/3. The cumulative average hours for 64 units are about the same as the unit hours of the 21st (64/3) unit. This approximation has saved me several hours of computations over the years. To review the math associated with improvement curves, refer to Appendix A.

This is the appropriate point to address a fashionable term that cropped up some time in the 1990s to describe the working relationship between an organization and its suppliers and customers.

SUPPLY CHAIN MANAGEMENT

Like many such concepts, supply chain management began with noble objectives pertaining to selecting suppliers, establishing a working relationship with them, and creating clear lines of communication.[3] Unfortunately, this philosophy seems to have made an illegal left turn somewhere along the way. One of the key ingredients, the "human aspect" of the relationship, has played second fiddle to speedy electronic links that enable communication between an organization and its suppliers — it has turned into a software project. While the ability to communicate promptly is certainly a vital ingredient, a basic building block of this philosophy has to be a mutual and honest working relationship between an organization and its suppliers. Regardless of the name used to christen this philosophy, there are four key issues that must be established to ensure a healthy, long-lasting relationship between any organization and its suppliers.

Supplier Selection

Logically, the first order of business must be to select the right group of suppliers. At the very least, a potential supplier must be able to meet the following basic requirements.

Capability

A supplier must have the capability to perform the required job. This includes expertise, facility, equipment, and people. This may seem obvious, but there have been instances where suppliers lacked some or all of these characteristics and strictly played middleman between an organization and yet another supplier. All that is achieved in such cases is an additional markup.

Of course, there are exceptions to this. Suppliers whose expertise lies in assembly-related work could justifiably subcontract machined or fabricated components that they do not have the capability to build. This is what creates the "supply chain."

Another exception occurs when an existing supplier is asked to act as a "broker" for select components. This is usually done as a convenience so as to avoid having to set up a new supplier in the computer system for a relatively trivial component.

Stability

Stability in this context refers to suppliers' financial stability and their customer base. This is crucial in ensuring a long-lasting working relationship. An organization looking for a stable supplier must also ensure that the work to be subcontracted does not constitute a very large percentage of the supplier's total business. This can be quite subjective. Some organizations try not to have their work constitute more than 10 to 15% of their suppliers' business; others may settle for a higher percentage. The objective is to ensure that a potentially significant reduction in work due to an economic downturn does not put the supplier out of business.

Willingness and Flexibility

Given that the main objective is to find a supplier with which an organization can enter into a long-term relationship, both parties must be willing to work with each other. The colloquial term that is often used to describe this is "going to bed with a supplier." A good working relationship between an organization and its suppliers is akin to a marriage, and many of the societal norms and expectations associated with a marriage apply, as will be explained. It is important that the relationship be consensual.

Flexibility is another key ingredient in such a relationship. This applies to both parties. The organization and the supplier must be willing to give a little, based on changing needs and circumstances. Sometimes large organizations tend to forget this and expect their suppliers to jump through hoops in the name of flexibility, without even considering alternatives that may require them to bend a little. Generally speaking, people who are rigid in their ways seldom make good marriage partners.

Proximity

Whenever possible, preferred suppliers should be in close geographical proximity to the subcontracting organization. This is no different than wanting to shop at a grocery store that is near your house. The ideal situation would be to choose suppliers that have a facility in the same town as the organization doing the subcontracting. In addition to the obvious convenience, it provides for closer interaction and communication and helps to reduce freight bills. While this is not critical for suppliers of relatively small commercially available items, it is especially true for suppliers that build large, bulky components and also for those that assist with building prototypes.

Having said that, it is not always possible. For example, the grocery store where you usually shop may not carry the kind of bread you prefer. You may have to drive a few miles to another store for that bread. So too, some suppliers may be geographically "scattered."

Proximity to a commercial airport is another key factor in deciding on a supplier. This is particularly important for a supplier that assists with building prototypes. During the initial design phase of a product, several visits to the supplier's facility may be necessary, and being close to an airport would certainly make life much easier.

Expectations and Negotiations

The next logical step after selecting a supplier is to establish a clear set of expectations between both parties. The expectations should be negotiated and must pertain to factors such as cost, quality, schedule of deliveries, and performance measurements.

Cost

Depending on the nature of parts furnished by a particular supplier, the cost-related negotiations might call for different approaches. For instance, negotiations pertaining to commercial items for which the supplier is a distributor would not require as much analysis as would value-added parts such as machined or fabricated components and assemblies.

At the initial stage, it is more important to establish the "ground rules" pertaining to how the suppliers cost and price their products and services than to jump into negotiations pertaining to a particular part (or set of parts). Again, this takes on greater importance for suppliers of value-added components.

The key is to understand a supplier's cost structure and markups. This includes the supplier's material burden for components that may have to be purchased, as well as the supplier's fully burdened labor rate and expected profit margin. The underlying assumption is that enough knowledge exists within the subcontracting organization to be able to reasonably estimate the material cost and labor hours involved.

One way to achieve this is to ask the supplier for the information. Once the supplier's pricing on labor and markup on material are known, a determination can be made as to whether the supplier's quotes are reasonable. Again, this assumes that there is enough knowledge within the organization to estimate the amount of material dollars and labor hours associated with the job. If the supplier's quote seems out of line, then it must be questioned and further negotiations may be warranted.

Such discussions would also provide a good indication of the suppliers' willingness to share information. Suppliers that are reluctant to share such information may not be the right candidates for a long-term working relationship.

Quality

Quality is something that we often take for granted. It is commonly assumed that suppliers should know that the components they provide must be of high quality and meet specifications. If this were true, then the concept of receiving inspection would never have been born.

Another common fallacy is to associate the word "quality" with only the quality of products and components. No doubt, good product quality is critical to the success of any organization, but "good quality" as a concept must encompass all possible deliverables by suppliers, such as packaging, care, commitment, communication, and service.

The initial phase of establishing expectations with potential suppliers must include the assignment and delineation of responsibility and accountability. Suppliers must clearly understand what is expected of them and what they should expect in return if they fall short of those expectations.

Timeliness of Deliveries

Suppliers must understand and accept the fact that the "due dates" specified on purchase orders are to be met. By the same token, the subcontracting organization must ensure that the dates are legitimate and the suppliers are allowed enough time to deliver the goods.

Some organizations establish a range of dates within which deliveries are acceptable. For instance, a delivery may be considered to be on time if it is no more than three days before or one day after the due date specified on the purchase order. While early deliveries (within reasonable limits, of course) are generally not much of a problem, late deliveries can cause much disruption on the production floor. It may be better to treat the due date on the purchase order as the drop-dead date. What is really needed is a date that can absolutely, positively be relied on — a date by which delivery is *expected*. This would have to be the due date on the purchase order and not the day after. Again, the inherent assumption is that the due date on the purchase order is legitimate and the supplier has agreed to meet it.

Performance Measurements

The expectations pertaining to cost, quality, and timeliness of deliveries must be measurable and quantifiable. Very simply, if someone can't measure something, they probably don't understand it. Without quantifiable metrics, rating a supplier's performance is reduced to subjective interpretation and often results in ill feelings between the two parties. It is important to note here that the metrics should apply to both parties. Very often, organizations tend to get carried away with metrics to measure their suppliers' performance, but ignore the metrics that would measure their own performance. It is rare for an organization to establish measurements for the timeliness of order placement or the number of supplier invoices paid late.

Of course, certain aspects of the relationship between an organization and its suppliers are subjective by nature. It would be virtually impossible to quantify the quality of the working relationship between the two organizations or the level of trust between them. These issues can only be "sensed," and a gut feel is all one has to go by. But such issues should be resolved before embarking on a long-term relationship. Why would anyone want to enter into a relationship that is not based on trust and good rapport?

Relationship

As mentioned earlier in this chapter, the relationship between an organization and its suppliers is a marriage of sorts, and as in any marriage, respect, honesty, trust, fairness, and sharing are qualities that are crucial to a long-lasting, successful business relationship.

The analytically inclined may say, "Here we go again with the intangible soft stuff." Well, without such soft stuff, the analytical and "touchy-feely" stuff is reduced to a mechanical exercise. Besides, without open, honest, and trusting lines of communication between the two parties, they would constantly be suspicious of the analytically derived numbers anyway.

Sometimes the relationship between an organization and its suppliers can become adversarial. In most such cases, either the suppliers feel "used" or the subcontracting organization feels as though it is being gouged. In many instances, the Golden Rule is rephrased: *Do unto others before they do unto you!* Such behavior does not lend itself to a long-lasting relationship; it is equivalent to a one-night stand.

The subcontracting organization must recognize that while beating up its suppliers may result in short-term gains in purchasing costs, no supplier will tolerate that kind of treatment for long. Eventually new suppliers must be sought, and if the cycle repeats itself, the organization can get a bad name in the marketplace. One of the basic objectives of establishing a relationship with suppliers is to keep from having to "shop" for components every time the need arises. Mistreating suppliers not only puts a company in the position of continually having to shop for parts, but also sets the company up to have to shop for new suppliers — an expensive proposition.

Likewise, suppliers that believe in gouging their customers cannot expect to do so for very long. In order to stay in business, they need to be competitive and serve their customers well.

Mode of Communication

How an organization communicates with its suppliers is less important than the need for communication. Whether by personal visits, telephone, or e-mail, it is important to have open lines of communication between an organization and its suppliers. Changes in component design, quantities, schedules, and pricing must be promptly communicated to avoid unpleasant surprises.

Depending on the types of components or products that are subcontracted, and the volume of transactions, the preferred mode of communication may vary. Intricate assemblies that are prone to design changes might merit a more personal touch, whereas revisions to documentation can be transferred back and forth via computer. On the other hand, for established commercial items with a frequent demand pattern, transferring purchase orders solely via computer may be all that is necessary.

It is important that an organization does not get carried away with computerized links with its suppliers. They must be used as required, but not at the expense of properly communicating vital information. As mentioned earlier, supply chain management is *not* a software project! Selecting the latest and greatest software package should not take precedence over conducting proper and efficient communication.

Some buyers print reports from their requirements planning system and send them (usually by fax) to suppliers without analyzing them. If that is all that a buyer is going to do, it can be done much less expensively with a telephone line and a modem! It is imperative to study the recommendations of the planning system in order to decide on the most applicable order quantities and delivery dates. Computers can only follow the rules laid down by people, but they cannot analyze exceptions — yet!

Much of what has been stated here is intuitive and within the precepts of common sense; in some cases, it may even seem obvious. However, these fundamental attributes for creating a healthy working relationship with suppliers are often ignored in the heat of battle, causing us to include Alka-Seltzer® as part of our daily diet and suppliers to make Preparation-H® an essential part of their toiletry.

NOTES

1. Eliyahu Goldratt and J. Cox, *The Goal: A Process of Ongoing Improvement*, North River Press, Great Barrington, MA, 1986.
2. Since the improvement curve is a logarithmic function, if the data in Table 7.1 had been plotted on a log-log scale (logarithmic scale on both axes), they would appear as a straight line.
3. While supply chain management involves interrelationships between all organizations, from suppliers to customers, I will concentrate on the suppliers in this chapter. The customer-related aspect is a part of the basic theme of this book.

This book has free materials available for download from the Web Added Value™ Resource Center at www.jrosspub.com.

SECTION III: PROCESSES

Everything should be made as simple as possible, but not simpler.

Albert Einstein

8

QUALITY

It's a funny thing about life:
If you refuse to accept anything but the very best,
you will very often get it.

W. Somerset Maugham

Although this chapter would have blended in quite well under any one of the three sections of this book, it is not by coincidence that it appears as the introductory chapter in the process-related section.

A PHILOSOPHY

Quality is a philosophy that pertains to the most fundamental process in which we engage — our thought process. The quality of our words and actions is a direct consequence of the quality of our thoughts. This holds true in our personal lives as well as our business lives. As an example, think about a person who normally cooks the meals for his or her family. If the person hates to cook, it is sure to be reflected in the food he or she prepares. More often than not, it will not taste very good. If by dumb luck a particular dish does turn out to be good, chances are that the person will not be able to repeat it in the future. It all depends on what is going on inside one's head. If you do not care about what you are doing, it is sure to show in the quality of the product. This goes back to the first of my five Cs — care (Chapter 3).

The same applies to one's business life. If you think of your job as nothing more than just a job, or if your mind is preoccupied with issues other than the work at hand, it will show in your output. When I was shopping for my first new car in the late 1970s, my friends told me to steer clear of cars that were built on a Monday or a Friday. The reason was that on Mondays, the autoworkers were believed to be getting over their hangovers from the weekend, and on Fridays, their thoughts were directed toward the activities planned for the coming weekend. The suspicion was that on both days, their minds were not totally on the work at hand. This is not to imply that all problems related to quality are a result of people not caring about what they do. Apathy is certainly one of the major contributors to poor quality in organizations, but there are a few others that give it strong competition. Ignorance, fixed mind-sets, poor processes, and fragile product designs are some of those issues. Ways to correct apathy and ignorance were addressed in Chapter 3 and product design was covered in Chapter 4. Addressing fixed mind-sets is a recurring theme throughout this book. The current section is dedicated to addressing ways to improve poor processes.

When people hear the word "quality," their minds subconsciously drift toward product quality. What else could it pertain to? After all, that is what customers see. When the quality of a product does not measure up to the customers' expectations, most questions are directed to the shop personnel and the group "responsible" for quality — the quality inspectors. The implication is that ensuring proper product quality is *their* job — and no one else's.

Until the early 1980s, quality control was a policing function within most organizations. When a finished product was completed, it was the quality inspector's job to verify that it was built correctly and that it worked. Likewise, when purchased components arrived at the receiving dock, the quality inspectors were charged with ensuring that the components were correct and would work. The tacit mind-set was, "We don't trust our employees and suppliers to build (and ship) good-quality parts repeatedly, so we will assign a group of individuals the task of checking their work and will call them quality inspectors." In the past, engineers designed the product, the people on the shop floor manufactured it, and the quality group made sure that it worked. Unfortunately, this mind-set is still prevalent in many organizations today, and a frightening number still have not realized that the concept of good quality extends far beyond product quality.

Good product quality is a result of doing the right things in the right manner, and ensuring good quality is the job of every individual in the organization, starting with the CEO all the way down the chain. This is a discipline and a new mind-set — a new jigsaw puzzle that must be solved with the help of everyone in the organization; it is not a spectator sport. Participation by everyone is perhaps the single most important piece of this puzzle. Everybody must believe in it and *live* it. The *only* way to ensure that this happens is for upper management to believe in it and to live it. If management cannot find the time to wholeheartedly participate in efforts to ensure good quality, it is because they do not believe in it. They are just mouthing the right words in the hope that the rest of the organization will comply and that the customers will be impressed. Such half-baked efforts are equivalent to slapping a fresh coat of paint on a corroded piece of steel; in time, the rust is sure to blister through.

Over the past few decades, several organizations appear to have been pre-occupied with and often completely absorbed by buzzwords and methods of the moment, all in the name of achieving "word-class" performance. Frequently, organizations tout their ISO certification or their efforts toward total quality management (TQM), zero defects, or a six sigma level of quality. On various occasions, I have had the opportunity to speak with some of the employees of such organizations. More often than not, when quizzed about the "world-class" objective, the response from the employees is, "Yeah, that's what they want to do," referring to the proverbial nameless and faceless "they" — management. It is very rare to get a response like, "Damn right! That's what we're shooting for."

This tells me that in spite of the mega-bucks invested in these efforts, somewhere in the fundamentals of their approach, management has missed a vital point: employee buy-in and commitment. Along the way, the horse and the cart seem to have switched places. Instead of soliciting employee buy-in and commitment in order to ensure a successful implementation of a project, the project is given a fancy name in the hope that it will help to gain the buy-in and commitment. The buy-in and commitment may not always materialize by purely democratic means; sometimes they may have to be required or demanded by the CEO of the organization. The unwilling constituents of the workforce always have a choice — participate or work for some other organization. In order to demand such compliance, however, the CEO must believe wholeheart-edly in the cause and must be willing to live the life that he or she promotes. In the 1980s, GE made significant strides toward improving the quality of its products and services under the umbrella of Six Sigma. Although Motorola is credited with pioneering such efforts and coining the term Six Sigma, GE is one of very few organizations that took it seriously. Let's face it, there is hardly an organization that would not want to emulate what GE achieved during the regime of Jack Welch. A fact of life is that not every organization is blessed with a CEO like Jack Welch.

Another stellar example comes from the U.S. Air Force. During the Gulf War, the late Four-Star General Bill Creech headed the Tactical Air Command (TAC) unit of the U.S. Air Force. He used the principles of TQM to turn the entire operation around. Operation Desert Storm is believed to be the first war that was won in the air. One of the several tributes to General Creech comes from the Arlington National Cemetery web site: "TAC, a sprawling command that at the time included 180,000 personnel in 46 states and five countries, had an 80 percent productivity improvement under Creech that resulted in savings of $12 billion to the government." Keep in mind, however, that the reason why Bill Creech was able to completely revamp the philosophy and organization of the TAC unit was not because of the simple fact that he had a good idea or that he talked a good line. He firmly believed in his convictions, lived by his principles, and led the TAC unit by example. He was also a four-star general with the necessary clout and support of his superiors, which helped him make it happen.

If you really think about it, every one of these methods has its roots in the teachings of Dr. W. Edwards Deming. With his fourteen points, along with statistical process control, he expounded and highlighted the *very same principles* that are being touted today, under different and sometimes ambiguous names. And he did it more than 50 years ago! After witnessing the trends over the past 30 years, my guess is that his teachings did not take a firm hold (except in Japan) because perhaps he did not dub them with a flashy name. He called them the "System of Profound Knowledge." To an average individual, this may sound a bit intimidating and is not as appealing as some of the newer buzzwords.

Every organization knows that in order to succeed, it must give its customers what they want. If you go to a steak house for dinner, you expect to get a juicy steak of your choice, cooked to your specification. When the steak is brought to the table, the accompanying sizzle enhances the anticipation of taking the first bite. In the world of quality and process improvement, however, the customers seem to be so enamored by the sizzle that they are willing to compromise on and sometimes totally forego the steak. It makes one wonder what customers really want — the steak or the sizzle?

Where quality and process improvements are concerned, I have developed a very simple, almost simplistic, philosophy: if we do the right things, good things will happen. This may seem idealistic to some, but over the years I have been able to prove it to myself repeatedly.

Before leaving the topic of TQM, zero defects, and Six Sigma, I recommend that you read Bill Creech's book, *The Five Pillars of TQM: How to Make Total Quality Management Work for You*. It provides an excellent practical application of the concept. It is full of valuable information for any company that wants to embark on the TQM journey.

ISO also merits some discussion. To date, it is perhaps the only globally recognized effort to develop a set of ground rules in the interest of standardizing policies and procedures related to quality.

ISO CERTIFICATION

Since the 1980s, ISO certification has gained a significant amount of popularity. The intent of ISO certification is to standardize the quality process within each organization from design through manufacturing, sales, and service. The assumption is that if the quality of the processes adopted by an organization is good, the quality of its products and services will also be.

The general approach requires an organization to set policy related to its quality objectives, establish sound procedures to support that policy, document the procedures in a quality manual, and follow those procedures. All that is really required is for an organization to say what it does and to do what it says. The policy and procedures are not dictated to organizations. Each organization is expected to set its own. The major ground rules only show up as broad guidelines pertaining to operational procedures. This is only reasonable. It would be impractical for the ISO body to dictate every minute procedure that organizations must follow. Plus, one size does not fit all. Organizations seeking ISO certification must make a concerted and honest effort to comply with the broad guidelines, as best suited for their particular business. The basic process of achieving and maintaining certification revolves around the traditional mind-set of inspection — third-party inspections performed by certified agencies and internal audits conducted by the resident ISO coordinator.

In several organizations, a key objective for most ISO coordinators is to make sure the company passes the ISO audit, although the means to that end have been left to individual interpretation. This simple fact, coupled with a few gaping holes in the ISO guidelines, seems to have turned a noble cause into a free-for-all. Anyone who has worked for an ISO-certified company has probably experienced a preaudit audit. For the better part of every year, work proceeds as usual, but a few weeks before a third-party audit, the proverbial sawdust hits the fan. Internal ISO auditors emerge from the woodwork to remind the rest of the workforce of the rules they are committed to follow. Everyone who has a copy of the quality manual dusts it off and ensures that they have the latest revision. Paper copies of drawings that people had religiously saved in their offices are carefully hidden from sight. A series of "coaching" meetings and rehearsals ensues.

I have always had a problem with this approach. It does not comply with the "say what we do, and do what we say" commitment that we made to ourselves as an organization. Perhaps the reason is just that — many organizations do not believe that the commitment they made is to themselves; they believe the commitment is made to a relatively faceless entity that appears at their doorstep once every year or so in the form of an independent auditor. That is when the internal auditors tell members of the workforce, "Yes, I know that is how you usually do it, but if you are asked by the third-party auditor, this is how you should answer." This happens when management takes a cavalier approach to ISO certification. It is simply contradictory to the original cause. When employees see that management is not taking this exercise seriously, why would they? And what message do they really receive about the quality of their work, their designs, their processes, and their products? It is ironic that some of these organizations also preach "lean manufacturing." Think of the hours wasted in rehearsing for audits.

A sad fact of life is that for several organizations, ISO certification has become a marketing tool to impress customers. This is not to find fault with the concept behind standardizing quality procedures, but some organizations have misused the trust placed in them by the ISO organization, the third-party auditors, and their customers.

I have participated in more audits than I can count, but not once have I (or anyone I know) been asked by an ISO auditor to comment on improvements in product quality, potentially resulting from years of being certified by ISO. Isn't improving product quality the driving force behind this whole rigmarole? Instead, the auditors' questions revolve around the corrective actions taken when poor quality is encountered. It is amusing that the measure of improvement from one audit to the next is tied to the number of major and minor infractions identified by the auditors — even though product quality could be down. There seems to be a mental disconnect between product quality and how religiously the procedures laid out in the quality manual are followed. We owe it to ourselves to ask, "Is this really working, or are we just going through the motions?"

One organization where I was employed decided to obtain ISO certification. I was the manufacturing manager for a certain product line, and it was my responsibility to ensure that the people in my group contributed to and practiced the procedures that had been laid out in the quality manual. My first statement at a kickoff meeting was: "If we sign up to do this, I want us to do so for the right reasons. This will change the way we conduct our business to some extent, and if we are not willing to abide by the procedures we set for ourselves, then I will gladly tell management that we are not ready for it." Of course, we all knew that if I had to say that to management, we could all end up at the unemployment office. But my group realized where I was coming from, and everyone agreed to sign up for the program. Things went quite smoothly after that, and we were spared the rehearsals. We just had to say what we did, because we were doing what we said we would do.

OUTLOOKS ON QUALITY

Anyone who has worked in the manufacturing discipline for a number of years has encountered a variety of individuals with perhaps an equally wide variety of approaches to quality. Some were passionate about achieving good quality in everything they did. Their motto was "perfection is the norm." It can be enjoyable working with such individuals if one prescribes to that philosophy. While these people expected perfection, they were cognizant of human frailty and the fact that errors can creep in now and then. As long as we learn from our mistakes and keep from falling prey to the same ones over and over again, we can chalk them up to experience. After all, "to err is human, but the eraser should not consistently run out before the pencil!" Others were passionate about *showing* how concerned they were about achieving good quality. Their motto seemed to be *"perception* is the norm." Of the people who fall in this category, one person stands out vividly in my mind. I'll call him Sam.

Most actions that Sam took were driven by how he would be perceived by his peers and those above him in the hierarchy. The fact that the people under him did not have much respect for him mattered little to him. Most organizations, good as they may be, have at least one such person in their employ.

Discussing perception brings to mind a particular episode of the sitcom *Coach* in which coach Hayden Fox hires an image consultant. The consultant coaches him in what to say and how to say it. After a day of this, Hayden goes home all excited and tells his friend Christine Armstrong (paraphrased): "Christine, all this time I've been going through life believing that there's truth and there are lies. Today, I learned about a huge gray area between them called perception!" That's just how it was with Sam. On his palette of life, gray was a primary color. In the following paragraphs you will see how a good idea can go bad if placed in the wrong hands.

A GOOD IDEA GONE BAD

During the course of manufacturing the initial units, several changes were made to the design of a new product XYZ, Inc. was introducing. Tom, the project manager, decided that if he did not keep track of the changes by serial number of each unit, it would be virtually impossible to know the "as-built" configurations once the units were deployed. He decided to use a three-ring binder for each unit built to compile the as-built configuration. Because he would have a book for every unit that was being built, he also decided to use the books to keep track of other pieces of information, such as serial numbers of major components and the results of tests that were performed during the manufacturing process. Tom did this to help maintain his own sanity and that of the person who stepped into the position after him. If a customer called about a malfunctioning generator, for example, he could thumb through the book and find the serial number of the component, which would help him with warranty issues with the supplier. This proved to be an excellent idea, and the books came in handy for several years after the units were sold to the customer.

Around the same time, our friend Sam was managing a different operation within the same company. When he heard about Tom's books, his eyes lit up. "This is a great idea," he said to Joan, a project manager who reported to him. "We will use professional-looking binders, so that when our customers or our vice president visit, we can show off the books to them." He dubbed the books the "quality books." While these books did help provide a quick response to some customer questions, they contributed absolutely nothing to the quality of the product. Yet, they were being advertised as an example of a concerted effort to improve product quality. The people to whom they were being advertised thought they were great.

Soon, maintaining the "quality books" in their completed form became a major objective for Joan. Periodically, Sam would meet with her to go over the books for the units that were recently completed. He actually performed quality audits on the books — but not on the product! While Tom was happy to maintain the books for his products, Joan hated them because they had been forced on her for the wrong reasons. Talk about a good idea gone bad!

CONTINUOUS IMPROVEMENT: PROCESSES

Several organizations and individuals take pride in the fact that they strive for continuous improvement. Usually, the hope is that the end result will be a favorable impact on the company's bottom line. Very often, small steps toward improvement do not have a significant impact on the bottom line, but a collection of such steps certainly could. In their zeal to show a positive impact on the bottom line, some companies focus their efforts on just that, the bottom line. They skip over the key ingredients that contribute to the bottom line. During such efforts, almost everyone agrees that revenue has to increase or profits need to be raised or costs must be cut, but they seldom know how to go about achieving it. Once the bottom line becomes the sole focus of attention, management's view tends to become myopic, and the knee-jerk reaction is often to raise prices, launch creative advertising campaigns, conduct motivational meetings, or reduce head count. Some companies even resort to creative accounting practices. These days, it is difficult to pick up a newspaper and not see such organizations make the headlines in the business section. This is *not* continuous improvement.

Where processes are concerned, efforts toward continuous improvement generally require studying each process and making modifications. The objective usually is to simplify the process to reduce cost and the time it takes to perform the process or to lower the amount of scrap and improve quality. In some cases where it is determined that the existing process no longer adds value to the operation, it may be possible to eliminate it completely.

Contrary to popular belief, the process of process improvement is an iterative one. It is not unusual for organizations to attempt to change a process, see that the expected results were not met, and then shelve the exercise, believing that they tried it, but it does not work in their industry. Dr. Deming is responsible for popularizing the change process that was originally introduced by Dr. Walter Shewhart. Deming called it the Shewhart Cycle, but over the years, it has come to be known as the Deming Cycle. The concept is simple and follows the precepts of common sense (Figure 8.1):

- Step 1. *Plan* the change: Decide what needs to be changed, what it would take to make the change, and what the expected effect of the change is. This is a critical step that is often ignored. As the saying goes, "If you fail to plan, you plan to fail."
- Step 2. *Implement* the change: Carry out the plan, perhaps initially on a small scale.

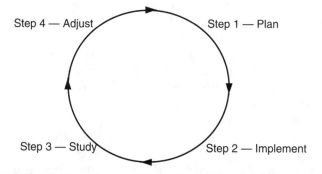

Figure 8.1 The Deming Cycle (Shewhart Cycle) (Based on W. Edwards Deming, *Out of the Crisis,* The MIT Press, Cambridge, MA, 1998, p. 88.)

- Step 3. *Study* the effects of the change: Test the results from Step 2. Were the expected results realized? Were sufficient resources allocated to the effort? Is a different approach needed?
- Step 4. *Adjust* as required: Make necessary adjustments to the design of the experiment.
- Step 5. Repeat the process until the expected results have been achieved.

Personal Experience

While many process changes require the iterative approach, some can be so trivial and obvious that they fall in the "no-brainer" category. In one such change, the finished product was a special-purpose heavy-duty truck. A customized body that was mounted on the frame rails of the chassis just behind the driver's cab served as the field engineer's office. After it was fabricated, the body was painted and then sent to the assembly station. As a new project manager for this product, I decided to observe the process to help me understand it, along with the intricacies of the product.

The first operation that the assembler performed on the newly painted bodies was to cut slots in the side and to install rivnuts. In order to do this, he used a power saw and a drill. Obviously, this caused the paint to chip off in several places, and the assembler would roll the body back to the paint shop for touch-ups. Once the touch-ups were completed, the body would be rolled back to the assembler and he would begin the assembly process.

"Dan, why are you drilling and cutting on the body after it is painted? Why aren't these operations performed prior to painting?" I asked the assembler.

"Because I know where to put the slots in the body and I also have a template that helps me position the rivnuts. I talked to engineering about this a long time ago, but they haven't implemented the changes on the drawings, so Bob cannot do this while he is fabricating the body," Dan said while showing me a crumpled page with a rough sketch and dimensions on it.

"Do the folks in engineering have this information?" I asked.

"No, but I showed Sam, the design engineer, what I am having to do and he said he would take care of it when he had some time," Dan replied.

"When was that, Dan?"

"Some time last year."

"Why don't we give the template and the sketch to Bob and have him perform these operations prior to the body being painted?" I asked Dan.

"That would be great! I wouldn't have to mess with cutting and drilling." Dan was thrilled at the prospect.

From the next body onward, Bob performed the cutting and drilling operations and also installed the rivnuts prior to the body being painted. A copy of the sketch was given to Sam, along with locations for the holes for the rivnuts, to help him make the necessary changes to the drawings.

How hard was it to move the operation from Dan to Bob? It certainly did not take an in-depth analysis to figure it out. Yet the people on the shop floor had been following this procedure for several months — just because *nobody* questioned it.

The quality of the product was really not affected by this change. The shop floor personnel always made certain that the paint was touched up prior to starting assembly. The improvement pertained to the quality of the process. The paint touch-up operation was eliminated, which saved several hundred dollars and a day or two (depending on how crowded the paint booth was) of process time.

UNDERSTANDING AND MANAGING PROCESS VARIATIONS

In his book *Out of the Crisis*, Dr. Deming provides an in-depth explanation of the causes of variation in any process. He credits Walter Shewhart for highlighting the difference between common causes of variations and special causes of variations. In lay terms, if the observations derived from a particular process are scattered around the expected average observation, then the process can be thought of as being stable, or in statistical control, and the variations are a result of common causes inherent to the design of the process. No amount of finger-pointing, threats, or motivational talks will make any difference in the outcome of the process. The only way to realize improvement is to address and modify the process itself. That responsibility sits squarely on the shoulders of management. If, on the other hand, the observations denote periodic wild swings from the expected average, chances are good that they are a result of a special cause — perhaps a new worker on the job, equipment in need of maintenance, or something else external to the process.

Dr. Donald J. Wheeler and David S. Chambers present a lucid explanation of and a variety of uses for control charts[1] to enable analysis of data retrieved from different processes. The key benefit of using control charts is that they reveal valuable information that is not intuitively obvious by just looking at the raw data. The information can be used to decide on the proper route toward improvement. The best way to show the importance and use of control charts is with an example. The one cited actually happened at a client's facility.

I decided to explain the theory behind control charts in the main body of this chapter and not in an appendix, as I believe it is important for everyone, regardless of position, to understand it.

Example: Use of Control Charts

During one of my meetings with Tom, the manager of the department responsible for the sale of spare parts at an automotive dealership, he mentioned that he was going to have to step up the volume of spare parts sales for the current year (2000). It was early February when we spoke. Tom showed me the sales data he had compiled for the previous four years (1996 to 1999) by salesperson. The department consisted of nine individuals, eight of whom were responsible for over-the-counter and telephone sales and one who furnished parts solely to the service shop. Since this person was not responsible for over-the-counter sales, he has been excluded from the analysis. Two of the eight, who had just started to work there in January 2000 and had no sales history, have also been excluded. I have adjusted Tom's numbers to account for these exclusions.

I asked Tom about his plans for increasing sales. He mentioned that he was trying to motivate the salespeople to do better than their prior performance and pulled out a memo (Figure 8.2) that he was planning to distribute to them.

To: All Parts Sales Personnel
From: Tom Smith
Re: Year 2000 Sales Plan

This is an exciting time for us as employees of Have Truck Will Travel, Inc. Within the last year, we have been able to be a part of a complete transformation of the dealership. Being witness to this allows you to see the commitment that has been given us. This commitment has been to provide the best possible working conditions. Your work in this transformation has been greatly appreciated and I believe makes this occasion even more special.

Now is the time for us to make a commitment as a team. This commitment is to become the best source of parts to our industry and provide the best customer service possible. With this new facility we have the opportunity to attack the new century as a real powerhouse in our business. In order to do this, there are certain changes that must be made. These changes must begin with us.

We are going to begin these changes with a simple, yet historically effective plan. We are going to set goals and then strive to achieve them. In business, as in life, goals are used as an individual measuring stick to challenge ourselves to become the best that we can be. Now we will use this same philosophy to improve and grow our department. Attached you will find a chart and graph depicting historical sales levels that you have achieved. These levels are of no relevance now, because of the many changes that we have been through. The reason I included them was to allow you to see how your personal sales advances have allowed us to increase and become more profitable as a department. The important

Figure 8.2 Tom Smith's Memo

Tom was an intelligent, caring individual with the best interests of the organization at heart. However, he was new to the job, and much of what he had learned in the way of management skills was a result of on-the-job training. This is fairly typical in industry. Regardless of his good intentions, Tom's memo wasn't going to get the job done. Rather than talking directly with the employees and soliciting their input, some managers choose to take a nonconfrontational approach, as in this case, and manage with memos.

Tom's memo alluded to changes that had occurred at the dealership. The major change was a new building, which housed the parts department and the warehouse. Other than that, the memo was nothing more than a "rah-rah" speech, but I would like to highlight a few key points that Tom tried to make.

In the third paragraph of his memo, Tom talked about setting goals as though this was the first year that they would participate in such an activity. It makes one wonder what was done in prior years. In the same paragraph, he said that he will distribute a chart and graph showing each person's sales history, but that

---

numbers on the chart are the expected sales level and the goal sales level. The expected sales level is not anything new to us; we have always had that as a part of our job descriptions. Except now, as professionals should be, you will be expected to hit those levels each month. What we will strive for is to achieve our goal levels.

To reach these goals we must become timely, accurate, and efficient. There are many things that we can do to accomplish this, the easiest being to sell more to existing customers (up-sell) and provide better customer service. I expect you to develop an individual plan to achieve your goals. Commission structures are to be reviewed soon based on this plan, so I want suggestions on how we can improve your sales as well as the whole team's sales numbers.

Remember, for one to be successful, we must all be successful. We are only as strong as our weakest link. With that in mind, we must work together not only as a department, but as a company. Do not look at other departments as the enemy; look at them as other team members. Help them as much as possible, just as you do outside customers. If other departments are excelling, this just means more opportunities for the parts department.

We will make the year 2000 the "Year of the Customer." Always remember that they are the ones who pay our salaries, and superior customer service will set us far apart from the competition. After all, that is our goal — to be the best source of parts to our industry and provide the best customer service possible.

Thank you,
Tom

it is meaningless because of all the changes that had occurred, yet the only change was the new building.

In the next paragraph, he proceeded to tell the workforce how to achieve the goals. His prescription was for them to be timely, efficient, and accurate and to sell more parts (up-sell) to the customers, but he left it to each salesperson to develop and present his or her own plan for achieving the goals. The feeble carrot of revised commissions is hard to ignore. This was Tom's way of ensuring that the plans would be submitted to him in a timely manner.

Paragraph five appears to be an attempt to promote teamwork, and the last paragraph is a final waving of pompoms.

In Tom's mind, his memo, along with the new goals, was going to motivate the sales force to raise their level of performance. Boy, was he in for a surprise!

Let's take a look at the raw data, then plot it in the form of control charts and see what unfolds. As one would expect, the raw data shown in Table 8.1 are just a collection of numbers and really do not reveal much. Now let's look at the control charts. The type of chart that is used here is the XmR chart.[2] X represents the monthly sales dollars for each salesperson, and mR is the moving range computed by taking the positive value (absolute value) of the difference between the sales dollars in a given month and the preceding month. The salespeople are labeled SP-1 through SP-6. In Figure 8.3, the moving range for SP-1 for April of 1999 is $21,533, which is the difference between the sales in April 1999 ($99,547) and March 1999 ($78,014). The X-chart shows a solid line at $75,550, which represents the average (or mean) monthly sales for SP-1 for the four years. Above and below this line are two dotted lines, which represent limits for the data being analyzed. These are referred to as the natural process limits. They are computed by moving away from the mean ($\overline{X}$) in both directions, by the equivalent of three sigma. While the mean is a measure of central tendency, sigma is a measure of dispersion in the data stream. Why three sigma?[3] Three sigma is used because 99 to 100% of the observations are normally expected to fall in that range.

The formulae[3] used to compute the upper and lower natural process limits for X are:

$$\text{Upper: UNPL(X)} = \overline{X} + 2.66 \; \overline{mR}$$

$$\text{Lower: LNPL(X)} = \overline{X} - 2.66 \; \overline{mR}$$

Similarly, the upper control limit for the moving range, mR, is computed using the formula:

$$\text{UCL(R)} = 3.268 \; \overline{mR}$$

Table 8.1   Individual Sales for SP-1 Through SP-6

Year	SP-1	SP-2	SP-3	SP-4	SP-5	SP-6
1996	68,608	43,337		25,813	30,297	35,813
	64,052	33,591		22,331	22,409	36,044
	46,821	40,477		26,970	39,283	55,369
	87,390	48,922		31,966	29,338	30,050
	74,847	61,674		32,614	29,725	68,812
	65,506	52,595		36,851	31,641	45,122
	81,159	63,863		36,609	27,346	73,154
	120,921	68,857		40,494	21,286	68,865
	66,488	50,070		33,285	33,400	50,739
	79,448	63,708		31,543	22,850	36,096
	56,179	46,725		33,443	11,467	43,456
	57,278	47,916		25,652	14,812	52,778
1997	76,941	46,953	24	36,875	24,224	65,783
	54,940	54,135	864	32,393	27,463	40,456
	90,895	45,624	4,947	32,028	17,103	59,253
	73,237	43,747	25,530	28,033	23,021	40,310
	76,815	47,159	36,537	40,177	27,917	29,040
	79,328	40,785	28,308	38,864	28,155	39,569
	65,284	59,322	51,429	62,592	31,273	35,269
	78,699	59,665	25,792	42,632	31,537	33,933
	77,287	69,175	24,582	43,283	26,356	37,844
	99,485	58,878	29,595	46,388	34,138	32,166
	86,444	52,019	22,425	28,181	13,774	20,477
	62,476	57,416	39,163	31,634	18,071	18,893
1998	84,854	61,048	36,585	36,218	30,044	29,183
	83,034	61,753	32,913	39,461	27,725	24,991
	73,825	64,601	30,815	45,896	37,314	34,007
	88,186	46,988	43,473	43,155	31,996	35,632
	80,280	74,209	35,947	47,181	31,212	38,510
	80,430	44,928	47,214	55,085	37,696	35,100
	58,776	66,963	34,535	49,571	32,023	42,890
	94,606	60,606	55,014	42,713	34,675	42,652
	102,192	57,252	46,001	32,325	32,029	51,830
	71,722	63,916	52,538	33,951	36,362	53,428
	62,644	57,723	20,503	35,401	17,286	51,775
	53,972	53,825	41,661	50,226	29,873	31,209
1999	98,400	65,110	37,559	33,698	29,180	40,653
	69,528	71,112	29,344	31,148	25,515	29,087
	78,014	73,753	36,756	43,623	27,031	58,522
	99,547	66,341	56,465	48,892	28,100	48,644
	79,318	64,354	49,382	34,244	30,374	43,379
	75,978	52,726	74,800	42,897	36,014	40,547
	79,298	77,813	37,769	54,591	34,662	38,033
	66,217	75,865	40,434	38,292	32,398	35,510
	78,103	73,899	47,513	41,572	33,394	26,629
	68,682	70,662	47,792	35,302	28,141	32,001
	55,127	57,112	39,725	36,448	24,281	41,746
	53,147	81,669	44,868	42,833	23,223	18,060

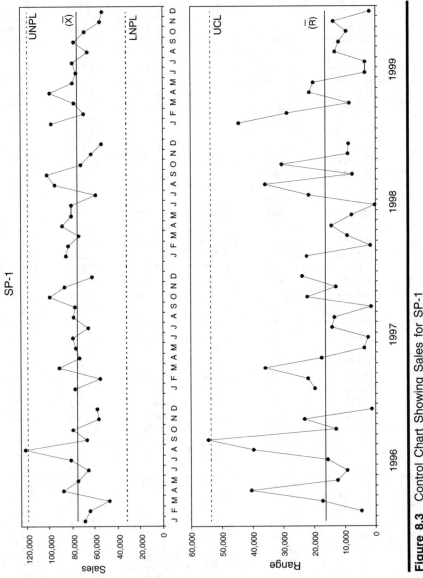

Figure 8.3 Control Chart Showing Sales for SP-1

Since the moving range is computed by taking the absolute value of the difference in successive values of X, a lower control limit does not apply here. Now let's analyze the control charts for each of the six salespeople:

- **SP-1**: The sales chart (X-chart) in Figure 8.3 shows that most of the data are randomly clustered about the mean, $\overline{X}$, and all data points, with the exception of August 1996, fall within the range specified by the upper and lower natural process limits. This is why the limits are called natural process limits. Dr. Wheeler refers to them as the "voice of the process."[3] In the case of SP-1, the limits are $31,965 and $119,135, with a mean of $75,550. This tells us that any number between $31,965 and $119,135 can be expected, and if the process is not modified, nothing can be done to change that. The variations are a result of common causes, which are inherent to the process. No amount of motivational meetings and pep talks with SP-1 are going to help him perform any better than the process will allow. In order to change the results, the process must be changed. August 1996, however, shows that the sales were higher than the upper natural process limit. The moving range also shows a corresponding spike in that same period. This is not natural (in the current lingo), and it certainly was not expected. It was the result of a special cause — a cause outside the basic process. However, at a meeting in February 2000, it is highly unlikely that we would be able to recall what SP-1 did in August 1996 to achieve such a high sales figure. If the control charts were being used during the summer of 1996, this aberration easily could have been identified and built upon. But by the year 2000, it was just a lost opportunity.
- **SP-2**: While there are no significant aberrations (other than a low point in February 1996), there appears to be a general upward trend in the data (Figure 8.4). SP-2 started out in 1996, and as he learned on the job, his sales figures improved each year. This trend is certainly worth investigating in order to help him continue the improvements in the future.
- **SP-3**: This person (Figure 8.5) was hired in 1997 and, like SP-2, shows an upward trend in the sales figures, although it is more gradual than that for SP-2. June 1999 highlights an exception that could have been learned from but, again, falls into the category of lost opportunity.
- **SP-4**: An upward trend appears for the first three years, and then levels off (Figure 8.6). Again, it was too late to understand the special cause that resulted in the spikes outside or very close to the control limits.

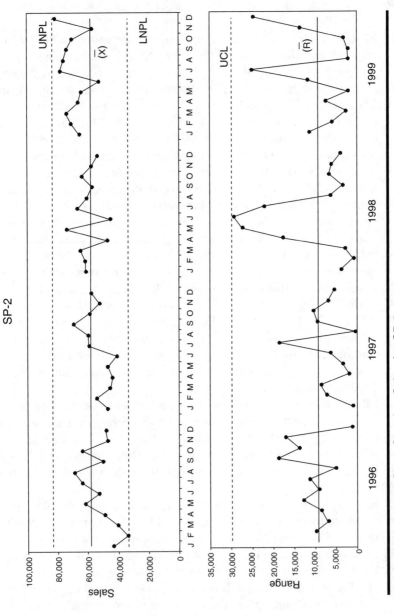

Figure 8.4 Control Chart Showing Sales for SP-2

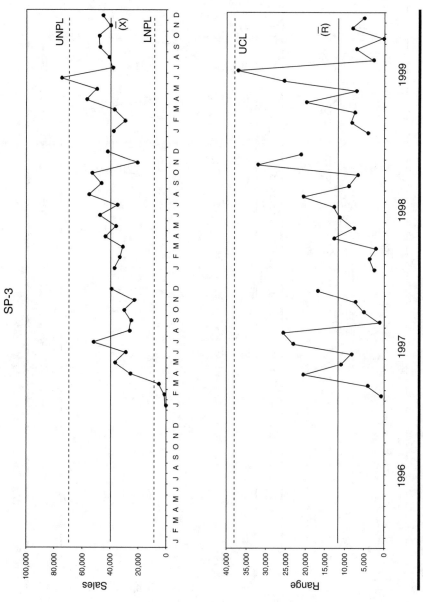

Figure 8.5 Control Chart Showing Sales for SP-3

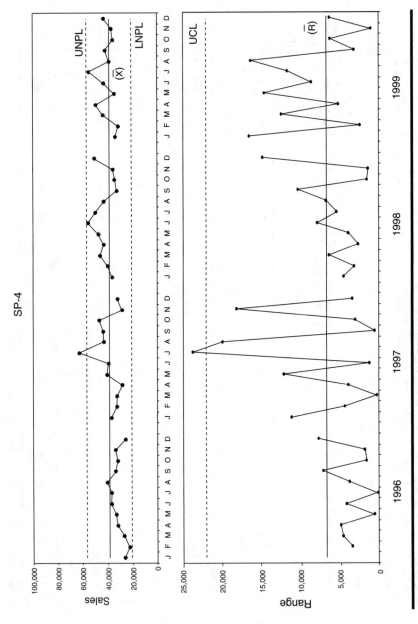

Figure 8.6 Control Chart Showing Sales for SP-4

- **SP-5**: A couple of interesting trends show up with SP-5 (Figure 8.7). For one, most of his sales figures are clustered quite tightly around the mean. However, a careful look at 1998, from March through October, reveals that all of the observations lie above the mean. According to statistical theory, this could be another signal. If eight or more observations lie on the same side of the center line (the mean), it may signal a special cause taking effect.[3] In fact, 1998 seems to be the best year that SP-5 had. Unfortunately, this also was not caught in time to be useful. Something else shows up. With the exception of 1999, every November shows a dip in sales. In fact, it is so pronounced in 1997 and 1998 that the moving range spikes above the upper control limit. This is not a result of natural causes. It signals a special cause. Sure enough, when I asked Tom what he thought might have caused the exceptions, he promptly said that SP-5 is an avid deer hunter and took time off every year in November to go hunting. During the same time in 1999, he was ill and did not go hunting, but he did come to work. This is exactly the point of using control charts. Special causes of aberrant data can be easily identified and explained if they are caught soon enough.
- **SP-6**: The data appear to be cyclical (Figure 8.8). In 1996, SP-6 appeared to be doing "reasonably" well and had a few good months. However, a third type of statistical signal is apparent from May through August. If at least three of four consecutive observations are closer to either control limit than they are to the mean, it could be the result of a special cause.[3] However, since more than three years had passed before the data were analyzed, it too was a lost opportunity. In 1997, a progressive decline occurs through the year, picking up in the spring of 1998 for most of that year and then declining again for the better part of 1999. The second half of 1997 and the first half of 1998 show enough points that are consecutively below the mean to suggest some special cause for the decline in performance. Once again, however, since management had not even heard of control charts, nothing was done about it.

So much for analyses based on control charts. Now let's see how they can be used to predict future outcomes. We will begin by recapping some of the historical sales data by salesperson. Table 8.2 shows the average sales per year, along with the grand average of monthly sales by individual.

It is reasonable to expect that the total parts sales in the year 2000 will be close to the sum of the average sales per individual, $280,805, if nothing is done

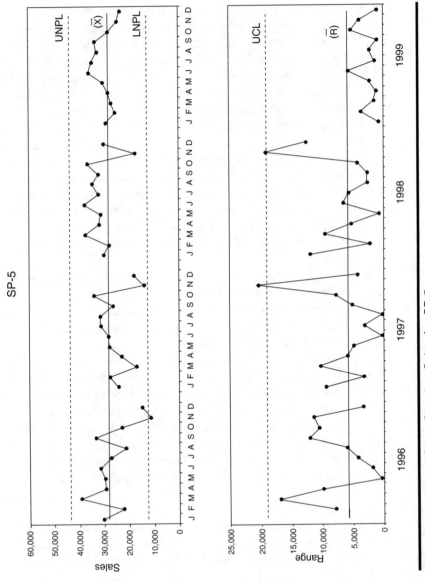

Figure 8.7 Control Chart Showing Sales for SP-5

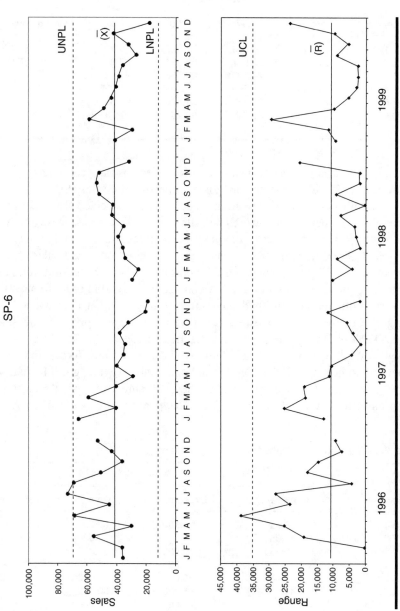

Figure 8.8 Control Chart Showing Sales for SP-6

Table 8.2 Average Sales for All Salespeople

| Salesperson | Average Sales | | | | |
	1996	1997	1998	1999	Grand Average
SP-1	72,391	76,819	77,877	75,113	75,550
SP-2	51,811	52,907	59,484	69,201	58,351
SP-3	—	24,100	39,767	45,201	39,484
SP-4	31,464	38,590	42,599	40,295	38,237
SP-5	26,155	25,253	31,520	29,359	28,072
SP-6	49,692	37,749	39,267	37,734	41,111
All					280,805

to change the basic process that has been followed for the past several years. However, Tom decided that he was going to present the salespeople with two different numbers — one representing what he really expected from them and another, much higher number, which he called the goal. He based these numbers solely on his "gut feel" after "studying" the individual averages for only the prior year (1999). Actually, there was a third number, budgeted sales, which was given to Tom by the owner and the controller. The new building for sales and the warehouse brought with it additional expenses, and in order to meet the necessary profit margin, the budgeted sales number is what they wanted the sales group to meet. The salespeople, however, were not privy to the sales budget. Table 8.3 shows the numbers described above.

Tom actually believed that his memo would get the sales force fired up to the point that they would work harder and come close to the "goal" he had set before them. And if they came close to the goal, surely they would meet the budget number. It was a disaster waiting to happen. I was concerned that Sam,

Table 8.3 Targets Compared to Average Sales

| Salesperson | Sales | | | |
	Grand Average	Expected	Goal	Budget
SP-1	75,550	65,500	85,000	
SP-2	58,351	65,500	75,000	
SP-3	39,484	50,000	65,000	
SP-4	38,237	50,000	65,000	
SP-5	28,072	50,000	65,000	
SP-6	41,111	45,000	50,000	
Total Monthly	280,805	326,000	405,000	364,833
Total Annual	3,369,660	3,912,000	4,860,000	4,378,000

the owner of the business, and John, the controller, may also prescribe to the same philosophy, so I decided to meet with the two of them and Tom.

At our meeting, I showed them the data in Table 8.3 and asked which number they would pick if they were to lay a large bet on predicting spare parts sales for the year 2000. All three picked the grand average and indicated that the number probably would be somewhere between $3.25 million and $3.5 million. Sam and John, however, were also quick to shake their heads and say that it would not be good enough, because the budget had to be met to recover the additional costs that resulted from the new construction and remodeling. The next logical question was to ask how they planned to reach the budgeted number for sales. They said that Tom wanted to hire a few more salespeople, but that would add to the expenses and the new hires may not be able to hit the ground running. Finally, I asked them whether they had asked the salespeople for their ideas. All three had perplexed looks on their faces as they said "no," but their looks said, "Of course not. How would *they* know?" Imagine that!

Keep in mind that these were intelligent, educated individuals, but they were ignorant about some things. I politely asked if I could spend some time talking to the sales force and offered to get back to them with my findings.

The common thread in the response I got from every salesperson was, "We just don't have enough time." Digging a bit deeper into the reason why they did not think they had enough time, I found the following gems of information:

- Each salesperson was required to pull parts for customer orders from the warehouse.
- Because inventory counts were not accurately maintained in the computer, the salespeople could not trust the system. They made special trips to the warehouse to ensure that the parts were physically there before committing to their customers.
- Some of the salespeople were notorious for "hiding" parts in case one of their favorite customers called for them. This added to the inventory inaccuracies. The parts would show up in the computer as being available, but other salespeople could never find them physically.
- The salespeople were required to place purchase orders for parts that were not available in inventory.
- A few months prior to my talk with the sales force, the ordering process had been computerized. Prior to that, each salesperson had to fill out a four-part form per component to place an order. However, since the manager of the department did not "trust" computers, the sales force was required to use both the new computer system and the four-part form — just in case the computer crashed.

- Auditing computer counts because of inaccuracies, pulling parts from the warehouse, and the duplicate system for placing purchase orders was taking up about a third of each salesperson's time each day.

The confusion that was created by all of this was unbelievable. This was a textbook example of a bad process that was taken for granted, but productivity was expected (hoped?) to improve as a result of pep talks and a memo. This is the way the manager had run similar operations for 30 years, and it was the only way with which he was comfortable. If the sales force did not meet the expected numbers, it was only because people were not working hard enough and had to be motivated.

My recommendations to Sam, John, and Tom were very straightforward:

- Hire a couple of people to pull and stock parts in the warehouse and to perform daily cycle counts (certainly a cheaper alternative than hiring more salespeople).
- Conduct a physical inventory and start over with a clean slate.
- Keep the sales force out of the warehouse (when everyone has a hand in the cookie jar, no one is accountable for the cookies).
- Establish proper procedures for backing up the data in the computer system.
- Discontinue the use of the four-part purchase order form.
- Educate the sales force in the art of selling (the current interpretation of "up-selling" was the equivalent of asking the customer, "You want fries with that?").

Disencumbering the sales force of all the nonvalue-added work that had to be performed was equivalent to adding two individuals. Instead of spending just two-thirds of their time tending to customers, the six individuals on the sales force could spend closer to 100% of their time.

None of this would have surfaced if control charts pertaining to the sales process had not been plotted and analyzed and the individuals who actually did the work had not been consulted. The business probably would have continued as it had in prior years.

An Analogy

When it comes to problem solving and process simplification, it is critical to address both with a definite sense of purpose. Taking wild swings at problems as they arise, only to see them raise their ugly heads again down the road, is not the right approach. The mission should be to "seek and destroy" the root causes of problems so that they do not recur. An analogy that applies to this situation compares street fighters to prizefighters. Street fighters repeatedly take wild swings, hoping to land a good punch, while prizefighters are trained to study the situation and to make every blow count.

PAPER IS CHEAP!

One of the keys to improving quality is process simplification. Elaborate, unwieldy processes lead to confusion and frustration within an organization. Such processes also lead to higher costs in the way of labor required to stoke them, reduced flexibility, and poor quality. An important point to remember is that any process is a means to an end. Performing and perpetuating the process itself is not why we wake up and go to work. The ultimate objectives usually are to reduce costs, improve quality, increase flexibility, improve customer service, and to be more competitive — all of which are expected to favorably influence the bottom line. The same applies to efforts directed toward process improvement and simplification. They, too, are just a means to the same end. It is important to keep this in perspective.

Many organizations are reluctant to utilize technology to simplify jobs. This is more prevalent among smaller, privately owned companies. Computers are utilized sparingly in favor of paperwork. Many use a computer as an expensive cash register. The mind-set is that "paper is cheap." While this is true, what some people do not realize is that the cost of managing, filing, maintaining, and retrieving the paperwork can be extensive. This also results in delays and lost records. Over the course of time, the focus of the organization shifts from serving customers to managing paperwork. The results can be disastrous.

It is not unusual to find organizations where employees are inundated with paperwork — sometimes to the point where they cannot think clearly about simpler alternatives. This is not to say that paper documents do not still hold a legitimate place in our daily lives. For instance, some people are more comfortable reading a printed document than a computer screen. That's fine, as long as they trash (or recycle) the document once they are done with it. But that is not what usually happens. Once they have read a document, they want to "file" it someplace safe, where they can get their hands on it at a later date. The fact that the document still resides in the computer from which it was printed falls by the wayside; psychologically, they feel that it is much easier to find a paper document than an electronic one. Once this practice sets in, it begins to snowball. The next step is to requisition file folders, labels, filing cabinets, and perhaps the most expensive commodity, office space. Now that this filing "system" exists, people have to be hired to maintain it. Yet another large expense. Think about all the various documents that people end up filing and the costs associated with doing so — monthly status reports, financial reports, customer orders, purchase orders, invoices, packing lists, receiving reports, etc.

PROCESS EVOLUTION — THANKS TO TECHNOLOGY

The following example helps to put in perspective where we are compared to where we were 30 years ago, all thanks to technological developments. Not all that long ago, different colored multipart paper forms interleaved with carbon paper were used. A typewriter or a #2 pencil was used to complete those forms. Either way, people's hands got dirty. Then came NCR (no carbon required) paper. The same implements were used to fill out the forms, minus the dirty hands. Soon after, with the advent of mainframe computers and dot-matrix printers, the same NCR paper was available in fan-fold form. Even then, however, each sheet (usually at the foot of the page) indicated the color of the paper and its eventual destination (for example, "white copy — customer," "pink copy — accounting," "yellow copy — originator," and so on).

When laser printers came on the scene, they presented a major problem. While they were much faster than dot-matrix printers and the quality of the print was far superior, the multipart forms could no longer be used. With a laser printer, the same document had to be printed four times, and even though the information on every sheet was identical, the nomenclature was still printed at the bottom of every page. People could not let go of the color-coding concept. As a result, each sheet was forced to be unique by adding a note that read, for example, "yellow copy — originator," even though every sheet was white. While it may have been useful to indicate the department where the document was to be delivered (accounting, purchasing, etc.), it was not really necessary to assign a color to every page. Old habits die hard!

Not until the advent of electronic mail did people feel comfortable eliminating the paper form completely and performing the same activity on-line. A remnant from years gone by and something we see every day but do not give a second thought to is the ability of most e-mail programs to send a copy of a message to several individuals using the label "cc." This term originated perhaps before most of us were born and really is a misnomer in the high-tech age, but it helps get the message across — it stands for "carbon copy."

It is important to look back once in a while. It makes us realize how far we have come and helps to alleviate fears and concerns about how much further we can go.

These habits were developed over the years, because in the past there were no plausible alternatives and they made sense. These days, a 40-gigabyte hard drive costs about the same as a filing cabinet, and the hard drive can store multiple filing cabinets worth of documents. Good-quality scanners are also available at reasonable prices, allowing digitizing of paper documents and storage of the electronic version. Until a few years ago, a legitimate reason to file contracts was that signatures could not be transcribed to an electronic format. With the advent of reasonably priced electronic signature pads, that excuse has also fallen by the wayside. The real problem is that we are not able to wean ourselves from old habits. Storing documents and holding on to information provides some people with a false sense of purpose and comfort in the knowledge that they have a paper trail. God forbid someone should accuse them of something and they cannot whip out a stack of documents to support their actions. This is self-preservation in action. Another reason why people hoard paper documents is that they have not taken the time to learn how to use computer systems. The net effect of this is that some employees relate their jobs to the paperwork; in fact, it is because of the excessive paperwork that some of them were hired in the first place. When management begins to look at ways to alleviate the paperwork, some employees see it as a threat to their jobs and find ways to defend its legitimacy. Once again, it is management's job to educate the employees and help allay their fears.

LOOK MA, NO HANDS!

At the other end of the spectrum are organizations that automate for the sake of automating. They talk about their plans for a "paper-less" office or factory. They are too eager to switch key processes and decisions to an imaginary autopilot — the "system." Often, the hope is that the "system" will show them how to set up their processes, thus avoiding the trouble of actually thinking through them. Automating processes that have not been manually defined can be the kiss of death. Sometimes "less paper" is a better alternative than "paperless."

NOTES

1. Portions based on Donald J. Wheeler and David S. Chambers, *Understanding Statistical Process Control*, 2nd edition, © copyright 1992, SPC Press, Knoxville, TN. Used by permission. All rights reserved.
2. I could have used the average monthly sales figure for all six individuals and plotted what is commonly called the $\overline{X}R$ chart. The results of such a chart would lead to similar

conclusions. I decided to use XmR charts because they facilitate a comparison among the different salespeople.

3. Portions based on Donald J. Wheeler, *Understanding Variation: The Key to Managing Chaos,* © copyright 1993, SPC Press, Knoxville, TN. Used by permission. All rights reserved.

This book has free materials available for download from the
Web Added Value™ Resource Center at www.jrosspub.com.

9

ENGINEERING PROCESSES

*Much progress can be realized if we only allow
our "cannots" and "do nots" to give way to "why nots?"*

Soli J. Engineer

Most engineering groups are involved with activities that revolve around designing parts and products, configuring them, and laying out detailed specifications pertaining to them. Implementing changes is, of course, an integral part of these activities.

In the "old" days, the design of parts was represented in the form of drawings, which were created manually, and the bill of material was displayed as a list of parts or a table on the face of a drawing. Depending on the circumstances, the specifications were included either on the drawing or in a separate document. The drawings usually were furnished to the shop floor and suppliers in the form of "blueprints," which were disposable copies of the originals. The originals were carefully guarded by a group called engineering records. The records group would make copies of the originals for manufacturing and would allow design engineers to "check out" originals if changes had to be made.

Technological advances over the past several decades have enabled us to perform these functions far more easily. Now we have access to software that allows designers to create a three-dimensional model of a component, and drawings, part numbers, and bills of material are generated at the touch of a button. Product Data Management (PDM) systems act as an interface between engineering and manufacturing groups and allow the storage of any and all information for a given component or finished product. PDM systems have also rendered the engineering records function obsolete. Engineers who want to modify documentation can "check out" the appropriate document and make the necessary changes. Once the changes have been made, the software requires the proper hierarchy of approval signatures before the modified version can be made available for use by manufacturing. Individuals in manufacturing can print the required drawings at will and, more often than not, transmit electronic copies to suppliers.

Thanks to such technological advances, the tools of the trade have come a long way from what they used to be. For many of us, however, our inherent mind-sets have been slow to follow suit. We still struggle with and sometimes argue about elementary issues, such as when to change a part number and when to change the revision level. We still look for shortcuts to documentation, even though they may complicate the lives of the people in manufacturing. And we still believe that engineering and manufacturing can continue to work independently of each other and still create a cost-effective, good-quality product of which any customer should be proud.

These mind-sets are the focus of this chapter. They will be blended into discussions of engineering-related software systems and the process of managing engineering changes.

DESIGN SYSTEMS

The generic name for computer systems that facilitate the design process is computer-aided design (CAD). These days, state-of-the-art CAD software packages allow designers to create 3-D models of components. Several suppliers of commercially available parts provide such models of their components, making it easy for designers to simply plug the model into their designs of assemblies. What a great convenience and time-saving tool! Once the designer is satisfied with the 3-D model, the required drawings are a cinch to generate.

Regardless of the level of sophistication of the CAD software that is used, the single most important requirement for the design of any product is that it conforms to specifications. This aspect of a product's design is not dependent on the software; it is totally dependent on the individuals involved with the design process. For products that are produced in volume and sold commercially, the design must conform to specifications that are advertised to potential customers. Similarly, for custom-designed products, the design should conform to the specifications laid out by the customers. The specifications provide customers with data pertaining to key aspects of the product. They include information relating to the size and appearance of the product, its configuration and functions, the environment within which the product can be used, power and/or fuel requirements if applicable, safety requirements, and the expected life of the product, just to name a few. The bottom line is that customers must know what to expect and be confident that the finished product meets their expectations. Such customer-related specifications are an integral part of the design of any product.

To actually build the product, however, a far more detailed set of specifications is required. These come in the form of drawings with associated material call-outs, dimensions and tolerances, bills of material, and specific instructions pertaining to issues such as metal coating, testing, and calibration.

With the advent of sophisticated design software, drawings are created from a three-dimensional model of the component being designed. Many of these software packages are capable of assigning unique part numbers and generating a series of single-level bills of material. Specific instructions are documented using word-processing programs, which come in a variety of flavors.

The design stage, the first in a series in the life of any product, is where significant strides can be made to ensure a low product cost, a high level of quality, and greater flexibility to handle changing customer requirements. In order to realize these benefits, it is important to keep the design simple and to resist specifying materials and components that are difficult to procure (unobtainium). Experience has shown that in many instances, just the opposite is the case. The product is overdesigned, sometimes calling for difficult to procure components or material, and the bills of material are oversimplified. Tolerance specification usually is one of the biggest factors in the "overdesign" category. Designers tend to specify tolerances that are tighter than necessary, just to be on the safe side. Sometimes this is done by design (no pun intended), but at times it is unintentional. Although this topic was covered in Chapters 4 and 7, an experience from many years ago is relevant.

The part in question was a tabletop made of marine-grade plywood, which was to be laminated with a plastic sheet. The supplier trying to build the tabletop noticed that the drawing called out a tolerance of ±0.015 inches. Knowing that he could not possibly hold such a tolerance on a part made of plywood, the supplier called the designer to see if he would loosen the tolerance. The designer must have been preoccupied at the time and rather tersely told the supplier to build the part per the drawing. Frustrated, the supplier brought the drawing to me, asking if I could get the tolerance changed. I met with the designer and facetiously mentioned that he was missing a couple of pieces of information on the drawing — the temperature and humidity at which he expected the part to meet the tolerance that he had specified. He got the message, and the tolerance was changed to ±0.125 inches, the thickness of a table-saw blade.

PRODUCT DATA MANAGEMENT SYSTEMS

PDM systems are not cheap. The basic software alone can cost upwards of $100,000. Tack on additional computer hardware requirements and user training, and the resultant cost puts them well beyond the reach of most small businesses. This is unfortunate, because a good PDM system can add significant value to the engineering effort of any organization involved with product design. In fact, for large organizations, especially those with multidivision operations that are geographically scattered, a good PDM system is a requirement. Some of the key functions that a PDM system can serve are:

- Repository for engineering information
- Data library
- Engineering change management
- Buffer between engineering and manufacturing data

Repository for Engineering Information

The database associated with a PDM system can serve as a repository for any and all engineering information. The data can be tied to a specific part number or to a project code. For organizations that design custom products to customers' specifications, the project code could be replaced with a contract number or a sales order number. The information tied to a project or a contract can be generic and varied. It can include an electronic copy of the contract, various communications to and from the customer, and other miscellaneous information pertaining to the project or contract. When it comes to information related to a specific part number, certain pieces of information are mandatory. The type of information depends on the type of part; of course, revision level and description are always required.

Commercial Parts

For commercial items, two pieces of information must be specified in order to facilitate procurement: the manufacturer of the part and the manufacturer's part number. All too often, designers specify the distributor and the distributor's part number instead of the actual manufacturer's data. Although sometimes this is the simpler route to take, it is wrong — it is an accident waiting to happen. For seemingly trivial commercial items, designers are prone to use major distributors' catalogs to locate parts. Once the part has been found, it is all too easy for the designer to specify the distributor and the distributor's part number from the catalog. Distributors are prone to substitute parts, sometimes based on which manufacturer offers the best pricing. When that happens, the "new" part may not serve the purpose for which the designer had specified the original part. This can cause havoc downstream in manufacturing.

Custom-Designed Parts

These could be components that are designed by an engineering group to use in the finished product, or they could be components designed by the customer. In either case, the bare minimum information that is required includes drawings, bills of material, and specifications. In a PDM system, the drawings and specifications have their own unique part numbers that are attached to the component's part number. While drawings normally reside in the CAD system, they can be retrieved via the PDM system. Specifications and bills of material would reside in the PDM system in a separate database.

Kits

This refers to a special case where several components are grouped together under a parent part number, which is called a kit. A kit would not have a drawing or specifications, just a bill of material. The components of the kit would have the necessary information pertaining to them, as described for the previous two part types.

Data Library

Anyone who has worked for a large organization, particularly one with a gigantic engineering database, has experienced difficulty finding a part if the part number is not known. Although some software packages allow database searches on the description of the part, it can still be a hit-or-miss proposition, depending on the discipline that went into specifying the description in the first place. This is especially the case if parts have not been catalogued in an organized manner, but sometimes it is a result of sheer laziness and lack of discipline. The net result can be a part with multiple part numbers.

Let's say a designer wants to spec a particular component, a valve for example, into an assembly that he or she is designing. The proper approach for the designer would be to check the list of valves that are currently in the database and pick one that will serve the purpose at hand. In order to make it easy for the designer, the database should be properly catalogued, so that an individual can easily search for all valves specified in the database. If the parts are not catalogued, the designer may have to try alternate methods of searching for the valve. In such cases, a designer is prone to take a shortcut and create a new part number for a valve that may already exist in the system.

In organizations that have several divisions, this problem is multiplied. In cases where the divisions are scattered internationally, a false sense of "patriotism" kicks in, which makes the problem still worse. For example, one organization had two design and manufacturing divisions, one in the United States and the other in a Western European country. The American division had been using a particular model of a hydraulic pump in its products. Along the way, the European division experienced a need for the same pump, and the designer decided that he would issue a different part number. Not only was this the same pump that was used in the United States, but the European division was planning to procure it from the same supplier with which the American division was dealing. When I asked the designer why he wanted to create a new part number instead of using the same one that the American division used, he said, "Because this is a part for a European product, made by the European division." My response was very simple: "Who gives a damn?"

After I was able to explain the pros and cons of his decision, the designer reluctantly agreed to use the American part number. Just think of the potential confusion with the supplier. It was not hard to figure out the root cause of the designer's mind-set. Europeans use the metric system, but Americans do not. As a result, there was very little commonality of components between the two divisions, and each division had developed its own part numbering scheme. Although most pumps used by the European division had metric threads, that was not the case with the pump in question. The European division was going to use the same pump as the American division.

Such problems can be avoided if parts are catalogued in an organized manner. Although PDM systems do not come with this as a standard feature, any PDM system can be used to create and maintain a library of parts and products. Conceptually, think of a series of group codes. For example, a group code could be "Valve — Hydraulic." All hydraulic valves used by an organization (regardless of the number of divisions or their geographical location) could be categorized under this code. When designers need to spec a hydraulic valve in their designs, they should first look at the ones that are available in the system. If an existing valve will serve the purpose, then it should be used. If not, a new part number is merited and it should be catalogued under the "Valve — Hydraulic" group code. If your PDM system does not allow for such coding, an alternative method could be to create a part number for each group code. For example, "Valve — Hydraulic" could be a part number with all hydraulic valves as its single-level components. This would work just as well.

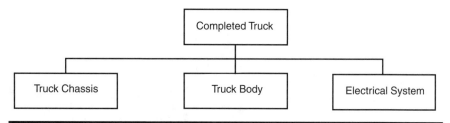

Figure 9.1   Generic Single-Level Bill of Material for "Truck — Model 123"

The same methodology can be used for finished products, with several options from which a customer can choose. For example, consider a special-purpose truck, "Truck — Model 123," which is built in two basic versions. One version is for use in North America and the other is meant for European operations. Again, in the interest of simplicity, let's assume that there are just two differences between the rules and regulations of the two continents — emission and voltage requirements. Figure 9.1 shows a greatly simplified, generic version of this product's single-level bill of material. It consists of a truck chassis, a body, and the electrical system. Now let's add the available options. Figure 9.2 shows the same bill of material with the options. In this case, "Truck Chassis — Model 123" and "Electrical System — Model 123" could either be project codes or unique part numbers (alphanumeric), with their respective options coded as single-level components. Depending on the options selected by the customer, the salesperson would check off the appropriate boxes on the order form. The designer would configure the bill of material within the PDM system for a specific truck by selecting the appropriate options reflected on the order form. The resulting "Truck — Model 123" would be assigned a unique part number.

You may have noticed that the bill of material for "Truck — Model 123" in Figure 9.2 does not represent a "working" configuration of the truck; it calls out two chassis and two electrical systems. That is okay. What is important is that the bill of material of the truck ordered by the customer is easy to configure and represents a working model. Figure 9.3 shows such a bill of material for the European version of the truck.

A logical question that arises is why a specific bill of material for the two different options is not created in the first place, instead of creating a seemingly unusable bill which includes all possible options. In cases where the bills of material are as simple as the one used in this example, that is a valid point. Once the options start adding up, however, a multitude of bills of material could result, each representing a specific mix of options, many of which may never

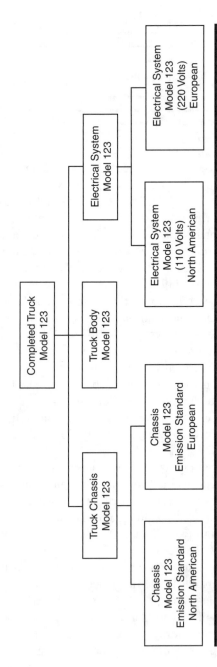

Figure 9.2   Bill of Material for "Truck — Model 123" with Available Options

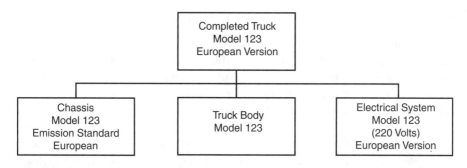

Figure 9.3 Single-Level Bill of Material for "Truck — Model 123 — European Version"

be ordered. Think about a car that could be ordered with options such as an eight-cylinder engine, power steering, power brakes, power windows, air conditioning, heated seats, heated mirrors, premium sound stereo, etc. If one tried to configure every conceivable mix of options as a unique bill of material, it could result in several hundred, if not several thousand, bills of material.

This is one of the more powerful ways in which a PDM system (and bills of material) can be used. What is required is an understanding of the benefits, education for all involved, and enforcement of proper discipline.

Engineering Change Management

This is a process that has repeatedly been "combobulated" beyond belief, in the interest of simplifying the work for engineers and designers. Let's first look at the theory and principles behind engineering change management.

The underlying objective should be to minimize, if not totally eliminate, vagueness and uncertainty. This should not come as a surprise — it is a recurring theme throughout this book.

Changes to an existing component or assembly can result from several sources. Technological developments may enable engineering to upgrade certain components, or manufacturing may decide that changing a component's design will make it easier to manufacture, thereby reducing its cost. Another source could be the customer, who may want to make revisions to the original specification after having used the finished product for some time. Before going into the details of the engineering change process, let's get one nagging point of confusion out of the way. Any time a component or assembly is to be changed, a decision must be made: Should the part number be changed, or should the revision level of the existing part number be bumped up?

Change Part Number or Revision Level?

Most of us who grew up in the engineering and manufacturing world are familiar with the three fs: fit, form, and function. The rule of thumb is that if any one of the three fs is altered as a result of changes made to a part, the part number must be changed. If, on the other hand, none of the three fs is affected, then it is okay to just bump up the revision level. Over the years, I have learned the hard way that a fourth characteristic must be factored into this decision-making process: specification. The rule of thumb that I believe is safer to live by is: if the fit, form, function, or specification changes, then the part number must be changed.

To explain why I include specification in the rule of three fs, I would like to share an experience. This example also highlights the importance of the manufacturer's part number as opposed to the part number specified by a distributor. The finished product was a special-purpose truck, and one of the components mounted in the ceiling of the truck body was a fluorescent light fixture. The designer had located the light fixture in a distributor's catalog, bought a sample, and tested it to see if it would work in a rugged environment. Once satisfied that the fixture would work, he spec'd it into the truck's design. Since the manufacturer's part number was not available to him, he used the distributor's name and part number to define the part. A few months later, the distributor found a better deal with another manufacturer of a similar light fixture and switched to the new manufacturer. However, since the fit, form, and function of the part remained the same, the distributor did not change the catalog number of the fixture. The next batch of fixtures that was received was of the new kind — and they did not work in the truck. The previous lamp fixture was made for mobile operations and consequently could withstand vibrations when the truck was running, while the new one could not and developed problems with loose contacts and a loose shade that kept falling off. While the two lamps were virtually identical in fit, form, and function, each had a different specification.

Another question that we sometimes struggle with is: If the part number of a component is changed because of significant changes made to it, should the part number of the parent assembly be changed or just the assembly's revision level? Once again, relying on the rule of thumb will help to answer this question. If the fit, form, function, and specification of the assembly do not change as a result of changes to the component, then simply change the revision level of the assembly; if one of these does change, then change the part number.

A third decision point on which we sometimes stumble is whether the revision level of a part and that of its corresponding drawing must always be the same. The answer is that they do not have to be the same. Of course, when a part and its drawing are first created, they will both be at revision A. For a two-letter revision system, when a part and its drawing are first created, they will both be at revision AA, although I would suspect that if a part has gone through 25 revisions (from A to Z), it is probably a good idea to change the part number. Yet, some organizations use a two-letter revision system, which would allow for 675 revisions!

Usually, when a drawing is created for an assembly, the individual component part numbers are not specified on the face of the drawing. The components are shown on the drawing as item numbers, sometimes referred to as balloon numbers, which are sequentially numbered starting with one. The bill of material ties each item number to a specific part number under the parent assembly. For example, to know what item 5 is on a drawing, one would look at the bill of material to find the part number. This is a good practice to follow, because unnecessary changes to drawings do not have to be made.

Let's look at an example where a component on an assembly's bill of material is changed. Part number XYZ, which is coded as item 3 on the bill of material and the drawing, is changed to part number UVW. The item number remains the same. Let's assume that the change in component does not affect the fit, form, function, or specification of the assembly, and so the revision of the assembly is bumped up instead of changing the part number. Does this change affect the drawing for the assembly in any way? No, it does not, because the drawing only refers to the component in terms of item 3, which was not changed. In this example, the revision level of the part number is changed, but it is not necessary to touch the drawing. The assembly can now be at revision B, while the drawing is still at revision A.

Conversely, let's look at an example where a change is made to a drawing that does not affect the part, such as correcting a spelling mistake on the drawing. Since the drawing is changed, its revision must be changed. But the part is not affected. In this case, the drawing can be at revision B, but the part is still at revision A.

Most good PDM systems allow a specific part revision to be tied to a specific drawing revision, and that makes it okay for the two revisions to be different. If the software used does not allow for this, then it would be mandatory to keep the two revisions in sync. Some would suggest that it would be much easier to keep the two revisions in sync, whether or not the software allows it. I disagree. For one thing, it would entail a lot of unnecessary ongoing work just to make some people feel more comfortable that everything is okay.

A few years ago, one of the designers at a client's facility showed me a multipage drawing that was sent to him by a customer. Pages 1 and 2 of the drawing were at revision C, but the rest of the pages were at revision B. The drawing details that were modified actually were on page 2, so naturally, it was revised up to C. A box on page 1 displayed the summary of changes in the top right-hand corner. Since the summary was updated as a result of changes to page 2, page 1 was also bumped up to revision C. When I first realized what I was looking at, I was speechless. I thought this was a case of ignorance being surpassed by laziness. You can draw your own conclusions.

The Process of Managing Engineering Changes

Regardless of the source that initiated the change, once the need for a change is acknowledged, it is up to the engineers and designers to implement it. The first step usually is for the designer to issue an engineering change notification (ECN) number, also known as an engineering change order (ECO). This is also the time when the decision is made to change the part number or just the revision level. The designer then "reserves" a copy of the documents to be changed (drawing, bill of material, specification) within the PDM system. This act of reserving a copy is the same as creating a backup copy of the latest effective revision of the part, drawing, or specification to which the changes will be applied. Once the documents have been reserved, the PDM system will assign a promotion level of "development" to the ECN. The promotion level is the equivalent of a status code. Different software may use different terminology, but the purpose is generally the same. A promotion level of "development" will signal anyone in the organization interested in the status of the ECN that it is being worked on by a designer. The details of the ECN document indicate who the designer is.

Once the designer is done with all the changes, the promotion level is changed to "complete." This means that the designer is done with his or her work and the ECN is now ready to go through the approval cycle. This is where the process can really get bogged down. Some organizations require approvals from the responsible engineer, the engineering section manager, the department manager, a person dubbed the "engineering records" checker, and a representative from manufacturing, usually the manufacturing engineer. This is too much pomp for the circumstances!

More often than not, the section manager and the department manager let ECNs stack up on their desks until somebody asks about them. All of a sudden, they approve a pile of ECNs in an hour. If that is the case, how much checking do they really perform? The managers do not need to be involved in the approval process.

The "engineering records" function is nothing more than a remnant of the old policing philosophy. Some organizations just cannot seem to wean themselves away from the philosophy of "final inspection." Are the designer, engineer, and manufacturing engineer really likely to slip through some shoddy work, so that a records function is needed to police them? If they really cannot be trusted, and if that is because there is good reason not to trust them, then they should be counseled and the problem must be corrected.

The simple fact is that if the designer and design engineer are responsible for implementing a change, they should also be responsible for implementing it correctly. The reason why a manufacturing engineer should be included in the approval cycle is not to police engineering, but because he or she is the manufacturing representative who is part of the team responsible for the change process. The manufacturing engineer is expected to be more in tune with the current events in manufacturing and can make logical decisions pertaining to the effective date for implementing a change in manufacturing, along with whether to use, rework, or scrap existing inventory.

The approval hierarchy should be limited to the design engineer and the manufacturing engineer. Once the designer is done with the changes and the promotion level of the ECN is changed to "complete," the design engineer must sign off on the changes. This is only logical because the design engineer shares ownership of the design. When the design engineer signs the ECN, the status is changed to "approved," and when the manufacturing engineer signs off, the status changes to "released," signifying his or her authorization to release the changes for updates to the manufacturing system.

Changes associated with "released" ECNs are transferred from the PDM system to the manufacturing system periodically (usually daily) by a batch program. Once the transfer is complete, the promotion level of the ECN changes to "synchronized," indicating that the manufacturing data for the part are in sync with the latest engineering change.

Buffer Between Engineering and Manufacturing Data

This is a significant benefit of having a PDM system because it allows engineering development and changes to progress without impacting the manufacturing or business system. As we saw in the previous section, once the changes have been completed and the ECN has gone through the various promotion levels, the changes are transferred to the business system in an organized manner. In order to really appreciate this feature of PDM systems, consider what could happen if a PDM system is not implemented.

Without a PDM system, engineering changes would have to be made directly to the live data within the business system. This can be a dangerous proposition, especially if the business system does not allow for proper engineering change management. The following examples highlight why making changes to live manufacturing data on the fly can often create more problems than it solves.

Examples

In an effort to save on expenses, a small company implemented a rudimentary business system. The system did not allow for proper engineering change management. Often, when changes needed to be made, the single design engineer on the staff would play judge, jury, and executioner. Although the designers implemented most changes, the engineer called the shots. This, coupled with the fact that the engineer and designers were not familiar with manufacturing business systems, made life very interesting for the manufacturing employees.

On one occasion, the engineer decided that the change he was implementing was significant enough to change the part number. He also decided that since the superseded part would never be used again, he could delete it. It did not occur to the engineer to look at inventory or open orders for the part prior to deleting it from the system. As luck would have it, there was an open purchase order for the part. For obvious reasons, serious confusion ensued. Had there been a change control mechanism in place along with the proper software to support it, this would not have happened. In any case, there was no justifiable reason for the engineer to delete the part from the system. He could have coded it as "obsolete," and life would have been much simpler for all concerned.

On another occasion, the same engineer created a part number for a certain type of glue that he decided to try in the assembly of a product. When the initial tests looked promising, the buyer placed an order for several gallons of the glue. A few days later, the engineer, with input from the assemblers, decided that the glue was not such a good idea after all and chose an adhesive tape instead. The engineer promptly went to his office and changed the description and unit of measure of the part number he had issued earlier for the glue to reflect the adhesive tape. The look on the buyer's face was priceless when a week later several gallons of glue were received as so many feet of tape.

SYSTEM COMPATIBILITY AND INTERFACES

The preceding discussions referred to three separate types of computer systems: CAD, PDM, and business systems. Naturally, compatibility is one of the critical issues that must be considered and ensured during the selection process. The CAD system must be able to feed data to the PDM system, which in turn should be able to transfer data to the manufacturing business system. While it is not a trivial effort, it is certainly simpler to ensure system compatibility for a single-plant operation. The compatibility objective becomes more complex for organizations with multiple plants or divisions that are geographically scattered. When some divisions are located in different parts of the world, this can be an especially daunting task.

Let's look at a multinational organization. The ideal situation would be for every division to implement the same CAD, PDM, and business systems that are compatible with each other. Such a situation would greatly simplify the tasks of data transfers and reporting among the various divisions. For a variety of reasons, things do not necessarily pan out that way. While in most instances the parent organization employs a central information technology group to ensure consistency in the selection of software systems, this is not always the case. Sometimes, the different engineering groups will select the CAD system that is "best" for their purposes and, likewise, manufacturing and accounting will favor different business systems.

If the design groups in different divisions share responsibility for designing components and assemblies of similar products, it is crucial for them to use the same CAD software to enable a smooth transfer of data back and forth. If, however, the end products are significantly different and the chance of designing similar components is slim, they could get by with different, even incompatible CAD systems. Even in such cases, however, this is not the recommended route.

The PDM system, as stated earlier, is the repository of all engineering data pertaining to components and products and, by definition, must be the same for all divisions. In fact, the database must be common to and shared by all divisions. Every authorized engineer and designer must have the ability to search and modify the data contained in the central database.

In the interest of sharing common data and consolidating divisional reports for corporate reporting, the manufacturing or business system also should be common to all the divisions. In this case, however, separate databases for each division can work just fine. While employees in each division should have the capability to search any other division's database, they would seldom have the need to update the information pertaining to other divisions. This information relates to inventory, open orders, production plan, component cost, and the like. Figure 9.4 shows a pictorial view.

In the scenario just described, it is important for the PDM system to be able to signal (based on specification by the designer) which manufacturing database needs to be updated, when data are ready to be transferred from the PDM system to the manufacturing system. While on some occasions just one division may require the manufacturing data to be updated, two or more divisions may build the same components or products. This would require the data to be transferred from the PDM system to all of the pertinent manufacturing databases.

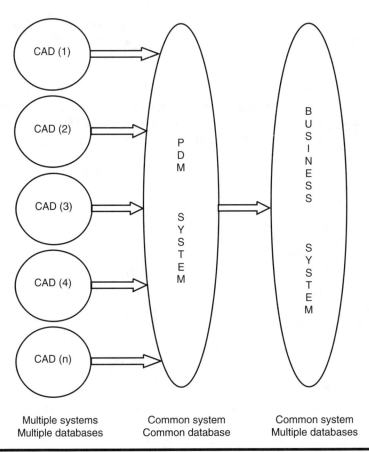

Multiple systems   Common system   Common system
Multiple databases   Common database   Multiple databases

Figure 9.4 Information Flow from CAD Systems to PDM System to Business System

DATA TRANSFERS BETWEEN PDM AND BUSINESS SYSTEMS

The previous section briefly alluded to the direction of the flow of information from one system to the next. The CAD system feeds the PDM system, which in turn feeds the business system. Sometimes, engineering groups may ask for information that resides in the business system (information pertaining to component costs, inventory, and suppliers) to be transferred to the PDM system. Not only is this unnecessary, but if this request is implemented, it can result in confusion. Some of the manufacturing data, such as inventory balances, can be so fluid that real-time updates would be required from the manufacturing system to the PDM system, This could be a costly and risky proposition. The reason for such requests is usually the mind-set that "We are engineering and we need some of this information to be available to us in *our* system. We should not have to spend time learning to look it up in *their* manufacturing system." The engineers and the manufacturing employees must be well versed in using both the PDM *and* the business system, in order to access the information they need. Both systems are part of the same organization, just as both groups are. The engineers need to know how to search the manufacturing database, and the planners, buyers, and manufacturing engineers need to know how to retrieve information from the PDM system.

About the only piece of information that may merit archiving in the PDM system from the business system could be the "as-built" configuration of the finished product. Many business systems available today allow for the as-built configuration to be captured, which renders the feedback of data to the PDM system unnecessary.

ESTABLISHING A WORKFLOW — THE MANUAL SYSTEM

Prior to shopping for a new computer system, a workflow document should be created. A workflow portrays a sequence of events that have to occur, from the design phase of a new product all the way to invoicing the customer for completed units. It is equivalent to creating a process that would be followed manually in the absence of software. Once the workflow has been established, the next logical step would be to shop for a system that will support it. Of course, there is always the potential need for some give and take between the manual system and what the software will allow, but this should be kept to a relatively small scale. A sample workflow is presented in Figure 10.1 at the end of the next chapter.

Embarking on the implementation of a new system without a realistic workflow is equivalent to launching a new business without a realistic business plan — both can be suicidal.

This book has free materials available for download from the
Web Added Value™ Resource Center at www.jrosspub.com.

10

MANUFACTURING PROCESSES

It takes as much energy to wish as it does to plan.

Eleanor Roosevelt

Most manufacturing processes can be classified into three broad categories: planning, execution, and reporting. Planning processes are required to help set targets based on anticipated customer demand and to evaluate the level of resources required to achieve those targets. The quality of the planning processes dictates the probability of success during the execution phase; it also helps to minimize ugly surprises. Execution processes enable us to implement the plan. Simple and elegant processes contribute toward greater agility and flexibility during the execution phase. Such processes also serve to increase the probability of delivering a good-quality product in a cost-efficient and timely manner. Reporting processes highlight what was done. While many such processes revolve around the financial performance of an organization, some of them are used to monitor and improve product quality, productivity in the shop, timeliness of deliveries, and overall performance to the plan. Within each of these categories, the level of detail ranges from broad to the nitty-gritty, depending on the process.

If we were to evaluate each of these processes with a cool, calm, and collected mind, with a logical thought process and common sense as our guides, we would find that every one of them makes perfect sense. Even the interrelations between the various processes would fall into the no-brainer category.

However, when ambiguous buzzwords, methods of the millennium, and creative marketing campaigns are thrown into the pot, they serve to cloud the simplest of issues and cast a veil of mystique over the entire effort. In this respect, certain self-proclaimed gurus, latter-day experts, and some software houses have done our industry an injustice. Even some professional societies have opted to hitch a ride on the buzzword bandwagon in lieu of taking a stand and setting the record straight. Instead of highlighting the simplicity of these processes, along with emphasizing the important issues required for implementing them, such as organizational education, discipline, responsibility, and accountability, they have taken the approach of glorifying the processes, and introducing unwarranted vagueness, thereby complicating them still further. It is no wonder that several organizations embarking on the implementation of such processes and systems often find the perceived magnitude of and costs associated with such efforts overwhelming.

Let's begin by looking at some of the processes that are encountered in manufacturing. This will be followed by an analogy to certain activities with which we are involved in our personal lives. The intent is to make the manufacturing processes seem less complicated. The following discussion includes most of the major processes, but is by no means comprehensive.

PLANNING PROCESSES

Business Planning

This is usually the starting point for most organizations. It is a way to chart the course that the organization expects to take for the next few years. This is the stage at which decisions are made to add to plant and equipment based on the projected rate of growth.

Sales and Production Planning

The sales plan is an aggregate list, usually stated in terms of currency, of what a company expects to sell during the planning period. The planning period is invariably a year. It includes firm customer orders for the near term, along with forecasts for periods out into the future. It should be realistic and achievable, in terms of available financing, size of the facility, amount of equipment, and strength of the workforce. If an organization does not have the capacity to meet the production demands required to support the sales plan, something has to give. Either the capacity should be increased, the sales plan trimmed down, or some of the work subcontracted.

The production plan is a more discrete version of the sales plan. It is usually stated in terms of units and takes into account any finished goods inventory that may already exist.

In some production and inventory management circles, the process of developing sales and production plans is referred to as Sales and Operations Planning.

In terms of planning meals for one's family, this type of planning is equivalent to creating a budget. Most families develop a monthly or annual budget for food, depending on their household income, their lifestyle, and the size of the family. The intent is to try to stay within the budget and to keep from overextending the resources.

Common Pitfalls

Perhaps the most common pitfall is the cavalier approach taken by many organizations. They tend to overload the sales and production plans. One of the most difficult things for any organization is to turn down work from potential customers. Very often, not enough attention is paid to the organization's capacity and other limitations.

Master Schedule

The master schedule serves as the drumbeat of a manufacturing organization. As a result, we need to really sharpen the pencil before developing a master schedule. It consists of a list of every item that has an independent demand, whether actual demand or forecast. The list must include finished products as well as lower level components that are expected to be sold as spares.

Notice that I did not say that the master schedule is a list of everything that is expected to be *produced* and sold. I said "expected to be sold." Over the last several years, a paradigm shift has occurred in this respect. More and more companies are outsourcing their production to auxiliary suppliers. Sometimes, finished products are completely subcontracted, and the parent organization does not actually produce them; instead, it *procures* them to eventually be sold to its customers. It is important to include these items on the master schedule. When the term originated, it was called a master *production* schedule. These days, it could just as well be called a master *procurement* schedule. Perhaps the "P" should be dropped from MPS and it should be called a master schedule. It is just a giant to-do list.

One of the more daunting aspects of the master schedule has always been managing variations in customer demand. How is an organization expected to react to varying customer demands? Uncertainties in customer demand have an adverse impact on an organization's ability to orchestrate the availability of components and shop capacity. This is especially true for organizations that "build to order." The logical consequence of this problem has been to freeze a portion of the master schedule. This is equivalent to creating a fence in time. Products that are scheduled to be built beyond the time fence can be considered to be fluid and subject to change, while those that fall within the time fence are considered to be unchangeable.

The next issue is to decide just how far out in time the master schedule should be frozen. Where should the fence be built? The answer to this depends mainly on a particular organization's mind-set and culture. Some organizations prefer to freeze the master schedule for an arbitrary number of months (three to six months, for instance) regardless of the products that are contained within the frozen window of the master schedule. Needless to say, this could introduce a high degree of rigidity in an organization's planning cycle and the resultant ability to react promptly to changing customer demands. Other organizations take the approach of not freezing any portion of the master schedule, in the name of being *totally flexible* to their customers' needs. Unless an organization is truly equipped to handle fluctuations in demand effectively, this can lead to a different kind of mess. It is the equivalent of trying to please all the people all the time, which has obvious repercussions.

Managing the master schedule poses a bit of a dichotomy. Freezing a portion of it helps to stabilize production and procurement efforts, but the frozen period should be kept as short as possible, so as to be able to please customers. It seems logical that changes to the master schedule should be permissible before actually embarking on the production and procurement of any product. However, once an organization is committed to building a product and the procurement activity has started, the customer is obliged to purchase the product. The safe and courteous approach would be to inform the customer of the "commit" date, after which changes could be considered, but only on a case-by-case basis.

If this approach is taken, the cumulative lead time (explained in Chapter 6) begins to play an important role. The assumption is that everything that is financially feasible has been done to reduce the individual lead times of the components. Referring back to the bill of material presented in Chapter 6 (Figure 6.1 and Table 6.1), if none of the components of product A is available in stock and we are starting from scratch, it would take 26 days to deliver product A. Therefore, it would make sense to freeze the master schedule for a period of 26 days for product A. However, it does not have to be that way. Depending on the cost of some of the components, we may choose to carry a few in inventory, thereby reducing the effective cumulative lead time. For instance, we could decide to carry a few units of the casting G in inventory. If we were to do that, the effective cumulative lead time would be reduced to 15 days. We could also consider carrying some of part F in inventory, resulting in the cumulative lead time being cut to just 10 days. To further shorten the cumulative lead time, we would need to carry parts D and E in inventory, and the result would be a cumulative lead time of just eight days. Keep in mind that both parts D *and* E would have to be carried in inventory, because carrying just one and not the other does not change the cumulative lead time from the previous value of 10 days. All of a sudden, by deciding to carry parts D, E, F, and G in inventory, we are able to shrink the cumulative lead time of product A from a bit over 5 weeks (26 workdays) to just over a week and a half (8 workdays). This is something customers would greatly appreciate. Of course, such decisions have to be made on a product-by-product basis, and the objective should be to achieve the biggest bang for the buck while keeping the organization from being exposed to too much inventory.

In general, a few select purchased parts are the culprits that add a significant amount of time to the cumulative lead time of an end item. The first step should be to talk to the suppliers of such parts and see if they can help with reducing the lead time. After all efforts to reduce the lead times have been exhausted, the next option is to carry a few of these parts in inventory. The quantity would depend on usage; a number can be chosen and then changed later if necessary. This effectively would reduce the cumulative lead time of the end item. If the resultant cumulative lead time is still too long, the next purchased component with the longest lead time should be identified and some of it carried in stock. Carrying these components in inventory brings up an interesting question: Is this philosophy in keeping with just-in-time manufacturing? The question here is: Just in time for *what*? If we have done a good job working[1] together with the suppliers responsible for providing the long-lead-time components and done everything that is possible to reduce the individual lead times, it is decision time. Do we bite the bullet and carry some components in inventory, or do we tell our customers that they will have to wait six months or a year for the end item?

Common Pitfalls

Given that the master schedule is the drumbeat of a manufacturing organization, it is critical for it to be realistic. After all, what good is a to-do list if it is not do-able? A common pitfall for most organizations is treating the master schedule as a wish list. It is important to ensure that the proper resources are available to procure and produce the items on the master schedule. This brings us to the process of planning capacity requirements.

Capacity Requirements and Shop Floor Scheduling

This process could merit a book of its own, but to stay within the framework of this book, the discussion will be limited to a section within this chapter.

Before getting started on the process of planning capacity requirements, it is important to state that *the capacity of every production shop is finite*. There is no such thing as infinite capacity. This is the most common pitfall when it comes to scheduling production. Intelligent, educated professionals talk about infinite capacity when it comes to production planning or scheduling. If the shop had infinite capacity, why would we even bother to schedule production? We could just toss the work to the shop, twitch our noses, cross our arms, blink our eyes, nod our heads, and *voila*! The finished product would appear just when needed. A fact of life is that shop capacity is *finite*.

Finite does not necessarily mean that the capacity cannot be tweaked. It certainly can be tweaked, because it is elastic to some extent. Capacity can temporarily be stretched to suit specific needs by working overtime, adding another shift, or bringing on a temporary crew. If after doing that the capacity of the shop still falls short of what is needed to build to the master schedule, then something has to give. Some of the work could be subcontracted, or the master schedule could be pared down. If that does not help level the load in the shop, more drastic steps may have to be taken, such as buying more equipment, hiring more permanent workers, or building another manufacturing facility. Of course, cross-training employees is always a good idea. It ensures that more people are capable of performing a variety of jobs on the shop floor, and that has a favorable impact on increasing shop capacity.

When it comes to planning for capacity and scheduling production, the common methods practiced in industry for the past several decades are, at best, suspect. Let's take a conceptual view of what is frequently preached.

The first serious attempt at capacity planning occurs at the master schedule level. It is usually referred to as rough-cut capacity planning. The assumption at this stage is that capacity is infinite, and the rough-cut scheduling method is called infinite loading. This implies that the work to be performed is shown as a "load" in appropriate time buckets, on the various work centers, regardless of the available capacity of the work centers in those time buckets. The result is usually a histogram, which shows the load versus the available capacity for each work center. The intent is that periods of overload would require some of the work to be pulled in or pushed out in time and moved to time buckets that are underloaded. Since this is normally done for individual work centers, the rescheduled work may create capacity conflicts at other work centers, which in turn would need to have their loads balanced with available capacity. This can be a tiresome, iterative process. The frustrating part is that it seldom facilitates achieving the goal of leveling load with available capacity.

The next step is to use firm work orders, along with planned work orders suggested by material requirements planning, and perform what is commonly termed capacity requirements planning. Capacity requirements planning is a more detailed version of rough-cut capacity planning, but it too assumes infinite capacity, and the scheduling method is infinite loading.

Finally, during the execution stage, the profound conclusion is reached that capacity is *not* infinite, and if work is to progress on the shop floor with a reasonable chance of success, we will have to bite the bullet and get serious about things. This is when methods such as input-output control are used to perform finite loading of the different work centers in order to execute the plan.

The problem with this approach is that during the planning phase, capacity is assumed to be infinite. Finally, during the execution phase, when crass assumptions can no longer be justified, reality is faced and the original assumption of infinite capacity is refuted. This is equivalent to planning as though one is Superman, but executing like Clark Kent. Very simply, if one starts out with absurd assumptions, one should expect to end up with absurd results. Yet people who work with such assumptions wonder why they are not able to bring their plans to fruition. Fortunately, many organizations have realized the fallacy of this approach and have moved to finite capacity planning; several others, however, have not.

It is imperative for an organization to have a good feel for the feasibility of the master schedule. For this to happen, people must recognize and accept the fact that capacity is finite from the start of the planning process — at the master schedule level.

Material Requirements

Once the master schedule has been created and obvious capacity constraints have been alleviated, the next major manufacturing process involves planning for the components and subassemblies that will be required for the finished products; it is equivalent to planning for the replenishment of ingredients used to prepare one's daily meals.

Before getting too deep into this topic, it is appropriate to establish a few definitions.

Dependent Demand

Demand for a component that arises as a result of a demand for its parent part is considered to be dependent demand. In the bicycle business, for example, demand for 100 bikes would create a demand for 200 wheel rims. The demand for the wheel rims is dependent on the demand for bikes. If there were no demand for bikes, the wheel rims would not be needed.

Independent Demand

If the demand for a component or a finished product is independent of the demand for another component or product, it is considered to be independent demand. In the preceding example, the demand for 100 bikes was independent of the demand for any other product. The customer simply wanted 100 bikes.

Mixed Demand

While this is not the term that is commonly used, it fits well in the current context. In the bicycle example, a customer could place an order for a few spare wheel rims. The demand caused by such an order would be independent of the demand for any other component or product. The demand for the spare wheel rims would be considered independent demand, while the demand for the 200 rims is dependent strictly on the demand for the 100 bikes. Thus, the wheel rim will have a mixed demand — dependent and independent.

There are only two ways to arrive at independent demand: a forecast and actual customer orders. For organizations that strictly manufacture to order, the independent demand is the list of customer orders. For those that build in anticipation of actual orders, a forecast for independent demand becomes necessary.

For dependent demand items, however, there is a simple way to compute the demand. In the 1960s, Joseph Orlicky presented a technique for doing this, called material requirements planning (MRP). Dr. Orlicky presented the fundamentals of MRP in his seminal book, *Material Requirements Planning: The New Way of Life in Production and Inventory Management.* He explained that for dependent demand items, there is no need to forecast the requirements because they can be computed. All that is needed is the bill of material for each independent demand item and the individual inventory and open order information for the items on the bills of material. If you have not already done so, I strongly recommend that you read Dr. Orlicky's book or George W. Plossl's updated version of the same book, *Orlicky's MRP.*

An example of the detailed workings of MRP is presented in Appendix B. The approach taken differs from the usual presentation because it is easier to comprehend. I encourage you to take a look at it.

Common Pitfalls

Over the past several decades, a few gurus have tried to use MRP to solve certain manufacturing problems for which MRP was never designed or intended. The net result was to create more problems and confusion — but that is fodder for the next chapter.

While MRP does a very good job of planning component requirements, it does not work very well with raw material, such as bar stock and sheet metal. Invariably, machined and fabricated components are made from portions of such material, and the amount of material that remains is put back in inventory. For example, starting with an eight-foot length of bar stock, three feet could be used to machine a part and the remaining five feet returned to stock. Since bar stock is usually inventoried in feet, it is virtually impossible for a computer system to determine whether the five-foot piece that was returned to stock is actually a five-foot piece or five pieces measuring a foot each. This requires a periodic visual review of raw material inventory.

Some organizations attempt to create different part numbers for different lengths of bar stock, but I do not recommend it. I recommend that such material be excluded from the MRP planning routine and replenishments planned manually, based on visual reviews.

EXECUTION PROCESSES

Issuing Work Orders

A work order is a document that authorizes work to be performed in the shop. The term work order is used here because it is perhaps the most commonly used terminology for such documents.

With the work order processes, significant reductions in nonvalue-added work can be made as described in Chapter 6. The real key to achieving these reductions lies in challenging traditional processes and, at times, deviating from the "accepted norm."

Over the past decade or so, the term "work order" has been treated as though it is a four-letter word. It does not seem fashionable anymore. It will be addressed in greater detail in the next chapter.

Common Pitfalls

When it comes to the work order process, three major pitfalls immediately come to mind:

- Placing orders for large quantities
- Releasing orders ahead of time, regardless of available capacity
- Laborious, nonvalue-added work (creating job packets, performing incoming inspections, and carrying inventory in centralized warehouses are just a few examples)

These issues were addressed in previous chapters and will not be covered further here.

Issuing Purchase Orders

This includes all activities pertaining to purchase orders — from negotiations with suppliers and issuing purchase orders to receiving the purchased parts and stocking them in inventory.

As with the work order process, efficient methods that minimize nonvalue-added work were presented in Chapter 6.

Common Pitfalls

The traditional mind-set of minimizing material cost is the reason for two of the most common pitfalls encountered in the purchasing activity. In an effort to get a "good price," sometimes much more than what foreseeable demand calls for is bought, resulting in excess inventory. The second pitfall is buying from the cheapest supplier. This results in the "get three quotes and buy from the lowest bidder" approach, potentially raising overhead costs. Yet another drawback, which is not a result of attempts to minimize material cost, is not holding suppliers accountable and responsible for the quality of the parts they furnish, which results in the policing function of incoming inspection. This also was addressed in Chapter 6.

Inventory Management

Typical processes relating to inventory management are cycle counting and an annual physical inventory. Timely issues from and receipts into inventory are necessary ingredients to assure inventory accuracy.

Common Pitfalls

Some software houses allow for the on-hand balance in the database to go below zero; a few even call this a special feature of the software. This is wrong. The on-hand balance is exactly what the name suggests — it represents what is *physically* on hand. While availability may fall below zero, the on-hand balance cannot. There is no way to physically count a quantity of minus five for any component.

The organizations that allow the on-hand balance to go negative are usually trying to take shortcuts. Often, this is a result of wanting to invoice a customer for a part that has not yet been placed in stock. The hope is that when the necessary paperwork to complete a work order is eventually done, the part will be placed in stock and the on-hand balance will correct itself. In reality, it usually does not happen that way, and errors in the inventory count are perpetuated.

Other Processes

While issuing and managing work orders and purchase orders are certainly two of the major processes involved in the successful execution of the master schedule, several others also play a significant role. Quality inspection, the methods for handling material, shipping, and invoicing fall into this category. The keys to gaining the maximum benefits from every one of these processes are to:

- Keep each process as simple as possible.
- Avoid *any* kind of nonvalue-added work.
- Solicit input from individuals involved with conducting the process.
- Make employees responsible and accountable for the quality of their work.
- Allow problems to be visible so they can be easily identified.
- Take prompt corrective action.
- Periodically review each process to identify potential improvements.

REPORTING PROCESSES

When it comes to processes pertaining to reporting recent performance, perhaps the first thing that comes to mind is financial reporting. Usually at the end of every month, the accounting department consolidates the results for the month and reports key performance indicators such as profitability, cash flow, and inventory investment. This is done in an effort to assist management review of financial performance, which may lead to adjustments for the future. For larger, publicly prominent organizations, these results are presented to stockholders and analysts on a quarterly basis. It would seem reasonable that the "simple" task of consolidating and reporting financial data on a monthly basis should not be very time consuming. These days, with access to high-power computer systems that can crunch large volumes of information in a matter of seconds, this would seem to be a very reasonable assumption. In spite of this, some organizations require two to three weeks just to close the books and report the events for the prior month. Part of the reason for this is the fact that the process of collecting and consolidating the data is unwieldy. This is usually the case when the resident computer system is not utilized to its full potential. However, another significant cause is the fact that this activity often goes beyond just reporting the facts as they occurred. It ventures into activities relating to *making* the numbers come out "right." As proof, hardly a week goes by without another corporation making the headlines in the business section of the newspaper.

Apart from the typical financial reports, the number and types of reporting processes can be virtually limitless. A few are listed below:

- Quality
- Labor hours
- Productivity
- Variance
- On-time deliveries
- Inventory accuracy
- Supplier performance

Once again, it is imperative that these processes be kept simple, easy to understand, and easy to execute.

Writing monthly status reports is a fairly common process. Most people don't give it a second thought (although few find it enjoyable). This ritual is followed to keep various levels of management apprised of the status of key projects and miscellaneous accomplishments. Ever wonder why it often takes almost a week to recap what was done in the previous month? It is absurd that writing monthly reports can become so tedious and time consuming that it might merit mention in the previous month's accomplishments. Think about the amount of time an organization spends on this activity.

Section managers ask their direct reports for status reports, which they consolidate and send to the department manager, who goes through his or her own consolidation ritual, before submitting a report to the division manager, and so on up the chain of command. At each stage, the respective "authors" add their own spin to the actual events that took place during the prior month, just so that everything sounds okay to the next person up the organizational ladder. By the time the person at the top gets the "final" version, it is a thick report that is no fun to read and probably gets set aside. It is amusing to read about efforts to cut costs and go "lean" in such tomes — and verges on being an oxymoron.

The similarities between certain activities and processes that are followed in one's personal life and in the manufacturing processes just covered are striking. The following analogy highlights the simplicity and common-sense nature of these processes.

An Analogy

Anyone who plans and cooks meals or shops for weekly groceries for the family logically follows the precepts of most of the seemingly complex processes associated with a manufacturing organization.

Let's say that you are the person who usually buys groceries and cooks the meals for your family and that Saturday is your normal shopping day. Your family probably follows certain eating habits. For instance, a barbecued brisket may be the traditional Sunday lunch for your family, and the leftovers usually end up as a meat loaf for Monday's dinner. Weekday meals might usually consist of sandwiches for the kids' lunches and something easy to fix, like roast chicken, for dinner. Dinner on Wednesdays is usually pizza, and Friday evenings the family eats out. A light lunch on Saturday is followed by thick, juicy steaks for dinner. Every morning, you and your spouse have coffee, orange juice, and toast with butter and jam for breakfast. Your son prefers a bowl of cereal, and your daughter will only eat cinnamon rolls. The stage has been set.

The first thing you do before you embark on your shopping trip is make a list of the items you will need for the coming week's meals. You probably know what ingredients you have and what you will need. For example, you know that you do not have chicken in the refrigerator, so you put a roasting chicken on your list. How big a chicken should you get? From experience, you know that a five-pound chicken serves the whole family. Fortunately, your spouse and daughter like dark meat and you and your son prefer white meat, so everyone gets what they want. If everyone in the family liked just dark meat, you would probably buy legs and thighs instead of a whole chicken.

You also know that you do not have steaks. You always buy steaks on the day that you are going to cook them, because you prefer them fresh rather than frozen. Since steaks are on the menu for Saturday evening and that is the day you shop, you put steaks on your shopping list. However, the grocery store where you usually do your shopping does not carry your favorite cut of steak, so you will need to stop at another store on the way home.

You make a mental note to take a brisket out of the freezer, so that it thaws in time for tomorrow's lunch. What about vegetables to go with it? You will need some fresh potatoes for baking. You usually serve canned beans and have a few cans in the pantry.

The next thing you would probably do is go through a mental list of the basic, everyday necessities. You check the pantry and refrigerator for daily consumable items, such as the amount of cereal, cinnamon rolls, salt, pepper, milk, butter, jam, and bread. Items that you may be running low on make your list.

Let's assume that on this particular Saturday, you are either very low on or completely out of some of the consumable items. How much of each of these items will you buy? Different people have different buying habits. Take bread, for instance. Some people buy several loaves of bread at a time and freeze them for future use, but this concept is not too popular with your family, so you will buy just enough bread to last you a week. In some cultures, even that would be heretical. The French, for example, buy fresh bread every day — sometimes twice a day. How much jam will you buy? One option is to go to a membership club and buy a gallon jar of jam. You would probably get a heck of a price break. You would probably also get a hernia! Besides, there isn't enough room in your refrigerator for such a big container. You will probably buy a few smaller jars, since jam has quite a long shelf life. The current jar, once opened, can stay in the refrigerator, and the others would be stocked in the pantry.

What about salt, pepper, and spices? It makes no sense to buy these items just when you need them. You keep a good supply in the house, because you never know when you will use them. But what constitutes a good supply? Will you buy a carton (12 containers) of salt, or will you buy just one container? Based on your family's eating habits and the amount of space in your pantry, you will probably buy a standard container.

Let's take a look at what you just achieved:

1. You planned the meals for the coming week; you established the menu for each meal, for every day of the week. You even took into account the personal likes of each member of your family. Hopefully, while doing so, you stayed within your family's food budget. This is equivalent to creating a master schedule. It is a list of end items (daily meals, in this case) expected to be delivered to customers (the family) when they need them (breakfast, lunch, and dinner). Furthermore, the meals that you planned took into account that you are usually tired after work and really do not want to be in the kitchen cooking something elaborate on weekdays. You respected the fact that you have a very limited amount of time and energy for cooking meals on weekdays, and you planned your meals based on your capacity to cook.

2. You went through the individual recipes to determine a list of all ingredients required. For those recipes that you are intimately familiar with, you probably did this in your head; for others, you may have referred to one of your cookbooks. The bottom line is that you referred to the list of ingredients (bill of material) for each recipe. Using these bills of material, you made a list of total requirements (gross requirements) for all ingredients (components).

3. Next, you compared the total requirements to what you already have in the house. The amount of each ingredient that you have in your pantry is the equivalent of on-hand inventory. This is determined by doing a stock check or a physical count. Based on the sum total of what you need (gross requirements) and what you already have (on-hand inventory), you made a list of all items that you need to replenish. This is the list of net requirements.

4. Depending on the type of ingredient, its shelf life, the frequency with which you use it, and the amount of storage space you have available, you decided on the replenishment quantity. For example, if your family's weekly consumption of milk has historically been a gallon, you would not buy five gallons, even if you got a good price break. It would only go bad, and that would be a waste of money. For ingredients such as salt and pepper, you would not buy exactly what you need for next week because these items are used on a regular basis. On the other hand, you probably would not buy a 100-pound sack of sugar no matter how attractive the volume discount because you just do not have the room to store it. You effectively established the lot size and ordering policy for each ingredient. Some items, such as steaks, are purchased just in time, and some, such as salt, just in case.

5. You also went through the exercise of supplier selection. You purchased most of your foodstuffs from the grocery store close to your house. You went to a specialty store to buy the kind of steaks you like. You probably also went to the neighborhood bakery for fresh bread.

6. Along the way, you made decisions to outsource some of the meals. For example, on most Wednesdays, you have pizza delivered to the house, and on Fridays the family dines at a restaurant. These are instances where the end item (the entire meal) is subcontracted. In some cases, you may decide to outsource just one component of the end item. Suppose that one of the meals on a weeknight is spaghetti and meatballs. You can make the sauce from scratch or buy a jar. This constitutes a "make" or "buy" decision. If you decide to buy the sauce premade, then a jar is all you would buy. If, on the other hand, you decide to make the sauce, you would need to go through the bill of material (the list of ingredients) for the sauce and purchase all components for which you had positive net requirements.

This concept is not all that difficult to understand. It is really quite simple. If most people can plan their weekly meals *so* effectively, why do they often find the task of planning production so formidable? The following are a few likely responses.

■ **"Surely, it can't be that simple"**: "What with concepts like dependent versus independent demand, forecasting, safety stock, order policy codes, 'make' versus 'buy' decisions, and long lead times, how can you possibly equate planning my production with planning a week's meals? My lead times alone are reason enough why the planning process becomes so involved. Some of my components have lead times ranging from 6 to 12 months. It's not like I can make a quick trip to the grocery store if I forget to buy a key component. I really can't afford the risk of stock-outs."

■ **"You obviously don't understand my objectives"**: "My job is to make sure that I deliver all products on time, *every* time. That's hard enough to achieve. To meet this objective, I have to carry a lot of inventory, and even then, I seldom meet the objective 100% of the time. With the uncertainty of demand from my customers and the really long lead times for my products, there is never a dull moment in my business life. We have to carry inventory to compensate for long lead times; that's the price we pay for doing business! My end product isn't bacon and eggs — it's a very sophisticated piece of equipment. Besides, my merit raise depends on delivering the goods on time, and if I don't, I could get fired. I'm not going to get a raise for keeping inventory low; that's not even part of my objectives. That's the inventory manager's problem; it's not my job."

■ **"We have a large enough warehouse"**: "We can afford to carry the inventory. We don't have a problem with warehouse space. Besides, our suppliers have agreed to carry the inventory with the understanding that we buy all of it by the end of the year. As long as we use up the inventory in a reasonable amount of time, why should anyone have a problem with it?"

■ **"I can't get wrapped up in details"**: "My job is to look at the big picture, not to worry about every single detail in the planning process. That's why we have this mega-dollar computer system. If a sophisticated computer system can't handle these problems, what makes you think I can?"

■ **The tune of the month**: "This month, our priority has shifted to component availability. We absolutely, positively must make sure that we have all required parts in stock. As a result, inventory levels have begun to rise. That's just a fact of life. We will address the inventory issue when the 'powers that be' holler from above."

Sound familiar? Now let's examine some of the differences between planning family meals and planning production.

Product Related

- It is a safe bet that you are more familiar with the meals that your family generally eats and their associated recipes than you are with the products that are built in your shop and their associated bills of material. Very simply, the bill of material for an intricate product is more involved than the one for spaghetti and meatballs.

- The frequency with which you repeat a given meal makes you more familiar with its configuration, and you are able to recognize most of the ingredients by sight. This creates a wider "comfort zone" than that associated with building a complicated product.

- Given that most ingredients are located either on the kitchen counter, in the pantry, or in the refrigerator, parts for recipes usually are close at hand and visible.

- Most ingredients that you would need for a recipe are readily available. The lead time associated with these parts is virtually zero. As a result, if you forget to buy an ingredient, you can always go to the store and make a last-minute purchase. There are, of course, exceptions to this. A recipe may call out for an exotic ingredient, such as foie gras or black truffles. Because run-of-the-mill grocery stores usually do not carry such items in stock, you may need to make a trip to a specialty store, and even then you may have to order the ingredient a few days ahead. A complicated product could have several exotic components that are not very easy to procure. These fall within the "un-obtainium" category. Obviously, such parts have to be planned more carefully.

Process Related

- By and large, the process of cooking a meal is much simpler than building a complicated product. An intricate product could require several different operations, such as machining, fabrication, metal coating, and assembly. More often than not, the various operations are performed in different shops or in different sections of the same shop. Some operations may need to be subcontracted to suppliers. In order for the product to be built on time, these operations require close coordination. In comparison, cooking a meal is much simpler. Fewer operations are involved, and most of the work is done by the person doing the cooking — the chef. Some operations may require someone else's assistance — help from a sous chef to, say, chop onions. In a production facility, the number of "sous chefs" can be staggering, and their activities need to be orchestrated. This is not a simple task.

■ Another process that plays a major role in both disciplines (cooking and production) is getting the right parts to the right place at the right time. In cooking a meal, this is relatively simple. Most of the ingredients are within reach, and it is not difficult to get them ready before starting to cook. French culinarians call it *mise en place.*[2] Selecting components to build a complicated product can take some doing. It requires organization. Someone, usually a warehouse clerk, needs to pick the parts called out on the bill of material, group them, and then deliver them to the assembly workstation where they will be used. This can take a considerable amount of time, and given the sheer number of parts involved, some components may be missed (or miscounted), causing disruptions in the production shop.

■ In-process inspection is yet another process that is simpler to follow at home than at work. Most people who cook meals for their families taste the food as it is being prepared. In a production facility, this process is usually more involved and instead final inspection is sometimes relied on more heavily.

People Related

Anyone who provides a product or service to others usually has to work with three categories of individuals: customer, supplier, and colleague.

■ **Customer**: A customer is a person or the people for whom a product or service is provided. When cooking meals for the family, the members of the family are the customers. In a production facility, customers are the people who buy the products and services that the organization provides. Sometimes customers can make unreasonable demands, which makes work life a bit more challenging. It is fairly easy to tell your children that they can't have ice cream for dessert because you are out of it and are too tired to drive to the store. It is not quite that simple to tell paying customers that they cannot have the product when they asked for it because you have other irons in the fire. With paying customers, you would be more willing to compromise and try to give them what they ask for.

■ **Supplier**: A supplier is a person or the people from whom component parts and some services are purchased so that an end item can be furnished to a customer. When shopping for groceries, you usually deal with a small number of suppliers. You probably go to a favorite grocery store where you do most of your shopping, along with a few specialty stores, such as a butcher shop or a bakery. However, when it comes to buying parts for production, many organizations deal with hundreds of suppliers. This makes life very interesting for most procurement groups.

■ **Colleague**: At home, it is quite easy to ask a family member to help you prepare a meal. However, it does not quite work that way at the office. The environment at work is quite different from home. At home, the environment is more relaxed and informal, and family members are usually willing to help out (although some may want to whine about it).

LESSONS FROM HOME

What have we learned from our experiences at home that we can use to make our work life simpler? We have learned that we should:

■ Know our products; we must be familiar with them
■ Stock parts at their point of use, within easy reach of the people who will use them, thereby eliminating wasteful material movement
■ Reduce lead times to be more flexible to our customers' demands
■ Plan ahead for items whose lead times cannot be reduced
■ Learn the process so that we can anticipate and ward off potential problems and devise methods for improving the process
■ Eliminate bureaucracy
■ Stay close to our customers so as to be able to anticipate their needs
■ Work with a small group of suppliers
■ Create and maintain a friendly and relaxed work environment

Access to accurate information in a timely manner is a fundamental requirement for good communication in any organization. This normally is achieved by implementing proper systems and processes. The word "systems" may conjure up thoughts of computerized systems. They do not have to be, but computer systems, if designed and implemented correctly, can certainly simplify life.

As much as most manufacturing companies would like to believe that they are "different" from the others, the type of data and the general flow of information through the organization are really quite similar from one company to the next. This should make it easy for any organization to implement a "canned" computer system, available from a reputable software vendor. I use the word "should" because it seems reasonable that this would be the case, if approached in the proper manner. Unfortunately, it seldom happens.

In a seemingly noble effort to improve their operations, some companies leap into the implementation of computer systems before they even have manual processes in place. The hope is that the "system" will establish the correct processes for them. Wrong move!

To make matters worse, many organizations do not spend the time and money to ensure that their employees have a working knowledge of basic manufacturing concepts and definitions before they embark on such a project. For instance, they must be familiar with a master schedule, work order, shop capacity, and the difference between a manufacturer's part number and a distributor's part number, to name just a few, before learning how to use a new computer system. The computer system is not the correct mechanism for gaining such knowledge.

Prior to shopping for a new computer system, a workflow document (Figure 10.1) should be created. A workflow portrays a sequence of events that have to occur, from the design phase of a new product all the way to invoicing the customer for completed units. Once the workflow has been established, the next step is to shop for a system that will support it.

Embarking on the implementation of a new system without a realistic workflow is equivalent to launching a new business without a realistic business plan — both could be suicidal.

Ideally, when a new system is implemented, the only education and training required for the workforce should pertain to learning the idiosyncrasies of the system. The employees must know how to navigate their way through the different screens, the causes and effects of transactions, and how to generate and interpret reports.

If basic knowledge of manufacturing concepts is lacking, my recommendation is to appoint a group of internal experts to educate the workforce. If this is not feasible, external help may be warranted. A knowledgeable consultant or a few APICS classes would serve the purpose.

NOTES

1. At face value, this statement may seem vague at best. The point is that if you work for a large organization, such as IBM, General Motors, or Boeing, your suppliers will be far more conducive to working with you to reduce lead times than if you work for Joe's Job Shop.
2. Meaning: setting up or organization (*Larousse Unabridged Dictionary*).

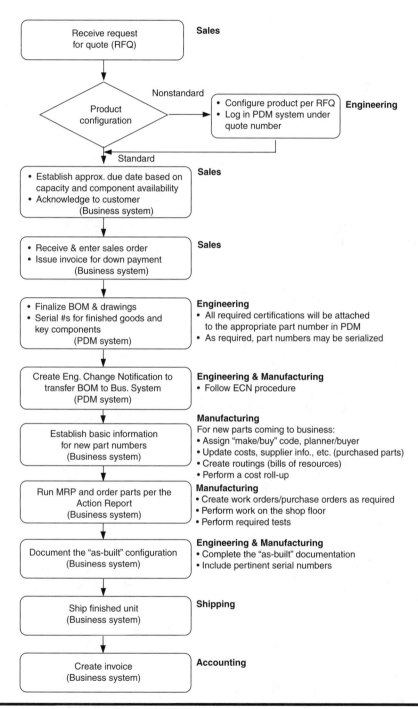

Figure 10.1 A Sample Workflow

11

MANUFACTURING PHILOSOPHIES

Nothing is more obstinate than a fashionable consensus.

Margaret Thatcher

A BIT OF HISTORY

Roughly 40-some years ago, manufacturing and materials management did not exist as an established profession as it does today. Individual organizations did what seemed appropriate just to get products out the door. Almost half a century prior to that, Fredrick Winslow Taylor published his Principles of Scientific Management, which eventually created the profession of industrial engineering, and Henry Ford proved that automobiles could be made more cheaply by using assembly lines. While several organizations began to follow the advice and example of these two individuals, elegant methods to plan production, manage inventory, and ensure good quality were noticeably lacking.

It was not until after World War II, when Dr. W. Edwards Deming presented his System of Profound Knowledge, that the importance of product quality began to be recognized as a vital ingredient in the survival of any organization. A few years later, George W. Plossl, Dr. Joseph Orlicky, Oliver W. Wight, and others began to promote the fundamentals of what today is known as production and inventory management (or manufacturing and materials management). All of these individuals were, in their own way, pioneers of the manufacturing and materials management profession as it now exists. Plossl, Orlicky, and Wight, along with a few others, blazed the trail and helped create the American Production and Inventory Control Society (APICS), the first professional society with a mission to educate professionals and to promote progress in this field.

Since those days, a plethora of philosophies, acronyms, and buzzwords have cropped up, all directed toward helping manufacturing organizations become more productive. However, the basic problems that most such organizations face continue to linger. The focus of this chapter is what has gone right and what has not.

In the 1960s, when many organizations were planning their material requirements for A[1] items manually, Joseph Orlicky presented the then fledgling profession of production and inventory management with a computerized technique that would be known as material requirements planning (MRP) to calculate the dependent demand for components of finished products. Dr. Orlicky also explained that dependent demand for items does not need to be predicted or forecast — it can be computed. All one would need to do this would be the bill of material for each independent demand item and the individual inventory and open order information for the items on the bill of material. That is all that MRP was intended to be. Replenishments for items with independent demand could continue to be prompted by the order point technique. This approach was promoted by a "crusade" in many chapters of APICS that led several organizations to adopt it.

Since that time, a few gurus (some self-proclaimed) decided that they would use the acronym MRP or variations of it to solve problems that it was never meant to address. This gave rise to MRP-II (manufacturing resource planning), BRP (business requirements planning), CRP (capacity requirements planning), and DRP (distribution requirements planning). Today, the name of the game is ERP (enterprise resource planning). Fortunately, the number of letters in the English alphabet limits the number of "xRP" permutations to 26. However, the ability to tack on a roman numeral suffix threatens an unlimited number of sequels.

While hundreds of thousands of dollars were being spent on computer hardware and software and consultants to help corporations become "world-class" users of convoluted interpretations of the term MRP, in a parallel development a multitude of new philosophies began to infiltrate business. The impact of the Japanese automobile manufacturers, particularly Toyota, on the American auto industry led to new words and acronyms, like just-in-time (JIT) manufacturing, total quality management (TQM), and kanban,[2] creeping into the business vocabulary. In the 1980s, Dr. Eliyahu Goldratt introduced the Theory of

Constraints, and companies like Motorola and GE began to tout their accomplishments toward achieving Six Sigma levels of quality. And let's not forget lean manufacturing, the lean supply chain, and the lean enterprise.

In an effort to help potential customers "see the light," some of the pundits of production and inventory management began to draw comparisons between philosophies like JIT and kanban and the "old" workhorse MRP, which never delivered all that was promised by underqualified experts. This is not to defend MRP or to make a case for it. It is, after all, just a simple, common-sense procedure that can be used to plan material requirements, regardless of an organization's manufacturing philosophy. Very simply, if you want to build 100 bicycles, you need "something" that tells you to order 200 wheel rims. This is a basic truism whether one's philosophy is to build just in time or just in case.

Several years ago, I decided to take an unemotional, common-sense approach to the basic requirements for a well-run production facility, in an effort to evaluate some of the differences between the methods adopted in the West and those followed in the East.

THE BASIC REQUIREMENTS

In the mid-1980s, my manager at the time told me that a well-run production shop is a very boring thing to watch. Of all the various descriptions I have come across, including "productive," "efficient," "organized," "world class," and even "lean," to me, "boring" says it all: level of excitement = zero! All activities happen as and when they are supposed to, and the people in the shop work at a steady pace without breaking a sweat. Noticeably absent are signs of hurrying and scurrying, expediting, rescheduling, and rework.

For any type of production system or philosophy to work smoothly, four basic requirements must be met:

- Demand must be stable, relatively speaking.
- Raw material and/or component parts must be available in inventory or easy to procure.
- Resources must be available.
- Some mechanism must exist as protection from ugly surprises — a stabilizer.

Let's take each of these requirements and see how the Eastern and Western philosophies address them. For purposes of this discussion, the JIT approach utilizing kanban will be used for the Eastern philosophy and you can plug in your favorite acronym for the Western philosophy.

Stable Demand

Stability implies that demand is known or that actual demand closely tracks the forecast. If demand were not stable, some compromises would be merited.

Perhaps demand is known, but it is uneven. In the interest of maintaining a relatively constant production level (always a good thing), some products may have to be built slightly ahead of when they are actually needed. This would result in a temporary buildup of finished goods inventory, especially if customers refuse to accept early deliveries.

While demand in the near term may be known, demand for products out into the future may be unknown. In this case, it would be necessary to build to a forecast in anticipation of firm customer orders. This would result in carrying not only some finished goods inventory, but also component inventory. However, if the forecasting technique used were appropriate for the business, the amount of inventory would not need to be excessive.

The simple fact is that when demand is either not known or is sporadic, some amount of "cushion" or "buffer" inventory is necessary. This is how business has been conducted for years in the West. If our demand is not stable, more inventory is carried. Not much more than casual attempts go into trying to stabilize demand through customer negotiations. For the Eastern philosophy to work effectively, demand must be stable. The term JIT implies that we *know* when the right time is — it implies that we *know* the demand. The Eastern philosophy works well when forecasts are managed closely, bills of material and inventory counts are accurate, capacity is available, and lead times are short. Eastern companies work hard to achieve this in many cases.

Raw Material and Component Availability

Regardless of which philosophy one pursues, there must be a mechanism to help plan the replenishment of the right components at the right time. The Western world generally uses computerized MRP, as developed by Joseph Orlicky. A master schedule is laid out for a period of time out into the future, and the quantity and timing of component replenishments are determined using a product's bill of material and the current inventory status of component parts.

In the JIT philosophy, kanban cards (or containers) are used. Conceptually, a product's bill of material is translated into a series of kanban cards. Each card "travels" (remember the "old" travelers in Western systems?) with its respective container of parts. When a container is empty, the kanban triggers replenishment. The replenishment can come from a stocking location via a "move" kanban or from a feeding work center via a "production" kanban.

Availability of Resources

Very simply, for any type of work to happen, the proper resources must be available. In a manufacturing environment, the critical resources are employees and equipment. This is true for the internal resources pertaining to a manufacturing shop. Suppliers that perform value-added work comprise the external resources.

In the Western world, resource requirements are sometimes treated in a cavalier manner. The traditional approach has been to perform some form of capacity planning on an aggregate level, assuming that the available capacity is infinite. The reason for this is twofold:

1. It is much easier to schedule production while assuming infinite capacity. Depending on the prioritizing rules that an organization chooses to follow, a program that does finite scheduling could require a multitude of algorithms. For the same reason, it is much easier to write scheduling programs that assume infinite capacity than it is to write programs that perform finite scheduling (assuming finite capacity). In fact, until a few years ago, most scheduling programs did not even offer a comprehensive finite scheduling option.
2. With infinite scheduling, an organization has the "perceived" luxury of delaying the prioritizing of jobs to a later date. The basic idea is that once a resource has been completely allocated to a job or a set of jobs during a particular interval in time, other "hot" jobs cannot be scheduled in the same time interval; they would have to be scheduled at a later point in time. This approach is often seen as requiring too much of a commitment — too final.

The key point that is often missed is that "hot" jobs become hot because some organizations still do not acknowledge the fact that capacity is finite during the planning stage. As a result, they tend to overcommit resources, which in turn forces them to juggle priorities at the eleventh hour.

Another trait that large Western manufacturers tend to lean toward is equipping their shops with complex machines — the "do everything" kind. By virtue of their capability, such machines are more expensive. In order to get the best return on the investment, manufacturers try to keep these machines busy making parts — often parts that could be made by a much simpler, cheaper machine that the company already has. This can *create* capacity constraints in that the "do everything" machine can become a bottleneck. Although alternate routings could be used to route certain parts back to the simpler machines, how often is that actually done? More often than not, scheduling problems are *created* that need to be resolved later. Some may rationalize that the extra parts could be used as safety stock. A better alternative would be to plan safety capacity, which avoids committing resources too early to specific items.

Eastern manufacturers take a significantly different approach to capacity planning. They actually recognize the fact that capacity is finite, and they plan their work accordingly. They also populate their shops with simple machines that are often inexpensive enough to dedicate each machine to a part or a finite group of parts. A concerted effort to minimize setup times is another trait that helps them keep the downtime of a machine to a minimum, thereby allowing more capacity to be available.

Stabilizer

Regardless of how well production is planned and how well the plan is executed on the shop floor, life by its very nature is uncertain, which means that some things will go awry. In order to minimize the "shock" resulting from unexpected, adverse events, many companies carry some inventory that acts as a cushion. What differentiates the Eastern methods from those practiced in the West is that the former use sharper pencils to help decide where they should carry extra inventory. The fact that there is such a thing as a "move" kanban implies that there are parts sitting somewhere, either at a storage location or at a feeding machine, waiting to be moved at the right time. The East also concentrates on the fundamentals, such as reducing lead times so that the level of extra inventory and the amount of time that it sits around are kept to a bare minimum.

The West takes a more broad-brush approach and often ends up carrying more inventory than necessary for longer periods of time. The mind-set is that it is always "safer" to carry more inventory than less, and often the added expense is considered to be a part of the "cost of doing business."

The differences between the methods used in the East and the West are mainly philosophical. The *symptom* of the differences may appear to be "system" related, but the system that each group adopts is dictated by the philosophy with which the job at hand is approached.

In an effort to promote the Eastern philosophy, several gurus have adopted the practice of comparing MRP with kanban, JIT, and TQM. While comparisons of philosophies are always healthy, there is a fundamental problem with the approach taken by some. It attempts to make the new philosophies look good by making MRP look bad. This only serves to muddle the issues. Often, it comes across as a high-stakes shell game and can become confusing.

Two of the more popular comparisons that have been floating around for the past several years are discussed in the following section.

"PUSH" VERSUS "PULL" SYSTEMS

This is one of the more absurd comparisons between MRP and philosophies such as kanban or JIT. The popular mantra is that MRP *pushes* parts and products through the shop whether or not they are needed, whereas kanban and JIT *pull* parts and products through the shop only as customers need them. This is a textbook case of deflecting blame to an inanimate entity, the "system," and it is espoused by many of the same people who were preaching the promise of MRP just a few years ago. But the MRP that they were expounding was not the one that Joseph Orlicky presented; it was a convoluted, cure-all, concocted version. The very same lot-sizing techniques, along with justification for building and buying in large lots, which were being taught several years ago (and still are today by many professionals) are part of this problem. Building parts regardless of need, just to use "economical lots" or to keep employees and equipment busy in a noble effort to improve resource utilization, is just another verse in the same mantra. Today, the mantra chants a lot size of one. The sad part is that large lot sizes are attributed to MRP and small ones to kanban. Few people stop to question why MRP cannot be used with smaller lot sizes. The problem is not MRP — it is *people*. Being the eternal optimist that I am, I look for the positives in this scenario. The one big positive is that over the years, we have learned that some of our traditional mind-sets were wrong and that there is a better way. The sad part is that many people are unable to admit that *they* were wrong — it is always the "system" that is at fault!

MRP does not push or pull components through the workshop — *people* do! Nothing but an inherent mind-set of building inventory prevents changing lot sizes to one. This same mind-set continues to cause work orders to be released to the shop prematurely.

WORK ORDER OR KANBAN?

In the category of absurd comparisons, this one qualifies for the winner's circle. Over the past several years, the term "work order" has come to be treated as though it is a four-letter word. "Work order = bad; kanban = good" is one of the verses in the modern manufacturing mantra.

A work order is a document that authorizes work to be performed. It usually contains information pertaining to what needs to be made (part number), how much of it needs to be made (quantity), when the part should be made available (due date), when the production work should begin (start date), and the destination of the completed part (deliver-to location).

A kanban is a document that authorizes work to be performed. It usually contains information pertaining to what needs to be made (part number), how much of it needs to be made (quantity), when the part should be made available (due date), when the production work should begin (start date), and the destination of the completed part (deliver-to location).

If both documents serve the same purpose, what makes one good and the other bad? Once again, *people* do. The good and bad come into play when we look at how each document is *used.*

Traditionally, work orders have become synonymous with piling work on the shop floor regardless of need or available capacity. Kanban, on the other hand, is synonymous with building only what is needed and only when it is needed. These are differences between two *philosophies* — philosophies that people choose to follow. It does not matter what these documents are called. What matters is how they are used. For instance, one could choose to release a work order when a bin is empty just as easily as when a kanban is empty.

HAVE WE COME FULL CIRCLE?

Some of the methods formerly used to help order parts include order point, ring-around-the-barrel, and the two-bin system. The inherent assumption with these methods was that if a replenishment order was placed at a point where there was just enough inventory to cover the demand for a part through its lead time, there would never be a shortage.

Some methods, such as ring-around-the-barrel and the two-bin system, were more obvious than others. With the ring-around-the-barrel method, for example, literally a ring was painted on the inside of a barrel. When the level of parts in the barrel fell to the point where the ring became visible, it was time to order more parts. The assumption was that the parts remaining in the barrel after the ring became visible would cover the demand until the replenishment order was received. The same concept applied to the two-bin system. When the first bin was emptied, it was time to place an order, and the second bin would cover demand until the replenishment order was received. Theoretically, the barrel or the second bin (depending on the method used) would be completely empty when the replenishment order was received, thus making room for more parts.

These methods seemed to require a lot of space and were a bit too time consuming to manage. When computers started to become affordable and popular, the "system" was used to indicate when orders needed to be placed. That gave rise to the computerized order point system, where a number that represented a part's demand during its lead time would be input, and when the inventory level reached or fell below that number, the computer would indicate that it was time to order more parts. What could be simpler?

In so doing, the one key element that was lost was visibility, in terms of how much inventory had to be carried just to last through the demand for parts through their lead times. There was a legitimate reason why people thought the manual system took up too much space: too much inventory was being carried. One of the reasons why inventory levels were high is because the lead times were lengthy. Instead of addressing the problem of long lead times, it was swept under the proverbial rug and computerized. The lead times were not shortened and the inventory levels remained high. Over the years, this mind-set did not change — regardless of which convolution of "MRP" an organization chose. After several futile attempts to address the symptoms and not the real problems, the hue and cry was that MRP just does not work and something different is needed. It is not that MRP does not work. It is just a technique to compute dependent demand, and it does that very well. The real problem is that the "MRP" tag is used to label traditional philosophy, and *that* is what does not work!

Enter JIT, kanban, and TQM. Among other concepts, these philosophies emphasize the importance of visibility pertaining to people, products, processes, and problems. A kanban, which can be a card or a container, is used to signal:

- The need to move parts from point A to point B
- The production of additional parts
- The replenishment of purchased parts from a supplier

When a kanban bin is emptied of parts, it is treated as a signal to refill it. How similar is that to the ring-around-the-barrel or the two-bin system, and what is the biggest difference between the kanban philosophy and the old ways? It is that the kanban philosophy goes way beyond just utilizing visible signals. It requires doing the preliminary groundwork to allow these visible signals to be used successfully. The preliminary groundwork consists of reducing lead times and lot sizes — a "minor detail" that many in the Western world have chosen to ignore.

EFFECT ON OUR INDUSTRY

In a nutshell, the "methods of the millennium" and associated buzzwords that potential customers are being bombarded with have succeeded in making even the most rational thinker's head spin.

Methodologies such as kanban owe their success to a basic philosophy, which stresses fundamental concepts such as simplicity, discipline, attention to details, and clarity of communication. Ironically, these very same methods are being presented to potential customers as nouveau cure-alls through the use of vague buzzwords. Of late, the approach taken by many latter-day gurus is "If I use a Japanese word such as *muda* to describe *waste*, it will give potential customers a favorable impression." These individuals have not done the manufacturing industry any favors.

To make matters worse, consultants and professional organizations, along with software developers, are too quick to focus on the technical and procedural aspects of these methods. They leave customers to fend for themselves when it comes to the basics — simplicity, discipline, attention to details, and clarity of communication.

There is no shortage of ads in which "professionals" offer to help with efforts to integrate kanban with MRP-II/ERP. Notice that I said MRP-II/ERP. This is to cover all the bases in case someone is familiar with one and not the other. Then there are ads that offer "automated" kanban systems. Now there is a good idea that is about to go to hell in a handbasket. While automation can be a very good thing, in the Western Hemisphere it is often confused with autopilot — a hands-off approach. Again, ironically enough, the Eastern methods preach against the hands-off approach.

It is amazing that more people do not see these contradictions, and if they do, that they do not speak up. The following experiences relate to these contradictions. If after reading them you find yourself letting out a chuckle or two, remind yourself that they actually happened. That is the sad part.

A FEW EXPERIENCES

We're Doing Just in Time

A midwestern heavy-duty truck manufacturer offered to take a few of my colleagues and me on a tour of the facility. When we arrived at the receiving dock, the tour guide very proudly pointed to a rather large room where new tires used to be stored. It was an open area, directly exposed to the outside environment.

The tour guide explained, "We used to store our tires over here, but since the area is not temperature controlled, the tires would dry rot. We used to experience a lot of scrap, but now we've taken the just-in-time approach. Only those tires that are required for the current shift are received at the beginning of the shift. The tires come in, we use them all during the shift, and then we get some more for the next shift."

I had to analyze what he said, and then I asked him, "This has got to be a scheduling feat! I'm sure that different customers want different brands of tires for their trucks. Also, depending on the type of truck, tire size would vary. How do you manage to plan such a wide variety and have them come in just in time for the appropriate shift?"

"That's the easy part," the tour guide answered. "We rented a four-story, air-conditioned warehouse down the road from here, and we bring only those tires that we need for the day. The air-conditioned warehouse solved the problem with dry rot."

That is what "just in time" meant to this organization, which it proudly advertised to its customers, expecting to impress them! Because the tires were dry rotting, an air-conditioned warehouse was rented. Dry rot was the *symptom,* not the real problem. The real problem was that several months worth of inventory was on hand and the tires were sitting around, exposed to the atmosphere.

Are You Familiar with Can-ban?

A few years ago, Jim, our buyer, and I were at a supplier's facility in Oklahoma. We had been having some serious problems with the quality of the supplier's work and late deliveries, so we decided to visit the owner personally. The supplier was building a special-purpose truck for us and had committed to ship one truck every month.

After we met with the owner and expressed our concerns to him, he offered to walk us through the shop so that he could show us what he was doing in the way of improvements. The first place he took us to was a vacant area of the shop where several containers of different sizes were stacked almost halfway up to the ceiling. When we reached this area, he proudly asked us, "Are you familiar with can-ban?" It sounded like he was referring to some ban on soda pop or beer cans.

This was just too tempting for me to let it pass. "A little bit, but why don't you tell us about it?" I asked.

"Those are can-bans," he replied, pointing to the containers. "We are going to use them to move parts through the shop. They will help us get organized."

"But the majority of the parts that go on our truck are too big for even the largest container you have," I mentioned.

"Yeah, we're going to have to use pallets or something else for the truck parts," was his response.

It was quite obvious what had happened with this supplier. Some enterprising person did a super job of convincing the owner to buy a bunch of containers. He had absolutely no clue regarding the "can-ban" philosophy. The very least he could have done was to learn how to pronounce the word correctly!

As we were driving away from the supplier's facility, I made a prediction to Jim. I told him, "My friend, we're going to have to find another supplier for this truck in a hurry. This guy's going out of business in about a year, 18 months tops."

As it turned out, I was wrong. The owner sold out about two years after our visit, and we had another supplier lined up by then.

We Can Help You with Just-in-Time Production

During the early 1980s, when just in time was starting to pick up steam in the United States, a group of consultants visited the company where I worked. They made a presentation to us, during which they expounded on the evils of cluttering the shop floor with parts, disruptions caused by shortages, and the benefits of just-in-time production.

At the end of their presentation, I asked them what we could do to achieve just-in-time production. They wanted us to give them our master schedule for the entire year, existing inventory balances, and all of the associated bills of material in an electronic format. Using this information, they would provide us with a list of all parts, along with the correct quantities that we should order right away. They would also help us organize our warehouse.

For a minute, I couldn't believe my ears. I had to ask, "So what you're telling us is that we must order all the parts that we're going to need for the entire year and keep them waiting in the warehouse. That way, whenever we need parts in the production shop, we can move them from the warehouse, just in time?"

Their response was "Yes — how else could we ensure just-in-time production?"

That did it for me. I thanked them for their time and told them to have a pleasant day. For the consultants to have made such an asinine suggestion with a straight face, they either had to be clueless or they must have thought that we were complete morons.

We Called It DQM

During the mid to late 1990s, when I was responsible for managing the manufacturing and subcontracting of a certain line of products, we were working with suppliers in the United States, France, and Scotland. Jim, one of the members of my group, who had recently transferred from another division of the same company, was stationed in Scotland. His job was to oversee production at the suppliers' facilities in Scotland and France. During the first month after he took the job, I asked Jim to take a tour of the suppliers' facilities with me, as part of his orientation.

While we were wandering through the French supplier's facility, Jim continuously bombarded me with his knowledge of and belief in "DQM." It turned out that the name of the division that he had transferred from started with the letter "D" and the president of the division had renamed TQM to DQM, in an effort to get the employees to accept ownership of the philosophy — a pretty neat approach, I thought.

All during the tour, Jim kept telling me how they did things to ensure "total quality" at the division where he used to work. One of the principles that he kept harping on was the importance of the urgency with which problems must be identified and resolved. I couldn't help but agree with that.

While I was familiarizing Jim with one of the products that was being assembled, I noticed a problem with a part that did not fit like it was supposed to and pointed it out to him. He agreed that it was a problem and that he would take care of it.

As I was about to start the car to head for lunch, Jim got into the seat next to me. I asked him, "Where are you going?"

"To lunch with you, and then to the airport," he replied. Jim was scheduled to fly back to Scotland later that afternoon, right after lunch.

"Have you resolved the problem we identified earlier?" I asked. I knew he had not.

"No, I thought I'd send the supplier an e-mail from Scotland," was his answer.

"I don't believe that you can explain the problem, let alone the solution, in an e-mail message well enough, given the difference in languages," I mentioned.

"You're right. I'll call him from Scotland," was his reply.

"Jim, when you're talking face to face with this supplier, you have to use hand gestures just to get your point across. How are you going to do that over the telephone?"

"You're right again. I'll call Pierre (one of Jim's colleagues in France) and have him call the supplier."

"Jim, let me make it easy for you," I said. "Why don't you stay back and resolve the problem while you're still here, and I'll bring you back a sandwich. You see, in this group, we do more than just talk about TQM — we *live* it!" Jim got the message.

The reason why I thought it important to include this experience is that such attitudes are not uncommon. New employees, along with prospective ones interviewing for jobs, are quick to toss out buzzwords that they do not necessarily understand but have picked up along the way in an effort to impress colleagues, managers, or interviewers. More often than not, when they are asked to follow through with their statements or are questioned further, the train quickly derails. What is even sadder is that managers and interviewers often shy away from challenging such statements for fear that they may come across as ignorant.

The dichotomy is that people often use ambiguous buzzwords and acronyms to describe philosophies that fundamentally preach against ambiguity.

WHAT REALLY MAKES JIT, KANBAN, AND TQM DIFFERENT?

Philosophies such as JIT, kanban, and TQM revolve around a few basic concepts:

- Communicate clearly.
- Minimize lead times and setup times.
- Order just what is needed only when it is needed.
- The workshop has a finite capacity.
- Strive for total quality in whatever you do.
- Work toward the elimination of waste of any kind.
- Maintain visibility pertaining to people, products, processes, and problems.
- Solve problems promptly — do not stop at addressing the symptoms.
- Emphasize problem prevention over repeated fire fighting.
- Involve the entire workforce in the effort toward continuous improvement.
- Pay attention to details.
- Measure progress.
- Use common sense.

Many of these concepts are diametrically opposite to traditional Western beliefs and thought processes. In the West, parts are built in large lots in order to spread out large setup costs, instead of concentrating on reducing the setup costs. Western manufacturers rely heavily on final inspection and rework to ensure the quality of a product before it is shipped to the customer. In the West, long lead times and high levels of inventory are ignored until someone higher up in the organization asks about them, and the general trend of management's thought process is that the workers are paid to do — not to think.

Some gurus have suggested that these differences could be a result of cultural influences and upbringing. Others have questioned whether the Western world is even capable of adopting the Eastern concepts. This is ironic, especially in light of the fact that it was an American (Dr. Deming) who first preached similar concepts to Japanese managers. He tried to do the same in the United States, but American management did not listen very well. It is also rumored that the roots of the famous Toyota Production System originated from what the then vice president of the Toyota Motor Company, Mr. Taiichi Ohno, observed while visiting a North American supermarket.

To some extent, the differences are cultural, but it is not that American or European workers are lazier or less conscientious than their Eastern counterparts. In fact, they are some of the most conscientious, hardest working people around. As the old adage suggests, there is a big difference between working hard and working "smart." This is where some of the cultural differences come into play, and they pertain to management style and not the workers. Traditional Western management style has been to get the workers to do what management deems to be the "right" things — a rather snobbish approach. Historically, Western management has failed to involve employees in the decision-making process, which is unfortunate because there is so much to be gained by helping them open up and by listening to their ideas. This is the biggest difference in philosophies between the East and the West, and the root cause is a cultural difference in management philosophy.

Philosophies such as JIT, kanban, and TQM emphasize the importance of being frugal, taking a disciplined hands-on approach, and paying attention to details, in the belief that these traits will pay dividends in the long term. "If you do the right things, good things will happen."

The traditional Western mind-set looks for instant gratification by throwing money (often in the form of expensive computer systems) at perceived problems and switching to an "autopilot" mode when it comes to managing activities — Look Ma, no hands!

NOTES

1. Pertaining to the traditional A-B-C classification of parts.
2. A Japanese word meaning a "signal" (loosely translated).

This book has free materials available for download from the Web Added Value™ Resource Center at www.jrosspub.com.

SECTION IV:
THE FUTURE

For any student of history, change is the law of life.
Any attempt to contain it guarantees an explosion down the road;
the more rigid the adherence to the status quo,
the more violent the ultimate outcome will be.

Henry Kissinger
Years of Renewal (Simon & Schuster)

12

WHERE DO WE GO FROM HERE?

The longest journey begins with a single step.

Chinese proverb

In numerous organizations, senior managers believe that they are doing fine and the company is in good shape as long as it is making money. It is not uncommon for management to be complacent as long as the company's bottom line is in the black. As soon as the bottom line changes color from black to red, the first impulse usually is to sell more products and to raise prices. If the economy is in a slump and the demand for products is low, the next knee-jerk reaction is to trim the workforce.

We must recognize that we are entering a new age where, in every type of business, customers expect goods and services cheaper, faster, and of exceptional quality. Because it is important for any business to price its products and services competitively, continually raising prices is not the preferred way to stay in business. In order to create more headroom, we must look at ways to drop the floor, instead of repeatedly raising the ceiling.

The best way to drop the floor is to eliminate every kind of waste and activities that do not add value to products and services. Reducing head count should be considered only as a last resort. Remember that a company invests a significant amount of time and money in developing the workforce, and the next time the market swings upward, the people who were terminated will be missed. The next market upswing would require hiring new people and reinvesting in them. In fact, downturns in the economy are an opportune time to redirect some of the "extra" personnel toward improvement-related activities.

THE TRADITIONAL TOOL KIT

The ideas presented throughout this book make use of tools from the traditional tool kit with which many of us are familiar. Tools such as bills of material and methods of maintaining inventory and managing production have been in existence since the pioneers in the field of production and inventory management introduced them several decades ago. Concepts underlying work breakdown structure and improvement curve theory have also been around for several years.

What I have attempted to do in this book is to present different ways in which the same tools can be used to help make significant strides on the road to improvement. Many organizations have stayed with the tried-and-true methods of running a business or a production facility, because those are the only ways with which they are familiar. It seems as though no one has granted permission to use the traditional tools in a different manner; it is a form of a paradigm that they are unable to snap out of. I prefer to take the approach that no one has said that the tools *cannot* be used differently. Some people may like to believe that the traditional tools are passé and it is time to adopt some of the more modern philosophies that have helped several organizations. Ironically, the modern philosophies are also quite heavily dependent on the old tools.

As mentioned in several places throughout this book, it is not important what the chosen method is called. What is really important is how the tools are used.

ONE SIZE DOES NOT FIT ALL

With the onset of the 21st century, it has become more important than ever for manufacturing organizations to be competitive in the global marketplace. To gain an edge on the competition, organizations need to change their ways of conducting business. While it is true that if we do the right things, good things will happen, what is right for one organization may not necessarily be right for another. One size does not fit all.

Senior management should decide on the proper path for its industry and organization. Employee participation is crucial to this effort.

I am a firm believer in Japanese manufacturing techniques, but I choose to practice them in English. What has made me a firm believer in Japanese techniques is the fact that they are all based on attributes that are near and dear to my heart — discipline, attention to detail, and common sense. However, the recent trend seems to be to adopt an esoteric-sounding philosophy, hoping to rally the workforce and impress customers.

Instead of making efficient use of traditional tools, many Western manufacturers seem to be on a constant quest for a magical "silver bullet" that will solve their problems and provide instant gratification. As a recent IBM advertisement suggests, "There is no pixie-dust." We must accept this and move forward.

An analogy about the jeweler and the blacksmith is appropriate here. The jeweler uses a small hammer to strike multiple, yet gentle taps to create a fine piece of jewelry. The blacksmith, on the other hand, beats an iron ingot into shape with a few good whacks, using a much heavier hammer. The approach toward continuous improvement must be similar to that of the jeweler — several small improvements over time.

CHERRY-PICKING IS NOT A GOOD IDEA

The secret to success for any organization lies in addressing three major constituents: people, products and services, and processes. Often, organizations pay attention to just one or two of these constituents; seldom do they concentrate on all three. People issues usually take a back seat. If all three constituents are not given due consideration, the entire effort toward improvement could tumble like a house of cards.

A FINAL EXPERIENCE

I adopted the jeweler's approach when I worked for a corporation in the late 1980s. The results were dramatic. By implementing the ideas compiled in this book, we were able to reduce the throughput time of our product from 66 days to 22 days and reduce the product cost by roughly 14%. Fourteen percent may not sound like much, but when the product cost is in the range of $300,000, the savings can amount to a significant piece of change. We achieved these improvements by the time we shipped the 15th unit.

Before we embarked on the road to improvement, the workshop was notorious for poor workmanship and missed deliveries. Management, not trusting the quality of the finished product, had installed a procedure called the "Red Box," which referred to a designated area on the shop floor. The shop supervisor would move each completed unit to the red box and then walk away from it. An independent team from the quality group would inspect the unit and note their findings. The goal was an average of less than one defect per unit. We achieved this goal within the first year. By the end of that year, the shop personnel were so certain of the quality of the finished product that they would dare the inspection team to find something wrong with it. Management noticed the change in culture on the shop floor and discontinued the red box ritual. Also, starting with the initial prototypes, all units were shipped on time.

Work breakdown structure and improvement curve theory were big contributors in the total effort. These concepts were new to me at the time, and although I was skeptical at first, I decided that we had nothing to lose by trying them. The results spoke for themselves and made a true believer out of me. I have used and defended these concepts and methods ever since.

The single biggest contributor to the improvements was teamwork. For the first time, engineering and manufacturing personnel were not at loggerheads — they worked together. Also, for the first time, key suppliers were part of the team and participated in weekly project meetings.

Were blood, sweat, and tears involved? You bet!

You may have noticed that I do not have a name for the methods described in this book. They are just results of a few good attributes: discipline, attention to detail, and common sense. And, of course, a good sense of humor.

I wish you luck on your journey toward continuous improvement and success in juggling without gravity.

This book has free materials available for download from the
Web Added Value™ Resource Center at www.jrosspub.com.

APPENDIX A: COST ROLLUP EXAMPLE

To illustrate how the costs of components are rolled up via the various legs of a bill of material, a simple bill of material for a finished product A (Figure A.1) will be used. The material cost of each purchased component (B, D, and E) is listed below the component, and the labor hours required to manufacture A and B are also noted. Let's assume that the total purchasing overhead, including an allowance for freight, is 8% of the material cost, the labor rate is $10 per hour, and the overhead pertaining to labor is $20 per hour. Let's also assume that making one unit of item A requires one each of items B and D, two of item C, and three of item E.

As the term suggests, a cost rollup requires computing the cost of the lowest level components and progressively moving up every leg of the bill of material until the cost of the finished product is computed.

Before getting started with the cost rollup, it will be helpful to establish some terminology.[1] Standard costing is assumed for this discussion.

- **Material standard this level (MSTL):** The material cost at the level of the part in the bill of material. This will have a value greater than zero for purchased components only.
- **Labor standard this level (LSTL):** The labor cost associated with making the part. It is the product of labor hours and labor rate for manufactured parts.

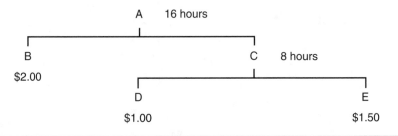

Figure A.1 A Sample Bill of Material

- **Overhead standard this level (OSTL):** For a purchased component, it is the purchasing overhead multiplied by the material cost of the part. For manufactured parts, it is the product of labor hours and the overhead rate.

The three cumulative costs described below apply only to manufactured parts. Because purchased parts have no components under them, their cumulative costs will always be zero.

- **Material standard cumulative (MSCU):** The total material cost of all purchased components below the component whose cost is being calculated. Multiple quantities of the same purchased component must be included in the computation.
- **Labor standard cumulative (LSCU):** The total labor cost of all manufactured components below the component whose cost is being calculated. Multiple quantities of the same manufactured component must be included in the computation.
- **Overhead standard cumulative (OSCU):** The total overhead cost of all manufactured *and* purchased components below the component whose cost is being calculated. Multiple quantities of the same component (manufactured or purchased) must be included in the computation.

Based on the above terminology, the total material cost of any item will be the sum of its MSTL and MSCU. Likewise, the total labor cost will be the sum of its LSTL and LSCU, and the total overhead cost will be the sum of its OSTL and OSCU. The total cost of a part will be the sum of the total material, total labor, and total overhead costs.

Now let's move on to performing a cost rollup for finished product A. Step one is to compute the costs of the lowest level purchased components in the bill of material for item A. These would be items D and E. Table A.1 shows the material cost for each of these two components, along with their purchasing

Table A.1   Cost Rollup Example

Part	Quantity	MSTL	MSCU	LSTL	LSCU	OSTL	OSCU	Total
A	1							
B	1							
C	2							
D	1	$1.00				$0.08		$1.08
E	3	$1.50				$0.12		$1.62

overhead. The total costs of items D and E are $1.08 and $1.62, respectively. Keep in mind that the unit cost for each component is being computed, so multiple quantities are not included in the computation.

The next step is to roll up these costs into their immediate parent, item C, as shown in Table A.2. Remember that it takes one D and three Es to make one C. The resultant MSCU for C is $5.50, which is the sum of the material costs of one D and three Es. Likewise, the OSCU for item C is $0.44. The labor and overhead costs for manufacturing item C still need to be computed. It takes 8 hours to make one C. A labor rate of $10.00 per hour = $80.00 of LSTL, and an overhead rate of $20.00 per hour = $160.00 of OSTL. The resultant total unit cost of item C is $245.94. Note that at the level of item C, there is no material, and so the MSTL for C is zero.

Moving up the bill of material, item A is the next manufactured component. Before beginning to compute its cost, the costs of all of its components must be established. We just completed rolling up the cost of item C. Item B is the only other component of A. Since item B is a purchased part, the procedure used to calculate its cost is the same as for items D and E. Table A.3 shows that the MSTL for B is $2.00 and the OSTL is $0.16, resulting in a total unit cost of $2.16.

Now we are ready to compute the total unit cost of product A (shown in Table A.4). As in the case of item C, there is no material at the level of item A. The MSTL for A is zero. The cumulative material cost (MSCU) is the sum of the material costs of items B and C. The total material cost for item B is

Table A.2   Cost Rollup Example

Part	Quantity	MSTL	MSCU	LSTL	LSCU	OSTL	OSCU	Total
A	1							
B	1							
C	2		$5.50	$80.00		$160.00	$0.44	$245.94
D	1	$1.00				$0.08		$1.08
E	3	$1.50				$0.12		$1.62

Table A.3 Cost Rollup Example

Part	Quantity	MSTL	MSCU	LSTL	LSCU	OSTL	OSCU	Total
A	1							
B	1	$2.00				$0.16		$2.16
C	2		$5.50	$80.00		$160.00	$0.44	$245.94
D	1	$1.00				$0.08		$1.08
E	3	$1.50				$0.12		$1.62

$2.00 and that for item C is $5.50. Since two of item C are required, the cumulative material cost (MSCU) for item A is $13.00. The labor (LSTL) for assembling item A is $160.00 (16 hours at $10.00 per hour). The LSCU for item A is the total labor associated with its components. In this case, it is the labor associated with assembling two of item C, which is $160.00. The OSTL for item A is the overhead associated with assembling it, which is $320.00 (16 hours at $20.00 per hour). Finally, the OSCU for item A is the sum of all overhead costs associated with its components, one of item B and two of item C; the OSCU is $321.04: {$0.16 + [2 × ($160.00 + $0.44)] = $321.04}.

The resultant true M-L-O cost of item A is:

$$\begin{aligned}
\text{Material} &= \$13.00 \\
\text{Labor} &= \$320.00 \\
\text{Overhead} &= \$641.04 \\
\text{Total cost} &= \$974.04
\end{aligned}$$

As mentioned earlier, standard costing is assumed for this discussion. The cost rollup described above is a standard cost rollup and theoretically would be performed at the beginning of a company's fiscal year. During the course of the year, as the costs change, the "standard" cost elements (MSTL, MSCU, etc.) would remain frozen, but a similar group of elements representing the "current" cost (MCTL, MCCU, etc.) would be updated and a current cost rollup would be performed. At the end of the fiscal year, instead of performing a standard

Table A.4 Cost Rollup Example

Part	Quantity	MSTL	MSCU	LSTL	LSCU	OSTL	OSCU	Total
A	1		$13.00	$160.00	$160.00	$320.00	$321.04	$974.04
B	1	$2.00				$0.16		$2.16
C	2		$5.50	$80.00		$160.00	$0.44	$245.94
D	1	$1.00				$0.08		$1.08
E	3	$1.50				$0.12		$1.62

cost rollup, another option could be to perform a current cost rollup and then transfer the "current" cost elements to the "standard" cost elements.

IMPROVEMENT CURVES

The mathematical formula pertaining to improvement curves is:

$$y = a * (x^f)$$

where y is the number of hours at the xth unit, a is the number of hours at the first unit, and f is the factor representing the slope of the curve.

Since the improvement curve shows a downward trend, the slope (f) of the curve will be negative.

COMPUTING THE SLOPE

If a table of improvement factors (Table A.5) is not readily available to you, it is quite simple to calculate the factor. Suppose that for a particular assembly, we wish to project a reduction in hours along an 85% improvement curve. The first objective, before we can use the above formula, would be to find the slope (f) pertaining to an 85% curve. Recall that the 85% means that the hours for the second unit will be 85% of the hours for the first unit. For the current purpose, let's assume that the first unit takes 1 hour. The second unit will take 0.85 hour. Figure A.2 depicts a plot of this line.

If you thought you would never have any use for calculus in real life, you were mistaken. The slope of a line is computed by dividing the "rise" by the "run." In this case, the rise is actually a drop, so the slope will be a negative number. Given that the improvement curve is a logarithmic function, the natural logarithm of each data point must be used to compute the slope of the line.

$$\text{Slope } (f) = [\ln(1.00) - \ln(0.85)]/[\ln(1.00) - \ln(2.00)]$$

$$= [0 - (-0.162519)]/[0 - 0.693147]$$

$$= -0.234465$$

Now that we know that the slope (f) pertaining to an 85% improvement curve is -0.234465, we can use the formula $y = a * (x^f)$. In order to ensure that the value of the slope is correct, let's assume that a, the observation at the

Table A.5   Table of Improvement Factors

Improvement %	Improvement Factor (f)
100	0
99	−0.014500
98	−0.029146
97	−0.043943
96	−0.058894
95	−0.074001
94	−0.089267
93	−0.104697
92	−0.120294
91	−0.136062
90	−0.152003
89	−0.168123
88	−0.184425
87	−0.200913
86	−0.217591
85	−0.234465
84	−0.251539
83	−0.268817
82	−0.286304
81	−0.304006
80	−0.321928
79	−0.340075
78	−0.358454
77	−0.377070
76	−0.395929
75	−0.415037
74	−0.434403
73	−0.454032
72	−0.473931
71	−0.494109
70	−0.514573
69	−0.535332
68	−0.556393
67	−0.577767
66	−0.599462
65	−0.621488

first unit, is 100 hours. Now we can use the formula to compute the hours for the second unit ($x = 2$). By definition (85% improvement curve), we know that the answer should be 85 hours.

$$y = a * (x^f)$$

$$= 100 * (2^{-0.234465})$$

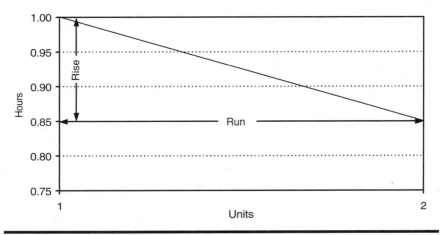

Figure A.2 Computing the Slope of an Improvement Curve

$$= 100 * (0.85)$$

$$= 85 \text{ hours}$$

This confirms that the value computed for the slope is correct. Using this value for the slope, we can compute the hours for any unit. For instance, what will the hours be at the 100th unit?

$$y = a * (x^f)$$

$$= 100 * (100^{-0.234465})$$

$$= 100 * (0.3397)$$

$$= 33.97 \text{ or approximately } 34 \text{ hours}$$

NOTE

1. I was introduced to this terminology and procedure while implementing IBM's IPICS software.

This book has free materials available for download from the Web Added Value™ Resource Center at www.jrosspub.com.

APPENDIX B:
MRP

THE LOGIC OF MRP

A word of caution before we begin: reviewing the inner workings of material requirements planning (MRP) does not share the spine-tingling suspense of a Hitchcock thriller, so please bear with me.

As mentioned earlier, MRP is a *technique*, not a philosophy. Based on the available information, the resulting recommendations are not forecasts, but *computed answers*. This technique is used to compute the *dependent demand* for *components* of end items.

Let's begin with a quick review of the inputs to and outputs of MRP.

INPUTS TO MRP

Master Schedule

The master schedule is usually the starting point of the whole process. In its simplest form, the master schedule is a list of products and components that have independent demand. It includes the quantity of each product as well as the date on which it needs to be completed.

Inventory Data

Once the master schedule has been introduced to the MRP process, the first step that MRP performs is to check how much of each item listed on the master schedule is available in inventory. If the master schedule quantity for an item is available in inventory for shipment, no further planning needs to occur for that item. However, if there is a shortage of a particular item in inventory, the planning routine is triggered.

The planning routine checks for the following parameters pertaining to the item being planned:

- How much is available for shipment from inventory?
- Is the item purchased or manufactured — or is it a phantom?
- What is the lead time required for procuring or manufacturing this item?
- Does the item have a value (greater than zero) specified for safety stock?
- Is a scrap factor or yield factor specified for this item? (As described in Chapter 5, using safety stock to compensate for scrap and yield is recommended.)
- Are there any open orders (purchase orders or work orders) for this item?
- How many of this item should be ordered each time (ordering policy)?
  - ☐ Order just enough to cover the next requirement (lot for lot).
  - ☐ Order x days worth of requirements (fixed period quantity).
  - ☐ Always order in lots of y each (fixed order quantity).
  - ☐ Always order a minimum of x units, a maximum of y units, and in multiples of z units (min, max, multiple).
  - ☐ A host of other algorithms.

Bills of Material

MRP uses bills of material pertaining to the products included on the master schedule to plan requirements for their components.

OUTPUT OF MRP

Based on the information provided to the MRP system, it could recommend rescheduling existing open orders (work orders and purchase orders) to match the need dates of requirements, or in the absence of open orders, it could suggest planned orders.

THE MRP PROCESS

Definitions

Before getting into the nuts and bolts of the MRP process, it will be helpful to clarify a few terms:

Figure B.1   Sample Bills of Material

■ **Need date**: The date when a component is needed. A planned order recommended by MRP will reflect this date as its due date. For an existing work order or purchase order, if the due date (or completion date) of the order does not coincide with the need date, MRP will recommend that the order be pulled in or pushed out.

■ **Due date**: Also known as the completion date, it is specified by a buyer or planner when placing an order.

■ **Release date**: The date on which an order should be released for work. It is calculated by subtracting the lead time of the part from the due date. The release date of a work order is also the date on which all components should be available.

■ **Low-level code**: The lowest level at which a part appears in *any* bill of material. In Figure B.1, part E appears at Level 1 in the bill of material for part X, and it appears at Level 2 in the bill of material for part A. Consequently, the low-level code for part E is 2. Table B.1 shows the low-level code for each part in Figure B.1.

MRP processes the parts in sequence of low-level code, from the lowest (Level 0) to the highest. Hence the term level-by-level netting. MRP does this to ensure that all requirements for a part have been included before beginning the planning routine for the part.

■ **Gross requirements**: The total of all requirements for a part. The requirements can originate from independent demand, dependent demand, or both.

■ **Net requirements**: The quantity needed after available inventory is netted out of the gross requirements.

Table B.1   Low-Level Codes

Part	A	X	B	C	V	D	E	W
LLC	0	0	1	1	1	2	2	2

Table B.2   Master Schedule in Tabular Format

	Period				
	1	2	3	4	5
Part A			2	3	2
Part X		1		1	
Part E	5	5	5	5	5

Now that the definitions have been established, let's begin with the example. Figure B.1 shows two products, A and X, with their respective bills of material, and Table B.2 shows the master schedule (independent demand). In the interest of brevity, the master schedule extends through just five periods, weeks in this case. This tabular format for displaying the master schedule is commonly referred to as the "bucketed" format, since the quantities are grouped into time buckets. A similar format is also a popular way of depicting the MRP planning grid. However, since MRP is a technique that is driven by specific dates, a different format will be used in this example. The format is commonly called the bucket-less format, but that is a misnomer; the time buckets are represented in days, instead of weeks or months.

Assumptions

In order to keep things simple, assume the following:

- Every part (A, C, X, V) with components uses a quantity of one of each component.
- Parts A, C, and X are "make" parts, V is a phantom (explained in Chapter 4), and the rest of the parts are purchased.
- Orders are launched (started) at the start of the day on the release date and completed at the end of the day on the need date (or due date).
- A work week consists of five workdays.

Since discrete dates will be used, the first order of business is to translate the master schedule to reflect a unique date for each requirement. Table B.3 displays the master schedule with specific dates.

Now we are ready to start planning material requirements.

GENERATING A MATERIAL REQUIREMENT PLAN

Imagine two tables for each part: a demand table and a supply table.[1] For items with independent demand, the demand table reflects the information contained

Table B.3   Master Schedule by Specific Dates

Part A		Part X		Part E	
Need Date	Quantity	Need Date	Quantity	Need Date	Quantity
05/15/00	1	05/09/00	1	05/05/00	5
05/18/00	1	05/24/00	1	05/12/00	5
05/22/00	2			05/19/00	5
05/26/00	1			05/26/00	5
05/31/00	2			06/02/00	5

in the master schedule. It shows the source of the demand, the required quantity (the demand), and the corresponding need date. It is sorted in ascending order by the need date.

The supply table lists all open orders for the same part. It contains the order number, order quantity, and due date. It is sorted in ascending order by due date. Table B.4 shows the demand and supply tables for part A.

The inventory data for part A are as follows:

On hand	= 0
Lead time	= 5 days
Ordering policy	= lot for lot
Safety stock	= 0
Open orders	= 2 work orders, A-1 and A-2, for a quantity of 1 each, due on 5/10/00 and 5/22/00, respectively

Now we are ready to create the planning table (also known as the material requirement plan) for part A. Table B.5a shows a blank planning table for part A.

The first step is to pull the first entry from the demand table and insert it into the planning table (Table B.5b). Since the on-hand balance for A is zero,

Table B.4   Part A Demand and Supply Tables

Demand Table			Supply Table		
Source	Need Date	Quantity	Order	Completion Date	Quantity
MS-1A	05/15/00	1	A-1	05/10/00	1
MS-2A	05/18/00	1	A-2	05/22/00	1
MS-3A	05/22/00	2			
MS-4A	05/26/00	1			
MS-5A	05/31/00	2			

Table B.5a Part A Initial Planning Table

Source	Release Date	Order Date	Need Date	Demand Quantity	Supply Quantity	Projected Availability	Action Message
On hand						0	

Table B.5b Part A Interim Planning Table

Source	Release Date	Order Date	Need Date	Demand Quantity	Supply Quantity	Projected Availability	Action Message
On hand						0	
MS-1A			05/15/00	1		(1)	

this causes the projected availability to become minus one, signifying that more As are required.

The MRP routine now checks the supply table for existing open orders. When it finds order number A-1, it pulls it out of the supply table and inserts it into the planning table, ahead of requirement MS-1 from the master schedule (Table B.5c). But since the due date for A-1 is May 10 and it is not needed until May 15, MRP suggests that the order be pushed out by five days.[2] The release date for order A-1 reflects a date that is five work days prior to when the order is actually needed. MRP keeps track of this revised release date because it is the date that it will use to establish the need date for the components of part A, if the order for part A has not already been released.

Now that the first requirement for part A has been fulfilled, MRP pulls the next requirement from the demand table and follows the same procedure (Table B.5d). In this case, the due date for order A-2 is beyond the need date of May 18, so MRP suggests that the order be pulled in.

Since there are no more open orders in the demand table, MRP suggests a planned work order[3] for a quantity of two of part A (because part A is coded as a "make" and its ordering policy is to order lot for lot). This is shown in Table B.5e.

Similarly, MRP goes through the remaining entries in the demand table until all demands have been accounted for. Table B.5f shows the completed planning table for part A.

Once the material replenishment plan for part A (which was the first part with a low-level code of zero) is complete, we move to the next part, part X. The inventory data for part X are as follows:

On hand   = 1
Lead time   = 15 days
Ordering policy = lot for lot
Safety stock   = 0
Open orders = none

Since there are no open work orders for part X, there will be no entries in the supply table. The demand table is shown in Table B.6.

The material planning process is similar to the one for part A, and the final planning table for part X is shown in Table B.7.

Table B.5c Part A Interim Planning Table

Source	Release Date	Order Date	Need Date	Demand Quantity	Supply Quantity	Projected Availability	Action Message
On hand						0	
A-1	05/08/00	05/10/00	05/15/00		1	1	Push out
MS-1A			05/15/00	1		0	

Table B.5d Part A Interim Planning Table

Source	Release Date	Order Date	Need Date	Demand Quantity	Supply Quantity	Projected Availability	Action Message
On hand						0	
A-1	05/08/00	05/10/00	05/15/00		1	1	Push out
MS-1A			05/15/00	1		0	
A-2	05/16/00	05/22/00	05/18/00		1	1	Pull in
MS-2A			05/18/00	1		0	

Table B.5e Part A Interim Planning Table

Source	Release Date	Order Date	Need Date	Demand Quantity	Supply Quantity	Projected Availability	Action Message
On hand						0	
A-1	05/08/00	05/10/00	05/15/00		1	1	Push out
MS-1A			05/15/00	1		0	
A-2	05/16/00	05/22/00	05/18/00		1	1	Pull in
MS-2A			05/18/00	1		0	
Plan-1A	05/16/00		05/22/00		2	2	Place W/O
MS-3A			05/22/00	2		0	

Table B.5f Part A Final Planning Table (Material Requirement Plan)

Source	Release Date	Order Date	Need Date	Demand Quantity	Supply Quantity	Projected Availability	Action Message
On hand						0	
A-1	05/08/00	05/10/00	05/15/00		1	1	Push out
MS-1A			05/15/00	1		0	
A-2	05/16/00	05/22/00	05/18/00		1	1	Pull in
MS-2A			05/18/00	1		0	
Plan-1A	05/16/00		05/22/00		2	2	Place W/O
MS-3A			05/22/00	2		0	
Plan-2A	05/22/00		05/26/00		1	1	Place W/O
MS-4A			05/26/00	1		0	
Plan-3A	05/25/00		05/31/00		2	2	Place W/O
MS-5A			05/31/00	2		0	

Table B.6 Part X Demand and Supply Tables

	Demand Table			Supply Table	
Source	Need Date	Quantity	Order	Completion Date	Quantity
MS-1X	05/09/00	1			
MS-2X	05/24/00	1			

Table B.7 Part X Planning Table

Source	Release Date	Order Date	Need Date	Demand Quantity	Supply Quantity	Projected Availability	Action Message
On hand						1	
MS-1X			05/09/00	1		0	
Plan-1X	05/04/00		05/24/00		1	1	Place W/O
MS-2X			05/24/00	1		0	

Notice that there are no more parts with a low-level code of zero. The process now moves to the first part with a low-level code of one. This is part B.

The inventory data for part B are as follows:

On hand	=	0
Lead time	=	5 days
Ordering policy	=	min = 5, max = 50, in multiples of 5
Safety stock	=	0

Open orders = 1 purchase order (B-1) for a quantity of 5,
due on 05/01/00

The next step in the process is to create the demand and supply tables for part B. Since it does not show up on the master schedule, we can assume that there is no independent demand for part B. So what causes a demand for part B to occur? This is where the bills of material come into play. Figure B.1 shows that part B is used to make part A. It stands to reason that it will be needed when we begin to assemble part A; this would be the release date pertaining to each order for part A. Table B.8 shows the demand and supply tables for part B. The need dates for the various demands for part B are the same as the release dates of orders for part A, from Table B.5f. The resultant planning table for part B is shown in Table B.9. Note that the ordering policy for part B required a planned order to be suggested for five units when just two are required.

The next part with a low-level code of 1 is part C. Like part B, the only parent that part C has is part A. As a result, the demand table for part C will

Table B.8   Part B Demand and Supply Tables

Demand Table			Supply Table		
Source	Need Date	Quantity	Order	Completion Date	Quantity
A-1	05/08/00	1	B-1	05/01/00	5
A-2	05/16/00	1			
Plan-1A	05/16/00	2			
Plan-2A	05/22/00	1			
Plan-3A	05/25/00	2			

Table B.9   Part B Planning Table

Source	Release Date	Order Date	Need Date	Demand Quantity	Supply Quantity	Projected Availability	Action Message
On hand						0	
B-1		05/01/00	05/08/00		5	5	Push out
A-1			05/08/00	1		4	
A-2			05/16/00	1		3	
Plan-1A			05/16/00	2		1	
Plan-2A			05/22/00	1		0	
Plan-1B			05/25/00		5	5	Place P.O.
Plan-3A			05/25/00	2		3	

Table B.10   Part C Demand and Supply Tables

Demand Table			Supply Table		
Source	Need Date	Quantity	Order	Completion Date	Quantity
A-1	05/08/00	1			
A-2	05/16/00	1			
Plan-1A	05/16/00	2			
Plan-2A	05/22/00	1			
Plan-3A	05/25/00	2			

Table B.11   Part C Planning Table

Source	Release Date	Order Date	Need Date	Demand Quantity	Supply Quantity	Projected Availability	Action Message
On hand						0	
Plan-1C	04/18/00		05/08/00		10	10	Place W/O
A-1			05/08/00	1		9	
A-2			05/16/00	1		8	
Plan-1A			05/16/00	2		6	
Plan-2A			05/22/00	1		5	
Plan-3A			05/25/00	2		3	

be identical to the one for part B. Since there are no open orders for part C, the supply table will have no entries.

The inventory data for part C are shown below:

On hand   = 0
Lead time   = 15 days
Ordering policy = order in lots of 10
Safety stock   = 0
Open orders   = none

The demand and supply tables for part C are shown in Table B.10, and the planning table is shown in Table B.11. Once again, because of the lot size of 10, 3 of part C will remain in inventory at the end of the planning cycle.

The next part with a low-level code of one in the planning process is part V. However, since part V is a phantom part, MRP will not plan its requirements. Instead, MRP will plan requirements for the components of part V (part D and part W). This is commonly referred to as "blowing through" the phantom, part V. As a result, there will be no inventory data, nor will there be planning tables for part V.

Table B.12 Part D Demand and Supply Tables

Demand Table			Supply Table		
Source	Need Date	Quantity	Order	Completion Date	Quantity
Plan-1C	04/18/00	10			
Plan-1X	05/04/00	1			

Table B.13 Part D Planning Table

Source	Release Date	Order Date	Need Date	Demand Quantity	Supply Quantity	Projected Availability	Action Message
On hand						5	
Plan-1D			04/18/00		6	11	Place P.O.
Plan-1C			04/18/00	10		1	
Plan-1X			05/04/00	1		0	

This brings us to the first part with a low-level code of two, which is part D. Notice in Figure B.1 that part D is a component of part C and part V. Since part V is a phantom, part X will replace it as the parent for part D. Consequently, the need dates for part D will match the order release dates for work orders pertaining to part C and part X.

The inventory data for part D are as follows:

On hand   = 5
Lead time   = 5 days
Ordering policy = 3 weeks worth (fixed period quantity)
Safety stock   = 0
Open orders   = none

The demand and supply tables for part D are shown in Table B.12, and the planning table is shown in Table B.13. Notice that the ordering policy calls for the replenishment order to include all requirements within a three week (15-workday) window. This creates the need for just one planned purchase order, Plan-1D, for a quantity of six.

The next part at low-level code two is part E. While part E will experience dependent demands resulting from demands for its parents (part C and part X), it will also experience independent demands resulting from the fact that it is included on the master schedule (Table B.2).

The inventory data for part E are as follows:

On hand   = 15
Lead time   = 5 days
Ordering policy = lot for lot
Safety stock   = 5
Open orders   = none

The demand and supply tables for part E are shown in Table B.14, and its planning table is shown in Table B.15.

Notice in Table B.14 that the safety stock requirement (SS-E) is the first entry in the demand table. This is because when a safety stock quantity is

Table B.14 Part E Demand and Supply Tables

Demand Table			Supply Table		
Source	Need Date	Quantity	Order	Completion Date	Quantity
SS-E		5			
Plan-1C	04/18/00	10			
Plan-1X	05/04/00	1			
MS-1E	05/05/00	5			
MS-2E	05/12/00	5			
MS-3E	05/19/00	5			
MS-4E	05/26/00	5			
MS-5E	06/02/00	5			

Table B.15 Part E Planning Table

Source	Release Date	Order Date	Need Date	Demand Quantity	Supply Quantity	Projected Availability	Action Message
On hand						15	
SS-E				5		10	
Plan-1C			04/18/00	10		0	
Plan-1E			05/04/00		1	1	Place P.O.
Plan-1X			05/04/00	1		0	
Plan-2E			05/05/00		5	0	Place P.O.
MS-1E			05/05/00	5		0	
Plan-3E			05/12/00		5	5	Place P.O.
MS-2E			05/12/00	5		0	
Plan-4E			05/19/00		5	0	Place P.O.
MS-3E			05/19/00	5		0	
Plan-5E			05/26/00		5	5	Place P.O.
MS-4E			05/26/00	5		0	
Plan-6E			06/02/00		5	5	Place P.O.
MS-5E			06/02/00	5		0	

Table B.16   Part W Demand and Supply Tables

Demand Table			Supply Table		
Source	Need Date	Quantity	Order	Completion Date	Quantity
Plan-1X	05/04/00	1			

Table B.17   Part W Planning Table

Source	Release Date	Order Date	Need Date	Demand Quantity	Supply Quantity	Projected Availability	Action Message
On hand						0	
Plan-1W			05/04/00		1	1	Place P.O.
Plan-1X			05/04/00	1		0	

specified for a part, MRP will normally reserve available inventory for it, prior to planning for other requirements for the part. This is also apparent in the planning table (Table B.15).[4]

The next and last part to be planned is part W. Since part W is a component of part V (Figure B.1) and part V is a phantom, part W is treated as a component of part X.

The inventory data for part W are as follows:

$$\begin{aligned} \text{On hand} &= 0 \\ \text{Lead time} &= 5 \text{ days} \\ \text{Ordering policy} &= \text{lot for lot} \\ \text{Safety stock} &= 0 \\ \text{Open orders} &= \text{none} \end{aligned}$$

The demand and supply tables for part W are shown in Table B.16, and the planning table is shown in Table B.17.

While the process of planning material requirements is tedious, it follows simple rules. This is where computers can help ease the burden, especially for products with large, multilevel bills of material.

NOTES

1. Many thanks to William G. Olsen, who used this method in an MRP program in 1981. This helped clarify my understanding of the MRP process.

2. Most software programs allow for tolerances that can be set to reduce the amount of "nervousness" in the MRP output. For instance, one could specify that MRP accept the order's due date if it is within x days after or y days before the actual need date.

3. The action message "Place W/O" (or "Place P.O.") will only appear if the release date of the order falls within a time window that can be set in most software programs. You would not want a planner or buyer to place a firm order based on a suggested planned order when the release date is outside the window.

4. Some programs may allow the safety stock quantity to be used to fill requirements and then create a demand record to replenish it when the on-hand balance goes below the safety stock level.

Web Added Value™

This book has free materials available for download from the Web Added Value™ Resource Center at www.jrosspub.com.

BIBLIOGRAPHY

Barker, J.A., *Paradigms: The Business of Discovering the Future,* HarperCollins, New York, 1993, pp. 15–19, 32, 163.

Coens, T. and Jenkins, M., *Abolishing Performance Appraisals: Why They Backfire and What to Do Instead,* Berrett-Koehler Publishers, San Francisco, 2000.

Creech, B., *The Five Pillars of TQM*, Penguin Books, New York, 1994.

Crosby, P.B., *Quality Is Free,* New American Library, New York, 1980.

Deming, W.E., *The New Economics*, MIT Press, Cambridge, MA, 1997.

Deming, W.E., *Out of the Crisis*, MIT Press, Cambridge, MA, 1998.

Engineer, S.J., Veterinary practice management: a different approach, *Texas Veterinarian*, 63(2), 22–23, 2001.

Engineer, S.J., Veterinary practice management: a different approach, *Texas Veterinarian*, 63(3), 24–25, 2001.

Engineer, S.J., Veterinary practice management: a different approach, *Texas Veterinarian*, 63(4), 30–31, 2001.

Engineer, S.J., Veterinary practice management: a different approach, *Texas Veterinarian*, 63(5), 30–31, 2001.

Gilley, K., *The Alchemy of Fear*, Butterworth-Heinemann, Woburn, MA, 1998.

Goldratt, E.M. and Cox, J., *The Goal: A Process of Ongoing Improvement*, North River Press, Great Barrington, MA, 1986.

Imai, M., *Gemba Kaizen*, McGraw-Hill, New York, 1997.

Jones, L.B., *The Path*, Hyperion, New York, 1996.

Kouzes, J.M. and Posner, B.Z., *The Leadership Challenge*, Jossey-Bass, San Francisco, 1995.

Lebow, R. and Simon, W.L., *Lasting Change: The Shared Values Process That Makes Companies Great*, John Wiley & Sons, New York, 1997, pp. 31, 51.

Orlicky, J., *Material Requirements Planning*, McGraw-Hill, New York, 1975.

Peters, T., *Thriving on Chaos*, Harper Perennial, New York, 1987.

Plossl, G.W., *Production & Inventory Control: Applications*, George Plossl Educational Services, Atlanta, 1983.

Plossl, G.W., *Production & Inventory Control: Principles and Techniques*, Prentice-Hall, Englewood Cliffs, NJ, 1985.

Plossl, G.W., *Orlicky's Material Requirements Planning*, McGraw-Hill, New York, 1994.

Scholtes, P.R., *The Team Handbook*, Joiner Associates, Madison, WI, 1988.

Scholtes, P.R., *The Leader's Handbook*, McGraw-Hill, New York, 1998, p. 295.

Schonberger, R.J., *Japanese Manufacturing Techniques*, The Free Press, New York, 1982.

Shingo, S., *Non-Stock Production: The Shingo System for Continuous Improvement*, Productivity Press, Cambridge, MA, 1988, pp. 8–9, 21.

Suzaki, K., *The Manufacturing Challenge*, The Free Press, New York, 1987.

Wagner, A., *Say It Straight or You'll Show It Crooked*, T.A. Communications, Denver, 1992.

Wheeler, D.J., *Understanding Variation: The Key to Managing Chaos*, SPC Press, Knoxville, TN, 1993, pp. 35, 39–41, 57, 60, 65–66, 79.

Wheeler, D.J. and Chambers, D.S., *Understanding Statistical Process Control*, 2nd ed., SPC Press, Knoxville, TN, 1992, pp. 43, 61.

Womack, J.P. and Jones, D.T., *Lean Thinking*, Simon & Schuster, New York, 1996.

INDEX